Russia and the European Union

Russia and the European Union explores the implications of EU enlargement in May 2004 for EU–Russia relations. The book presents the array of political, security, economic and social concerns that have been raised by the enlargement process and examines the opportunities and prospects for for EU–Russian cooperation. It incorporates different perspectives from existing and new EU member states, Russian scholars and politicians from Moscow and the north-western regions of Russia.

Key topics include:

- EU and Russia – developing priorities as neighbours.
- Russia's border regions – shaping policies.
- Kaliningrad – a Pilot Region for EU Russian cooperation?

This book is a unique collection of contributions from academics, praticioners and other analysts from Russia and from both existing and new EU member states.

Oksana Antonenko is Senior Fellow at the International Institute for Strategic Studies, London.

Kathryn Pinnick is Russia and Eurasia Programme Coordinator and Researcher at the International Institute for Strategic Studies, London.

Russia and the European Union

Prospects for a new relationship

Edited by Oksana Antonenko and Kathryn Pinnick

LONDON AND NEW YORK

First published 2005
by Routledge
2 Park Square, Milton Park, Abingdon, Oxon OX14 4RN

Simultaneously published in the USA and Canada
by Routledge
270 Madison Ave, New York, NY 10016

Routledge is an imprint of the Taylor & Francis Group

Publisher's Note

This book has been prepared from camera-ready copy provided by the editors.

© 2005 Oksana Antonenko and Kathryn Pinnick for selection and editorial matter; the contributors for individual chapters

Printed and bound in Great Britain by MPG Books Ltd, Bodmin

British Library Cataloguing in Publication Data
A catalogue record for this book is available from the British Library

Library of Congress Cataloging in Publication Data
A catalog record for this book has been requested

ISBN 0–415–35907–4

Contents

Contents

Maps and Tables

Contributors

Oksana Antonenko is a Senior Fellow and Director of the Russia/Eurasia Programme at the International Institute for Strategic Studies, London

Derek Averre is a Research Fellow, Centre for Russian and East European Studies, European Research Institute, University of Birmingham, UK

Katinka Barysch is Chief Economist at the Centre for European Reform, London

Timofei Bordachev is Deputy Editor of *Russia in Global Affairs* and Director of Studies at the Council for Foreign and Defence Policy, Russia

Bartosz Cichocki is an Analyst at the Centre for Eastern Studies, Warsaw

Piret Ehin is Deputy Director of the EuroCollege, University of Tartu, Estonia

Gennady Fedorov is Vice-Rector for Research, Kaliningrad State University and Director of EU–Russia Cooperation at BaltMION

Hiski Haukkala is a Researcher and Head of the EU Enlargement Project at the Finnish Institute of International Affairs, Helsinki

Hans Jeppson is Vice-President (Baltic Sea Region Contacts) at the Stockholm Chamber of Commerce, Sweden

Andres Kasekamp is Associate Professor at the EuroCollege, University of Tartu and Director of the Estonian Foreign Policy Institute, Tallinn

Andrey Klemeshev is Rector of Kaliningrad State University

Dov Lynch is a Research Fellow at the EU Institute for Security Studies, Paris

Vladimir Mau is the Deputy Director of the Institute for the Economy in Transition, Moscow

Vadim Novikov is an expert at the Academy of National Economy under the government of the Russian Federation, Moscow

Nikolai Petrov is a Research Associate at the Institute of Geography of the Russian Academy of Sciences and a Scholar-in-Residence at the Carnegie Moscow Center

Kathryn Pinnick is Russia and Eurasia Programme Coordinator and Researcher at the International Institute for Strategic Studies, London

Oleg Reut is an independent foreign and security policy analyst in Petrozavodsk, Karelia, Russia

Lev Schlosberg is Director of Vozrozhdenie Centre for Social Projects, Pskov, Russia

Natalia Smorodinskaya is Head of the Centre for Growth Poles and FEZ Studies at the Institute of Economics of the Russian Academy of Sciences, Moscow

Acknowledgements

This book is one of the outcomes of the Russian Regional Perspectives on Security and Foreign Policy project run by the International Institute for Strategic Studies from 2001 to 2004. This publication was made possible in part by a grant from Carnegie Corporation which supported that project. The statements made and views expressed are solely the responsibility of the authors. Many of the contributors to the book presented preliminary versions of their papers at a conference in Kaliningrad in February 2003 organised jointly by the IISS, the Carnegie Moscow Center and Baltic Centre for Advanced Studies and Education (Baltic CASE) of the Kaliningrad State University. The IISS thanks Robert Nurick, then director of the Carnegie Moscow Center, for his role as one of the conference organisers and for commissioning some of the papers in this collection. Amongst IISS staff who have been invaluable in the production of the book were Georgina Hounsome for research assistance, Simon Nevitt for the design and James Green for managing the publishing process. Thanks also go to Matthew Foley and Richard Jones for editorial assistance and to Gillian Kenyon for translating the Russian texts.

Glossary of EU terms

Tacis *(Technical Assistance to the Commonwealth of Independent States)*
The Tacis programme provides grant-based technical assistance to 13 countries in Eastern Europe and Central Asia. Its main aim is to aid the transition process. Tacis funding is allocated through national country programmes, regional programmes and small project programmes. It is due to expire at the end of 2006.

Phare *(Poland, Hungary: Assistance for the Restructuring of the Economy)*
Phare is an EU programme designed to assist the candidate countries of Central and Eastern Europe in their preparations for joining the Union. It is due to expire at the end of 2004. Funding has targeted institution building (adapting and strengthening democratic institutions, public administration and organisations that will enforce European Community legislation); and *acquis*-related investment (to help these countries comply with the *acquis* in areas such as the environment, nuclear safety, transport safety, working conditions and production processes).

InterregII (1994–99)
InterregII finanical instrument had three strands: A – cross-border cooperation; B – completion of energy networks; and C – cooperation in the area of regional planning, particularly management of water resources.

InterregIII (2000–06)
InterregIII superseded InterregII in 2000. Its aims are to stimulate interregional cooperation in the EU. It is financed under the European Regional Development Fund (ERDF), and is designed to strengthen economic and social cohesion throughout the Union through the three strands of: cross-border, transnational and interregional cooperation.

Schengen *acquis*
This is an area of 'free movement of persons' without internal border checks. It is based on an intergovernmental form of cooperation between the 15 member states prior to the 2004 enlargement. It is a body of law that could serve as a foundation for further cooperation, adopted on the basis of the EU's founding treaties (the Treaties of Rome, Maastricht and Amsterdam). All the new member states are obliged to meet all requirements set out in the *acquis* before becoming a part of the Schengen zone, which is unlikely before 2007.

Glossary of EU terms

Acquis communautaire
This is the concept, and body of law, that allows the EU to maintain its cohesion, despite the increased number of member states from May 2004. Each new member state was obliged to accept and effectively implement the *acquis communautaire* prior to accession.

The Schengen Information System (SIS) and SIS II
This network was set up to allow all police stations and consular agents from Schengen member states (and two non-members, Iceland and Norway) to access data on specific individuals, or lost or stolen vehicles and items. A second-generation SIS system is being developed with the capacity to cope with the size of the EU post enlargement. SIS II is expected to be operational by 2006.

ISPA *(Instrument for Structural Policies for Pre-Accession)*
The ISPA financially assisted the new member states in the period of preparing for accession, primarily in the field of the environment and transport.

Abbreviations

AC	Arctic Council
BEAC	Barents Euro-Arctic Council
BEARC	Barents Euro-Arctic Regional Council
CAP	Common Agricultural Policy
CBSS	Council of the Baltic Sea States
CEES	Common European Economic Space
CFSP	Common Foreign and Security Policy
CIS	Commonwealth of Independent States
ED	Eastern Dimension
EEA	European Economic Area (EU member states, Iceland, Liechtenstein and Norway)
ENP	European Neighbourhood Policy
ESDP	European Security and Defence Policy
EU	European Union
FEZ	Free Economic Zone
JHA	Justice and Home Affairs
MFA	Ministry of Foreign Affairs
MNEPR	Multilateral Nuclear Environmental Programme for Russia
NCM	Nordic Council of Ministers
ND	Northern Dimension
NDEP	Northern Dimension Environmental Partnership
OSCE	Organisation of Security and Co-operation in Europe
PCA	Partnership and Cooperation Agreement (between the EU and Russia)
SEZ	Special Economic Zone
SIS	Schengen Infomation Systems
WNIS	Western Newly Independent States
WTO	World Trade Organisation

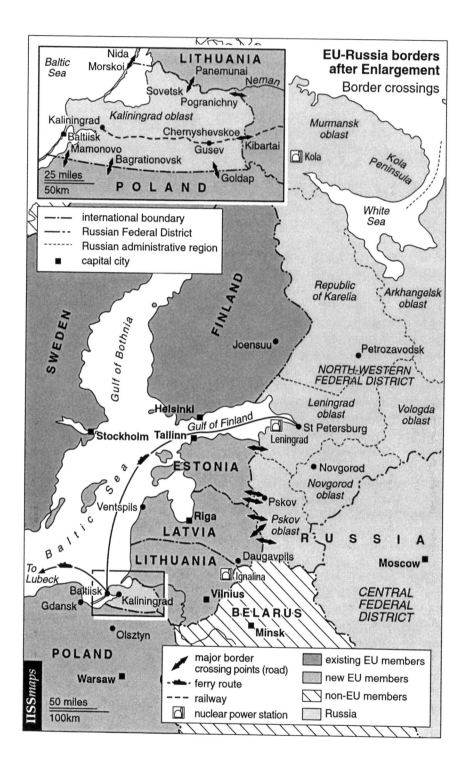

EU-Russia borders after Enlargement
Border crossings
Baltic Sea
Nida
Morskoi
LITHUANIA
Panemunai
Neman
Sovetsk
Pogranichny
Kaliningrad
Kaliningrad oblast
Baltiisk
Chernyshevskoe
Mamonovo
Gusev
Kibartai
Bagrationovsk
Goldap
25 miles
50km
POLAND
international boundary
Russian Federal District
Russian administrative region
capital city
Murmansk oblast
Kola
Kola Peninsula
White Sea
SWEDEN
FINLAND
Gulf of Bothnia
Republic of Karelia
Arkhangelsk oblast
Joensuu
Petrozavodsk
NORTH-WESTERN FEDERAL DISTRICT
Helsinki
Leningrad oblast
Vologda oblast
Gulf of Finland
St Petersburg
Stockholm
Tallinn
Leningrad
ESTONIA
Novgorod
Novgorod oblast
Baltic Sea
Ventspils
Pskov
Riga
Pskov oblast
LATVIA
RUSSIA
LITHUANIA
Daugavpils
Moscow
To Lubeck
Ignalina
Baltiisk
Gdansk
Kaliningrad
Vilnius
CENTRAL FEDERAL DISTRICT
BELARUS
Minsk
Olsztyn
POLAND
Warsaw
50 miles
100km
IISS maps
major border crossing points (road)
ferry route
railway
nuclear power station
existing EU members
new EU members
non-EU members
Russia

INTRODUCTION

The Enlarged EU and Russia: From Converging Interests to a Common Agenda

Oksana Antonenko and Kathryn Pinnick

In May 2004 the European Union (EU) finalised one of the most important and ambitious decisions in its history: to expand its membership from 15 to 25 countries by admitting ten new member states, eight of which – the Czech Republic, Estonia, Hungary, Latvia, Lithuania, Poland, Slovakia and Slovenia – are Central and Eastern European countries. Enlargement is bound to have profound ramifications for the EU – the largest single market in the world, uniting over 455 million people. Yet, the impact of enlargement outside of the EU, particularly on neighbouring nations and key partners, is equally significant.

Russia is the EU's largest neighbour: the Union's common land border with Russia now measures 2,257 kilometres. Russia has a population of 144m, and is an increasingly important source of energy for the European Union. The EU is Russia's principal trading partner: post-enlargement, the Union is set to account for over 50% of its external trade and to be responsible for 70% of foreign direct investment in the country. For Russia, the border with the EU is one of its most stable frontiers. A key foreign policy priority of Russian President Vladimir Putin is to achieve closer cooperation with, and some degree of integration into, the enlarged EU. However, Russia's prospects of formal institutional integration into the EU, or even membership, remain remote at best, or perhaps practically unattainable and mutually undesirable for the foreseeable future.

The EU and Russia are bound to be important neighbours, though, and the challenge in the post-enlargement period is to ensure greater convergence between them. Finding the appropriate strategy to do this will be the main goal of EU–Russia relations over the next decade. Russia has chosen not to join the EU's initiative – the European Neighbourhood

Policy (ENP) – which is being offered to other Eastern neighbours of the EU such as WNIS and South Caucasus states. However, at the St Petersburg summit in May 2003 the EU and Russia decided to enhance their partnership through an ambitious strategy of 'common spaces'. Russia and the EU are expected to adopt 'road maps' for these common spaces at the November 2004 summit. But implementing any new strategy in the short and medium term requires that the main challenge is addressed: the EU and Russia still have fundamental differences in approach to the main principles and objectives of their cooperative relationship. While enlargement implies that the EU's and Russia's interests are converging, we are still far from a common agenda for integration.

For the EU, the challenge is how to develop a strong set of incentives, short of membership commitments, that promotes political and economic reforms in Russia that could bring about increased convergence between the integrated EU area and its largest neighbour. This process should ideally cover all spheres – economic, political, security and social – leading ultimately to a free-trade area, shared economic benefits (particularly for the north-west regions of Russia closest to the EU), simplified movement of people across the border which will promote common democratic values, and effective joint protection against cross-border threats like organised crime and illegal migration and trafficking of all kinds.

The EU was slow to articulate and implement such a strategy in the period leading up to enlargement on 1 May 2004. The focus was understandably on preparing the new members for accession. In fact, the pre-enlargement strategy of the EU had the opposite impact on Russia. The result of its assistance programmes for, and provision of resources to, the accession countries was new disparities and divisions between Russia and its neighbours, rather than synergies. For Russians, enlargement has been associated with tighter border controls, more complicated procedures for citizens who wish to travel not only afar but also to neighbouring states, wider socio-economic gaps, and anticipated economic costs.

For Russia, the challenge of developing a strategy to achieve convergence with the enlarged European Union is even greater. The problem is how to reconcile the domestic economic modernisation and political agendas with the objective of integration with the rest of Europe. While Putin has declared Russia's relations with the EU to be a foreign-policy priority, he has also consolidated power to implement a different kind of domestic transformation than the Central European states which joined the EU. Far from aspiring to an EU-type decentralised, socially focused, and democratic system of governance, Russia is seeking to modernise through a strong state model, where elections co-exist with the increasingly authoritarian rule of the bureaucracy, and privatisation is followed by increased state intervention in the realms of business and private property. More importantly, this model is averse to pluralism and the devolution of power on the regional level; this has implications for Russia's relations with the EU. This domestic consolidation strategy is working against, rather than for, greater convergence with the EU.

If Russia's current rate of economic growth is to be sustained, it has to find ways to translate its new position of neighbour to the largest integrated and economically developed area in the world into practical benefits for its domestic reforms and for realising its aspirations as a European civilisation. In the period leading up to enlargement, however, Russia chose to highlight potential threats posed by the process to its economic interests, its European identity, and its historical relations with the countries of the Commonwealth of Independent States (CIS), now also part of the EU's 'near abroad'. As a result, all pre-enlargement negotiations were focused on Russia's long list of demands for compensation or pre-conditions, ranging from Kaliningrad transit to trade quotas to the rights of Russian-speaking minorities in the Baltic States. Russia's threatening rhetoric and zero-sum approach in the months leading up to enlargement provoked a negative reaction from the EU, particularly from its new members, and caused a six-month delay in practical work on developing road maps for the common spaces.

Neither the EU nor Russia could take their pre-enlargement policies vis-à-vis each other into the post-enlargement period. The EU's two-stage approach, focusing first on new members and second on new neighbours, was not sustainable, because in many areas, including energy exports, trade, migration, and even the European Security and Defence Policy (ESDP), it is increasingly difficult to promote these two sets of interests separately. Moreover, the new members themselves are likely to take greater initiative in developing relations with neighbouring countries, including Russia, particularly as far as cross-border issues are concerned. For Russia, pursuing a strategy of damage limitation which emphasises the threats posed by EU enlargement has proven to be detrimental to the advancement of its economic, political and security interests in relations with its neighbours and with established partners in the EU. Moreover, the perception that enlargement is a threat has complicated practical cooperation projects, particularly for Russian border regions and for Russian business. Russia's zero-sum approach, if continued, is bound to erase the political will in European capitals to move forward with its cooperative agenda with Russia, particularly since they are still preoccupied with integrating the new members. In addition, European governments are becoming more active at developing cooperation with the EU's other neighbours under the ENP and they are finding these new neighbours more willing than Russia to focus on the opportunities enlargement brings.

This book assesses the prospects for convergence between the EU and Russia, and attempts to identify areas where such convergence is possible in practice and desirable for both sides. Although the material centres primarily on EU–Russia relations in the pre-enlargement period, it also highlights practical opportunities for future cooperation.

The first part of the book examines the main objectives of EU and Russian policies in the political, security, Justice and Home Affairs (JHA) and economic spheres and the instruments used to fulfil them in the period leading up to enlargement. What were the fundamentals of EU–Russia relations on the eve of the enlargement? Why did existing mechanisms fail to address disagreements or to devise mutually beneficial outcomes in the pre-enlargement period? The book offers a balanced view, presenting European and Russian perspectives.

The second part looks more specifically at EU–Russia border areas. These are likely to be affected most by enlargement, and could become pilot regions for the testing of EU–Russia convergence strategies. The chapters on Pskov region and the Republic of Karelia look at how the regions of Russia that border the EU view the implications of enlargement. The perceptions of new member states on the other side of the border – Estonia and Poland – are also set out. How might their relations with Russia be transformed by enlargement? And what can be done to address the potential negative impacts of new border regimes? Also analysed are the political and economic limitations that Russia's regions confront in regard to participation in cooperation projects with EU partners.

The third part of the book contains a detailed special case study of EU–Russia cooperation, Kaliningrad. Can Kaliningrad – the exclave of Russia that is surrounded by the enlarged Union – become a pilot region where EU–Russia cooperation can be taken to a new level, or will it remain a centre of controversy and a source of problems for both parties? The section presents the different perspectives of scholars in Kaliningrad and Moscow, and a European expert.

The book is unique, since it offers a wide range of views: from regions and from capitals, from scholars and practitioners, from new and old members of the EU, and from specialists working in different fields – political science, international relations, economics and sociology. The book will be of use to policymakers, academics, analysts, researchers and students interested in the external policies of the EU, Russian regional studies, border studies and Russian foreign and security policy.

This collection of papers provides substantial material on policy areas and mechanisms which the EU and Russia might consider on their path from neighbourhood to convergence. The following factors should be taken into account in devising a new strategy for EU–Russia relations:

- **Convergence should be a mutual process.** Both the EU and Russia emphasise that their partnership is based on equality and mutual benefit, yet such 'equality' is difficult to achieve in practice. In particular, convergence means that both sides move towards adopting common norms and procedures and some elements of collective decision-making. The EU has engaged in a process of convergence with neighbours on two previous occasions: through the accession of new member states and through the establishment of the common European Economic Area (EEA) with selected non-member states. Neither, though, are appropriate models for EU–Russia relations. Instead, convergence should be the sum of two unilateral processes; each side commits to a realistic contribution towards creating common spaces instead of making demands of the other party. One-sided strategies, such as the EU's Common Strategy towards Russia and Russia's reciprocal Mid-Term Strategy towards the EU, were unsuccessful. These documents made unrealistic assumptions about the extent to which the other side could transform and they put forward demands and preconditions which were not in line with the other side's interests and capacities.

- The challenge now is **to transform these unilateral strategies into a common agenda,** under which both parties enjoy ownership of, and influence over, all stages of decision-making. A concrete and commonly agreed agenda should be underpinned by specific commitments from both the EU and Russia. On Russia's part, these commitments should include changes in its legislation, further market liberalisation and improving domestic and border security. Unlike the countries of Central and Eastern Europe, which implemented reforms with the clear prospect of EU membership, Russia does not have the same incentive and is likely to seek convergence 'à la carte' in areas where it sees clear short-term benefits, rather than striving to adopt the EU *acquis* in full. Russia should make it clear which aspects of the EU *acquis* it is prepared to adopt unilaterally and in what timeframe; it would be beneficial if this were to occur before the end of Putin's second term in 2008.

- On the EU's part, the commitments should include creation of a more favourable environment in which Russia can trade and promote its interests in EU member states and institutions and in which Russian citizens can travel with fewer restrictions.

- For Russia, which is economically weaker and has no prospect of EU membership, the principle of reciprocity in its relations with the EU is particularly important. **Russians resent the fact that, for the EU, convergence often implies that Russia move towards adoption of the EU** *acquis* **and norms.** Given that the EU is more developed economically and approves all of its legislation collectively, it could hardly be expected to borrow elements of the Russian economic, judicial or political system. Furthermore, the EU is justified in taking a strong position when its values are at stake and in applying conditionality to its assistance to, and cooperation with, Russia. Nevertheless, the EU can still move closer to Russia by offering a more favourable environment for Russia's legitimate trade and investment, facilitating the movement of people and goods, and welcoming Russia's interest in economic, cultural and regional cooperation with its neighbours.

- **The EU and Russia should clearly identify and convey to their publics and interest groups the specific advantages and new opportunities from enlargement and the new neighbourhood.** For the EU, this means that enlargement implies greater commitment to cooperation with Russia. For Russia, the enlargement should represent not a threat to its interests, but a source of economic, political and social benefits. Prior to enlargement, these benefits were poorly understood in Russia and the Russian government chose to highlight the anticipated costs. A joint assessment of the new opportunities for EU–Russia cooperation would be a positive confidence-building measure post enlargement.

- Another common challenge is **to focus on the short- and medium-term perspectives,** rather than on grand strategic designs that cannot be fulfilled in the foreseeable future. Ideally, **a mutual strategy should be developed based on the successful small practical projects** that have taken place with clearly identifiable stakeholders on both sides, rather than on grand strategic designs, such as Common Spaces, which are de facto substitutes for real commitments. Convergence should comprise small, measurable goals, focused on the short and medium terms, rather than on the long term, and hence, by definition, vague, declarations of intent. These goals should not necessarily be linked to high-level political dialogue between the European Union and Russia or to EU–Russia Summits, which are important for giving EU and Russian leaders political visibility, but have proven ineffective in regard to setting and reaching agreement on practical agendas. The newly created EU–Russia Partnership Council might prove more effective if it involves mid-level officials and regional representatives (modelled on the Barents Euro-Arctic Regional Council). However, a dispersed partnership strategy under which some EU–Russia cooperation programmes are attached to EU structures, such as JHA or regional-policy working groups, instead of the Partnership Council, might be more effective in informing the Russian side about the EU's current agenda and its decision-making mechanisms and in generating relevant ideas for cooperation (in parallel with the EU's own initiatives). This could be modelled on the initiatives under which Russian liaison representatives are attached to the EU Military Staff or to JHA liaison offices within embassies.

- The areas where 'bottom-up' convergence is most likely to succeed in the near term include the border regions, where cross-border cooperation projects are already being implemented. **North-west regions of Russia and the border areas of new EU member states** will be significantly affected by enlargement, yet, at the same time, they **will be the obvious locations for the testing of new cooperation initiatives.** The north-west regions of Russia are already becoming more important economically in regard to Russia's relations with Europe. Whereas in the Cold War period the location of regions like Arkhangelsk and Murmansk *oblasts* and the Republic of Karelia made them significant in geo-strategic terms (the Soviet bloc's northern frontier), now they are important in relation to the transit of goods and commodities between the EU and Russia. The challenge for them is to diversify their economic foundation: from resources and transit towards attracting foreign investment into manufacturing such as the timber and paper pulp industries and to increase trade with both other Russian regions and with the EU. New border regions such as Pskov and Leningrad *oblasts* should benefit from enlargement, when trade flows to and from the Baltic States increase with the lifting of double tariffs. However, these Russian regions need to invest in transit infrastructure, modernise border crossings, simplify customs clearances, and improve the local business environment in order to take full advantage of the economic opportunities. For Kaliningrad *oblast*, changes in the region's legislation might be required so that it is more integrated than the rest of Russia with European standards and legislation.

- The border regions are notorious for the **widening economic and social gaps that exist along the EU–Russia frontier.** At the moment, Russia does not see such developmental disparities as either a concern or as an opportunity to establish joint projects with the EU. For the EU, the asymmetry represents not merely an economic and social problem on its external borders, but also a potential security threat in terms of organised crime and illegal migration. In addition, the border regions have other characteristics that make them more attractive locations for the piloting of a convergence initiative. There are examples of historical, cultural and small-scale economic interdependence at the community level in the border regions that should be preserved and utilised. Some regions have re-orientated trade flows towards Europe. In Pskov region (one of the poorest areas in north-west Russia), in 1995, over 30% of regional trade was with the countries of the CIS. By 2002, though, this had dropped to 2.8%, while trade with the EU had increased from 34% to 48% over the same period (and from 20% to 37.5% with nations in Central and Eastern Europe). Furthermore, border regions have been the site of a plethora of sub-regional initiatives, including the EU's Northern Dimension and Euroregions. Although these have achieved mixed results to date, they have led to the creation of regional cross-border communities, better understanding of common interests, and experience of limited joint action. This is not the case for other areas of EU–Russia cooperation. Moreover, the case studies presented in this book from Pskov and Kaliningrad regions and the Republic of Karelia reveal that there are positive expectations, and that there is a greater desire to derive the benefits of EU enlargement compared to other parts of Russia, where the EU is still poorly understood.

- This book argues that the biggest obstacle to effective cross-border interaction is the **limited political and economic capacity of Russian regions.** Putin's federal reforms have resulted in greater centralisation, curtailing powers of individual regions to cooperate with foreign entities. The regions need the permission of Moscow to engage in such activities, even if they fall into the category of foreign economic cooperation, which, in principle, is within the scope of the regional administrations. Such permission is rarely granted on time or encouraged. The law on local self-government (the level within the municipalities at which grassroots initiatives usually occur) does not provide any powers for establishing foreign partnerships. The institution of the Federal Districts (such as the North-Western Federal District, comprising those regions of Russia contiguous to the EU), which was set up in 2000, has not been effective in elaborating a strategy for cross-border cooperation to benefit regional development;

rather, it has introduced an additional layer of control over regional and local government, particularly in the areas of foreign activity, 'soft security' and the environment. Yet these are the areas where cross-border cooperation was most advanced in the 1990s. Moreover, the federal reforms have redirected tax revenues to the federal budget, leaving the regions with fewer resources to allocate to cross-border programmes and without any special federal fund from which they can draw subsidies, even on the basis of open competition or tenders, to support initiatives with their EU neighbours. As a result, projects under the EU's Northern Dimension initiative are often delayed and cooperation under well-established cross-border programmes, such as Euroregio Karelia, have been downgraded from the original goal of promoting common practices and economic integration to merely local cross-border exchanges of officials and cultural groups. The challenge for new Euroregions involving Pskov and Kaliningrad *oblasts* (which are still at the planning stage) is to collaborate on common policy areas which bring economic benefits and improve understanding of the EU in Russian border regions.

- In north-west Russia, the goals of federal centralisation and convergence with the EU are increasingly coming into conflict. The Russian government should thus consider granting special powers and allocating resources to the north-west regions of the country that border prosperous and stable EU states. A special commission could be set up to examine three proposals. First, the granting of special powers to border regions and municipalities to allow them to enter into agreements with their foreign counterparts in particular policy spheres, which have been clearly identified as priority areas for EU–Russia cooperation. Such powers will not undermine Russia's sovereignty and territorial integrity, but, rather, will encourage the development of a strong and viable region along Russia's border with the EU. Second, the creation by the federal government of a special goal-oriented fund to support cross-border cooperation programmes in the regions (for example, Interreg or Euroregions) – to which the regions can apply to obtain additional funds. This would guarantee that the regions enjoy greater ownership of projects and more influence over the setting of the sub-regional cooperation agenda. And third, special attention should be given to 'soft security' issues in the regions, with more funds being allocated and institutions being created on the regional level. Meetings of border officials and customs and migration officers, for instance, should generate proposals to be considered at ministerial meetings under JHA or by special JHA sub-committees within the Partnership Council.

- **Kaliningrad is one of the natural candidates to become a pilot region for bringing Russian trade practices and legislation into line with EU standards.** The European Union is already offering some special arrangements for Kaliningrad in relation to the movement of people and goods. Major infrastructure and investment projects are being implemented in the region by the EU and more are planned in future. The Special Economic Zone (SEZ), which has existed in Kaliningrad since the mid-1990s, has not led to the development of a legitimate and sustainable economic foundation in the region and has failed to make it more compatible with the EU business environment. However, given Kaliningrad's special geographical location, the SEZ cannot be abolished completely. Instead, Kaliningrad should become a pilot region for EU–Russia cooperation and should be awarded special status by the Russian government that would allow its regional legislation to be brought into line with the provisions of the EU *acquis* before Russian federal laws do so. This status will not undermine Russian sovereignty over the region, but will respond to the need of Kaliningrad residents to move closer to the EU if the region is to be economically viable. The EU and Russia should develop a joint programme for regional development that does not include Kaliningrad alone, but also neighbouring states and some other North-Western regions of Russia. The EU and Russia should set up a special regional fund to finance regional development projects, particularly infrastructure projects, commercial port facilities and Europe–Asia transport corridors through Kaliningrad region. Finally, the EU and Russia should agree to extend simplified travel arrangements for Kaliningrad residents, as well as for residents of neighbouring EU states, beyond 2006-07 when Poland and Lithuania (and the other new members) join the Schengen *acquis*.

- **Obstacles confronting the EU in regard to bottom-up cooperation** with Russia include: an excessive focus on sub-regional cooperation on security and environment issues (favoured by EU member states), rather than on economic and infrastructure projects (favoured by Russia); too much emphasis on political dialogue with Moscow and poor knowledge of problems and actors in Russia's border regions; the introduction of tighter visa and border regimes, complicating cross-border trade (this could be addressed through the implementation of local traffic visas); the lack of funds available to EU and non-EU states for joint assistance programmes (this could be tackled via the new Neighbourhood Instrument, which is slated to come into effect in 2007); a shortage of political and financial support for the expansion of the Northern Dimension initiative; poor coordination between the EU and sub-regional programmes and actors, which has led to duplication and resources being wasted; disproportionate allocation of assistance to highly paid foreign consultants who sometimes do not understand the realities of Russia; and complicated application and decision-making processes for the award of project funds. (Perhaps in future a greater number of experts from new member states with an understanding of economic transition processes and experience of working with Russia should be included in bottom-up cooperation initiatives, as well as more representatives of grassroots institutions in Russia.) These obstacles should be acknowledged and addressed in future EU programmes.

* While to date enlargement has not significantly altered the **border and visa regimes that exist between Russia and the new EU members,** there is no doubt that the impact will be more profound after 2006–07 when the new members join the Schengen *acquis*. Consequently, it is important that a set of measures be developed and put into practice in the next two years to prevent the disruption of cross-border contacts and more economic hardship for the residents of the border areas. Time is short if substantial changes are to be implemented. While a visa-free regime remains a long-term goal, more realistic near-term objectives include: greater flexibility in regard to Schengen rules governing the issuance of multi-entry visas; cheap visas; the introduction of group visas for educational and cultural exchanges; a local visa for border residents; simplified application procedures for residents of regions without EU consulates (applications could be submitted by e-mail or post); the opening up of more consulates in Russian regions, particularly in the north-west; and the preservation of special arrangements for the transit of Russians to and from Kaliningrad. Many of these measures can only be implemented if reciprocal measures are introduced on the Russian side, which has so far failed to simplify its visa application and registration procedures for existing and new EU members. An EU–Russia agreement on simplified visa-application procedures might be the answer, rather than Russia and individual EU member states concluding bilateral visa agreements.

* The most significant impact of **tighter border regimes will be on small-scale cross-border trade.** Some of this shuttle trade is essential to the livelihoods of border residents in both Russia and neighbouring states. Although much of the trade is legitimate, the illegal part of the cross-border trade should be transformed gradually into legitimate tax-generating transparent business enterprises, as opposed to

activities taking place within the grey economy. These new legitimate businesses should be granted special privileges in relation to visas, travel and border-crossing logistics. Moreover, more investment in the economies of the border regions should take place to create new jobs in other sectors for people who are likely to lose income as a result of changes to cross-border trade. Other activities, such as the smuggling of high-excise goods or more dangerous items like drugs or weapons, and trafficking in human beings, should be tackled not by introducing tighter visa regimes, as experience to date indicates that many organised-crime networks can overcome these barriers, but through improved border infrastructure, the eradication of corruption among border officials, the creation of a joint database for tracking criminals, and the implementation of tougher penalties, particularly in Russia, for traffickers and organised-crime groups. EU assistance programmes for modernising border-crossing points should be expanded – for instance, the relatively small amount of resources expended on modernising the Svetogorsk and Salla crossing points has made a huge difference to cross-border flows between Finland and the Republic of Karelia.

- Russia and the EU continue to pursue different agendas regarding cooperation on JHA. For the EU **organised crime and illegal migration** are the most prominent concerns. For Russia, the main objective of a common space of JHA is to introduce visa-free travel between the EU and Russia. A common agenda has to be developed incorporating the interests of both sides. As a first step a joint assessment is required. It is important to define clearly to what extent Russia poses a major threat to the EU from the standpoint of organised crime and migration. Understandably, Russia is resentful of EU's stereotypes of the 'Russian mafia', which often includes citizens of other post-Soviet states. These stereotypes might be dispelled through joint monitoring of organised crime statistics and regular exchanges of data. Russia's membership of Europol can help in this regard. As for migration, statistics show that Russia is not the major source of illegal migration to the EU – indeed, it is a major target for illegal migration from the countries of the CIS. Moreover, Russia is not even the major transit route for illegal migrants from third countries who wish to enter the EU from the south. While enlargement could create more incentives for third-country migrants to use Russia to access the territory of new member states, internal border controls within the EU still constitute a barrier. Hence, the EU and Russia should develop a joint set of measures to prepare for 2006–07 when the new members join the Schengen *acquis* and internal border controls are to be eliminated. These measures should be based on the understanding that migration is a joint problem and that synergies are required if it is to be addressed effectively. The obvious recommendation for EU policy is to help Russia improve controls on its porous southern borders (which are notorious for third-country migrants and the trafficking of drugs destined for Europe). Other measures might include: joint training of migration officials; setting up databases to monitor migrant flows; and regular data exchanges between border officials and federal departments. Russia, for its part, has to sign and ratify border treaties with Estonia and Latvia and produce a clear road map for the signing of a readmission treaty with the EU.

As this book goes to press, the EU and Russia do not have a practical strategy in place for working together in the post-enlargement era. The material included in this collection highlights policy areas where practical cooperation can be expanded, building on experience gained in the period leading up to enlargement. Enlargement presents an appropriate time to focus on the challenges facing the EU and Russia and also to examine the opportunities. The new proximity between the EU and Russia has to be addressed. However, extended neighbourhood does not mean that convergence is inevitable. If it is to occur, it will be a long slow process and instant results should not be expected. But without convergence, the EU–Russia border will bear closer resemblance to a dividing line, a situation that both sides very much wish to avoid.

London
June 2004

PART ONE

1. From 'Frontier' Politics to 'Border' Policies Between the EU and Russia

Dov Lynch

Borders perform many functions. They are 'power containers' in so much as they mark the outer limit of an entity and of its identity. They are also 'power definers' in relation to entities that lie beyond that line. Borders are a means of protecting an entity from outside threats, and offer a way of defining an internal space. They revolve around notions of inclusion and exclusion: whatever lies within a border is defined as 'us', and whatever falls beyond is defined as 'them'. Compared to the concept of the 'frontier', which is, by definition, more vague, with unclear lines of demarcation, power and control, borders are tightly delineated and clearly drawn. One can cross a border; one passes through a frontier. Borders are lines; frontiers are zones.

After the collapse of the Soviet Union, and for much of the 1990s, a 'frontier' separated the European Union (EU) and the Russian Federation. The zone between the external border of the EU and the new borders of Russia was characterised by an enlarging but reluctant 'empire' (in the shape of the EU), which was slowly and with difficulty developing an accession strategy towards an arc of post-communist countries in the new Eastern Europe, and a retreating former empire, which was enduring a painful transformation process while seeking to fashion new relations with states that had previously been under its tutelage.[1] The outcome was a blurred area with overlapping interests and policies. The lines between the two parties were not clearly drawn. Furthermore, neither the EU nor Russia was particularly concerned about the other, as both were deeply engaged in their own internal reform processes.

This is changing. The EU and Russia have started a process to define the nature of their external borders with each other, and to fashion a 'border' policy towards the other. In the early years of the twenty-first century, the EU and Russia remain focused on their own internal development and transformation, which are all-encompassing processes that leave little time and energy for thinking about interests and requirements on their borders. Moreover, the process of defining appropriate relations between the EU and Russia is in an embryonic and fragmented state. Nonetheless, the nature of border relations between Brussels and Moscow is becoming clearer. The frontier days may be coming to an end.

A number of factors are likely to influence emerging border politics between the EU and Russia. First, the two parties are distinct entities. That is, neither one wants to integrate or join the other. In particular, President Vladimir Putin's Russia has declared that it is not seeking to accede to the European Union. Second, the two parties have separate interests, which they look to satisfy through their own means. At the same time, though, the EU and Russia recognise that they have numerous common interests. In regard to this third factor, Brussels and Moscow both realise that they cannot be entirely independent from one another. Consequently, EU–Russia relations revolve around a range of border questions. The EU has an interest in ensuring that enlargement is successful and in securing the transformation of Russia along 'European' lines. Russia, meanwhile, wants to prevent enlargement from undermining its political and economic interests, and to have an equal say on the continent.

The development of a smooth partnership between the EU and Russia has been delayed by numerous variables. First, there is the difficulty of establishing a relationship between a diverse group of states, within which sovereignty is pooled, and a traditional state that is deeply defensive of its sovereignty. Second, the EU and Russia have devoted most of their energies since 2000 to pressing internal questions; indeed, both have instigated a process of internal transformation. The focus of Brussels and Moscow on enlargement and state consolidation respectively has left little time and energy to concentrate on the other party.

This chapter is in three parts. The first examines the main elements that are forcing the EU to come to terms with Russia as a neighbour. The second analyses the evolution of EU thinking on, and policy towards, Russia, mainly through an examination of two important developments in 2003–04: the release in March 2003 of the European Commission's communication entitled *Wider Europe – Neighbourhood: A New Framework for Relations with our Eastern and Southern Neighbours*, representing a systematic attempt by the EU to define a neighbourhood policy;[2] and the review taking place within the European Council of the Union's Russia policy, launched in December 2003 as a result of the perception that significant failings have occurred. The third part of the chapter looks at the state of the EU–Russia political dialogue, before examining the problems that are holding back the process. EU–Russia interaction in regard to the conflict in Moldova is discussed in the conclusion, providing insight on the friction that characterises the current security relationship.

Forces pushing for definition of the borders

Various forces are driving the EU's new border relationship with Russia. It is not an overstatement to say that the EU is currently in the midst of a revolution, following the accession of ten new member states on 1 May 2004. The impact of enlargement on the internal and external dynamics of the Union is likely to be fundamental. Internal political dynamics that the EU has become used to, even reliant on, will change, and new constellations of actors with new interests and needs will emerge.

The impact of enlargement will be fourfold. First, the EU's new member states have different interests and priorities compared to the old members. In the run-up to accession, Poland, for example, was instrumental in pushing for a greater EU role in Moldova and Ukraine.[3] The new members bring a new urgency to border questions with the East, which have hitherto only been touched upon. Second, the enlarged EU has new borders, with Belarus, Russia and Ukraine (and, from 2007, following the accession of Romania, with Moldova and the Black Sea). These borders place new emphasis on EU thinking about the states on its periphery, and the policies that should be adopted in response to potential and actual threats emerging from these regions.

Third, partly as a result of these changes, the EU has started to think about new policies towards the states on its new borders. For much of the 1990s, EU 'foreign policy' revolved around the question of membership/non-membership: if the prospect of membership existed, then the EU had a policy towards that particular state; if accession was not an option, then the EU had little in the way of policy. This is changing. In a sense, we are witnessing the birth of the EU as a full foreign-policy actor, able to develop a variety of policies to promote its interests abroad.

Finally, despite all of the reports of the death of the EU's Common Foreign and Security Policy (CFSP), the crisis over Iraq saw the EU emerge as a security actor in 2003, now with military operations in Africa and the Balkans. The Iraq crisis also stimulated thinking on the development of an EU Security Strategy, drafted in June 2003 by the EU High Representative for Common Foreign and Security Policy, Javier Solana, and formally approved by member states in December 2003.[4] The Security Strategy stresses the need to have a belt of well-governed countries on the EU's periphery and to develop the strategic partnership between Brussels and Moscow. Although there are myriad problems, the European Security and Defence Policy (ESDP) is not dead. Far from it.

The forces driving the EU and Russia to consider their needs and the nature of their relations more intensely thus stem from internal developments within each of the parties. Russia, under Putin, has recognised the importance of the EU as its main trading partner, as well as the increasing role to be played by the EU not only in Europe, but also in relation to wider security developments. Russia can no longer afford to ignore or misunderstand the EU. As for the EU, although it underlined the importance of its relations with Russia throughout the 1990s, the imperative of enlargement, and the shifts associated with the process, have obliged it to start to consider seriously its interests and priorities with regard to Russia. For most of the 1990s, the EU remained distant from Russia, both in policy and geographical terms; enlargement has placed the Union on the doorstep of Russia.[5]

EU policy towards Russia has gone through two main stages. The first began with the Partnership and Cooperation Agreement (PCA), which was finalised at the European Council meeting in Corfu, Greece, in June 1994. (The Common Strategy on the Russian Federation was another feature of EU policy in this first period.) While the PCA remains the cornerstone of EU–Russia relations, the Union launched a new approach towards Russia in 2003 with the Wider Europe initiative and in 2004 with the comprehensive review of its Russia policy. This demonstrates that, throughout the 1990s and in the early twenty-first century, the EU has attempted to develop an appropriate mechanism for interacting with Russia. The internal review of EU policy undertaken in early 2004 is a sign that a satisfactory solution has still to be found.

The PCA and the Common Strategy

The PCA, comprising 112 articles, ten annexes, two protocols and a joint declaration, and running to no less than 178 pages, is mostly concerned with trade and economics.[6] The 'partnership' has numerous goals, ranging from increasing economic ties, to supporting Russia's democratic and market transition, to the eventual creation of a free-trade area.[7] Classifying Russia as a state with a transition economy, the PCA goes some way towards liberalising trade, based on the mutual exchange of most-favoured nation status. Despite having a strong technical focus, the PCA also sets the objective of developing a 'political dialogue' between the EU and Russia to 'bring about an increasing convergence of positions on international issues of mutual concern, thus increasing security and stability'. The PCA also determined a number of institutional mechanisms for EU–Russia interaction: biannual presidential summits; annual meetings of a Cooperation Council (at the ministerial level); biannual meetings of a Cooperation Committee (at the level of senior officials); and regular meetings of nine Sub-Committees, and a Parliamentary Cooperation Committee.

More than anything else, the PCA highlights the deeply technical nature of the EU–Russia relationship, which, notwithstanding a quick reference to political dialogue, remains overwhelmingly focused on trade matters. Moreover, the institutional layers of the dialogue underline the heavily bureaucratic nature of the relationship. The structure and pace of the dialogue are more a function of the internal requirements of the EU than of the relationship itself. For example, the biannual summits are determined by the rotating EU presidency and not by the need for continual high-level discussion.

The implementation of the PCA was soon undermined by developments within Russia. The governments that served under Russian President Boris Yeltsin throughout the 1990s never pushed for the full application of many of its terms. As a result, in the words of the former British Ambassador to Moscow, Sir Rodric Braithwaite, 'the practical results of the PCA have been disappointing'.[8] Moscow's reluctance stemmed from a desire to control the pace of reform and to protect certain sectors of the economy. Russian governmental inefficiency and lack of competence were additional factors. Furthermore, entry into force of the PCA was delayed until December 1997 because of EU concerns over the first war in Chechnya (1994–96). The Chechen 'irritant' forced the EU and Russia to approve an Interim Agreement, signed in July 1995, to regulate their relations.[9]

The Common Strategy on Russia, approved in Cologne, Germany, in June 1999, was the Union's first attempt to formulate a shared vision.[10] In some respects, the Common Strategy was a limited exercise: it remains underpinned by the PCA, and no additional resources have been dedicated to developing relations with Russia. At the same time, the stated goal of the Common Strategy is to assist 'Russia's return to its rightful place in the European family in a spirit of friendship, cooperation, fair accommodation of interests and on the foundations of shared values, enshrined in the common heritage of European civilisation'. To achieve this grandiose objective, the Common Strategy set forth four aims.

- To consolidate democracy, the rule of law and public institutions in Russia.
- To integrate Russia into a common European economic and social space.
- To increase stability and security in Europe and beyond through cooperation.
- To respond jointly to common challenges on the European continent, such as nuclear safety, organised crime and environmental hazards.

It is important to note three features of the Common Strategy. First, it called for a more efficient, operational and permanent political dialogue 'to bring [the EU and Russia] closer together and to respond jointly to some of the challenges to security on the European continent'. The document expressed specific support for joint foreign-policy initiatives. In addition, the EU allowed for the possibility of Russian participation in its operations 'when the EU avails itself of the WEU [Western European Union] for missions within the range of the St Petersburg tasks'. The Common Strategy envisaged cooperation with Russia in all areas of peace support, ranging from conflict prevention and conflict management to conflict resolution. The political and security dialogue was situated in the context of the development of a 'new European security architecture', which was to include the Organisation for Security and Co-operation in Europe (OSCE). These points laid the foundation for the security dialogue that was launched under Putin.

A second feature of the Common Strategy was its assumption that, for Russia to return to the 'European family', it had to become like Europe. The Common Strategy sought the full transformation of Russia.[11] The list of actions that Russia was required to carry out was dizzying. A few examples illustrate the point: 'In the first instance, an operational market economy needs to be put in place'; 'The rule of law is a prerequisite for the development of a market economy which offers opportunities and benefits to all the citizens of Russia'; and 'The emergence of civil society in all areas is indispensable for the consolidation of democracy in Russia'. The tone of the Common Strategy was at once condescending and vapid. It recognised that Russia would not become a candidate for membership, yet the Union's approach resembled the heavily conditional and interventionist one that it had developed for the accession countries. As a result, the Common Strategy demonstrated a tension between the comprehensive demands placed on Russia by the Union and the limited end game that was envisaged for the relationship.

A third feature of the Common Strategy that complicated relations between Brussels and Moscow was the emphasis on values. On the one hand, it stated that the EU had a 'strategic interest' in Russia. At the same time, though, it explicitly declared that a reinforced relationship between the EU and Russia must be based on 'shared democratic values'. The Common Strategy thus contained two gauges for considering a partnership with Russia: the 'strategic' and the 'democratic'. The tension between them has yet to be resolved.

The Common Strategy stimulated Russian thinking on the EU. In some respects, however, former Foreign Minister Yevgeny Primakov had already started to give serious thought to the issue in 1998. Indeed, entry into force of the PCA forced Moscow to formulate policy more clearly than it had done so previously.[12] The result was a more sober understanding of the EU among Russian officials, with increasing recognition that EU enlargement, in particular, might represent a cause for concern.[13] The Common Strategy led Moscow, in 1999, to commission a group of Russian experts from inside and outside of government to draft a response. The result was 'The Medium Term Strategy for the Development of Relations between the Russian Federation and the EU (2000–10)', written in mid-1999 and presented to the EU in October of that year by Putin (who was then still prime minister).[14]

Wider Europe and the Comprehensive Review

The prospect of enlargement in 2004 initiated a review of EU relations with Russia. The starting point for this review was the European Commission-led process to determine a strategy towards the new neighbours of the enlarged Union, including Russia. Then, in December 2003, the European Council called for a specific review of EU policy towards Russia.

A letter sent from British Foreign Secretary Jack Straw to the European Council in March 2002 instigated the process of formulating an EU strategy towards its new and old neighbours.[15] This was followed by a decision – taken in Luxembourg on 15 April 2002 – to task the EU Commissioner for External Relations, Chris Patten, and Solana with exploring further the notion of a 'Wider Europe'. During the summer, the Danish presidency organised meetings on the matter at the level of political directors. In September, Patten and Solana made a joint presentation to the European Council, in which they called for a new regional and national framework to underpin relations with Belarus, Moldova and Ukraine – at this stage they did not include Russia. The General Affairs and External Relations Council agreed on 18 November on the 'need for the EU to formulate an ambitious, long-term and integrated approach towards each of these countries'.[16] At the European Council meeting in Copenhagen, Denmark, on 13 December 2002, what was now called the 'Wider Europe–New Neighbourhood' initiative was expanded to include southern Mediterranean countries and Russia.[17] With this new mandate, the European Commission gathered information from future members, before finally presenting its communication on 11 March 2003.[18]

Twenty-seven pages long, the communication was designed to start a debate within the enlarged EU and between the EU and its neighbours about the new geographic reality and its consequences.[19] Its explicit premise is EU recognition of the interdependence of the Union and its neighbouring states. This is seen to impose a 'duty' on the EU to promote political stability, economic development and poverty reduction in a 'shared environment'. The new neighbourhood framework is targeted at states that do not currently enjoy the prospect of EU membership. The document is clear: 'A response to the practical issues posed by proximity and neighbourhood should be seen as separate from the question of EU accession.' Although eventual membership is not ruled out, the neighbourhood framework is not on the same track as accession. Also, with regard to Belarus, Moldova and Ukraine, the communication creates a new conceptual category: the 'Western Newly Independent States' (WNIS). Russia is seen as being distinct from these nations. Finally, the communication is founded on the concepts of 'differentiation' and 'progressivity'. Differentiation concerns the different levels of relations required depending on the state in question, while progressivity refers to the progress that this state has made in reaching agreed benchmarks of reform.

In order to meet its objective, the communication proposes that the EU offer incentives ranging from extending internal market and regulatory structures to offering preferential trading relations, raising the long-term possibility of the lawful migration and movement of peoples, and integration into EU energy, telecommunications and transport networks. These will be laid out in an Action Plan for each neighbouring state. In addition, the EU could become more deeply engaged at the political level in neighbouring states, including in crisis management, and possibly even 'internal security arrangements' (the Moldovan conflict is mentioned). The communication also proposes the creation of a new financial assistance programme – a Neighbourhood Instrument.

The communication is the first systematic attempt by the EU to consider a policy towards its new Eastern neighbourhood. It contains a number of interesting ideas that mark the birth of the EU as a more complete foreign-policy actor. Nonetheless, with regard to Russia, the communication fails to answer a number of important questions.[20] What does the new neighbourhood policy mean for relations with Russia? The EU already has a Common Strategy towards Russia – does the new approach override this? Are relations with Russia downgraded as a result? Being placed in the same category as Belarus and Moldova is unlikely to satisfy Moscow. More fundamentally, will Russia welcome the deep engagement in its internal affairs that the EU promises through its Action Plans? Again, this is unlikely. Finally, how will Russia respond to the EU's promise of greater security involvement in the WNIS?

By early 2004, it had become clear that the Wider Europe project was unlikely to satisfy the Russian leadership. The Russian government is uncomfortable with being included in the same group of countries as Moldova and Morocco, given that Brussels and Moscow have declared their intention to build a 'strategic partnership'. For Moscow, this implies the development of special relations with Brussels, reflecting the weight and importance of Russia as a European partner. Moreover, the Russian leadership has posited its objectives for the strategic partnership through the concept of common spaces. The EU accepted the form, if not the substance, of the Russian proposal at the St Petersburg Summit of May 2003.

The St Petersburg Summit determined the goals of the four common spaces. First is a common European economic space. Efforts in this area will concentrate on establishing a more open and integrated market between Russia and the EU.[21] On the one hand, Russia is seeking to offset the potential costs of enlargement to its national trade and to create mechanisms to manage its reliance on the EU. On the other hand, it is looking to create opportunities for greater European investment in the Russian economy. The Rome Summit of November 2003 saw agreement on a concept paper dealing with the setting up of this space.[22]

Second is a common freedom, security and justice space. In non-EU parlance, this means initiating discussions on the long-term prospects for visa-free travel. Due to the enlargement of the EU, Russian citizens have lost the right to visa-free travel in the countries of Central and Eastern Europe, because new member states are required to assume the obligations established by the Schengen regime, currently regulating the control of external borders and the issuance of visas within the EU. Moscow refers to the Schengen zone as a new 'Berlin Wall', believing that it will divide the European continent into insiders (in an integrating union that takes up most of the continent) and outsiders (those relegated to the sidelines of Europe). Putin has gone to great pains to put the question of visa-free travel on the EU agenda and has achieved some success. Resolution of the matter is a long way off, however, as the EU is unsatisfied with the state of border control and migration management in Russia and the countries of the Commonwealth of Independent States (CIS), and Russia has still not signed a Readmissions Agreement with the European Union.

Third is a common space for research and education. The EU and Russia have signed a number of agreements that allow Russia access to EU educational exchange programmes. This common space is seen in Russia as a sign of EU recognition of the shared cultural and historical heritage of Russia and Europe.

Fourth is a common space for external security. This implies cooperation in the realm of international relations and crisis management, including the maintenance of peace and stability in the Balkans, and collaboration within the Quartet to promote a settlement of the Israeli-Palestinian conflict.

However, by January 2004, the EU had carried out a comprehensive review of its Russia policy. This was triggered by three factors. First, the prospect of enlargement carried with it the objective requirement that both Brussels and Moscow review its impact on their relations. In January 2004, the Russian government put to the EU 14 concerns about enlargement, ranging from the quantitative limits on Russian steel exports, Russia's grain quota, tariff questions, and barriers to Russian agricultural exports, to the non-application of restrictions on Russian energy supplies and the sustainable development of Kaliningrad. EU member states were concerned that Russia would refuse to extend automatically the PCA to the ten newcomers from 1 May 2004.

Second, EU member states had become increasingly concerned about developments in Russia that called into question the existence of shared values as a foundation for the strategic partnership. In early 2004, the list of EU concerns was long, ranging from the arrest of Mikhail Khodorkovsky to the conduct of parliamentary and presidential elections and the continuing low-level conflict in Chechnya.

Third, in late 2003, many EU member states called for a review of the Union's internal mechanisms for formulating and implementing its Russia policy. For many, the EU–Russia Summit in Rome in November confirmed the need for a clear and accepted common policy towards Russia – in which EU interests would be clearly defended – in order to minimise the ability of certain member states to hold Union policy hostage to their own inclinations. This perception coincided with general recognition that the 1999 Common Strategy had failed.

The Irish presidency took up the baton, and was instrumental in pushing through the review in early 2004, developing a presidency paper on the question in February. In the run-up to the meeting of the General Affairs and External Relations Council on 23 February 2004, the European Commission submitted its views in a Communication on Relations with Russia (dated 9 February 2004).[23] The communication stated that the increasing strains in EU–Russia relations necessitate a policy review and that the EU has not been effective in developing a common position towards Russia or in defending the interests of the Union. For an EU document, the communication is surprisingly blunt: 'Despite common interests, growing economic interdependence and certain steps forward, there has been insufficient overall progress on substance.'

Departing from these points, the European Commission has proposed a number of measures to ensure greater internal coordination and greater coordination between member states with regard to the making of policy on Russia, including the drafting of objective papers before summits. The communication also recommended that the EU start more actively to link issues on which Russia seeks progress with those that are of concern to the Union. Finally, the European Commission called for the development of a 'Permanent Partnership Council', which will serve as a key institutional mechanism to link Brussels and Moscow on a number of levels and to address different questions.

The conclusions of the meeting of the General Affairs and External Relations Council on 23 February 2004 signalled a hardening of the EU position on Russia, raising the prospect of a 'serious impact on EU–Russia relations in general' if Russia refused to extend the PCA to the new member states from 1 May. The council also agreed to strengthen the Permanent Partnership Council to make it a primary institutional link between Brussels and Moscow. Overall, EU member states seek more balanced and results-orientated cooperation with Russia, and have pledged to identify more clearly EU interests and priorities with respect to Russia and to pursue them more coherently.

The comprehensive review undertaken by the Irish presidency marks the end of the first phase of EU policymaking towards Russia and the start of a new period. The PCA remains the cornerstone of cooperation. However, the EU has also accepted the desire of Russia to develop four common spaces. With all of this, the Union's earlier Common Strategy has been quietly abandoned. Thus, the question of developing a fitting mechanism for EU–Russia relations remains open.

The first step was made at the EU–Russia summit in May 2004 when both sides managed to overcome these disagreements. Russia agreed to extend the PCA and the EU agreed to support Russia's application for WTO membership. Together the EU and Russia decided they would adopt a 'road map' on developing common spaces at their November 2004 summit.

Russia's role in the EU's neighbourhood policy was redefined. A new formula was adopted replacing the Wider Europe strategy. In May 2004 the European Commission released a communication on the European Neighbourhood Policy (ENP) which applies to the WNIS, the South Caucasus states (and non-EU Mediterranean states), but which excludes Russia. At the EU–Russia summit of the same month, the two parties agreed that the EU's neighbourhood policy towards Russia would be conducted within the framework of the common spaces.

The EU–Russia political dialogue
Dialogue dimensions
For all of its difficulties, political dialogue between the EU and Russia is more frequent than that between the EU and any other party. In addition to biannual summits, regular consultations take place between members of the EU's Political and Security Committee (COPS) – the main EU body concerned with security decision-making – and the Russian Ambassador to Brussels. Meetings between the chair of the EU Military Committee and officials from the Russian Ministry of Defence first occurred in May

2002. Later that year, Russia assigned a liaison officer to the EU Military Staff in Brussels.

The political dialogue has five dimensions.[24] First, the EU and Russia have looked to coordinate their positions on wider foreign-policy issues. In the Balkans, the EU has taken the lead with Russia's tacit consent, while there has been greater and more equal cooperation in the Middle East, even if both stand in the shadow of the US. Dialogue on the former Soviet Union has been limited. The EU has sought to use the political dialogue to influence Russian policy on the conflicts in Moldova and the south Caucasus and to address the question of Belarus, but to little avail. Despite similar views on a number of international security questions – ranging from the role of the United Nations (UN) to that of the Quartet in the Israeli–Palestinian conflict – the dialogue thus far has produced few meaningful joint positions.

Second, Brussels and Moscow have exchanged views on concepts of conflict prevention and crisis management. In 2001, the Russian Ministry of Defence developed proposals for joint military crisis-management activities with the EU, and, in 2002, Russia's Ministry for Emergency Situations presented to Brussels a concept for civilian crisis management. Direct contacts have been established with both departments in Moscow, but the fact that the EU has not yet developed its own concepts has prevented cooperation from advancing in this area.

However, the EU has worked out modalities for the participation of Russian forces in EU crisis-management operations.[25] After the formulation of a 'concept of operations', Russia may be invited to participate and attend a force-generation conference, which would bring together potential contributors. If Russia provides 'significant forces', Moscow will have the same rights as participating EU member states in the so-called Committee of Contributors, the body responsible for managing the ESDP mission in question. The possibility of Russian involvement emerged in 2002 during planning for the European Union Police Mission (EUPM) in Bosnia-Herzegovina. Russia sent five officers to participate in the operation, which was launched in January 2003. Russia's involvement in the EU's first crisis-management mission, even if civilian based and limited, is significant in that it signals Russia's willingness to work under EU command in the Balkans.

The terrorist attacks of 11 September 2001 brought the third topic – counter-terrorism – to the fore. In October 2001, the EU and Russia agreed: to exchange information on terrorist activities and networks; to ban such groups from their territories; to block terrorist groups' sources of finance; and to swap intelligence on dubious transactions.[26] In late 2002, the EU and Russia pledged to cooperate in bringing to justice the 'perpetrators, organizers, and sponsors of terrorist acts'.[27] Cooperation between the EU and Russia to combat organised crime, including money laundering and arms and drug smuggling, may be seen as an indirect facet of cooperation in the sphere of counter-terrorism. There had already been some cooperation on this prior to 11 September 2001; a joint Action Plan to counter organised crime in the Russian Federation was launched in 2000.[28] Although cooperative efforts got off to a slow start, meetings of the Russian and EU Justice and Home Affairs Ministers are now becoming routine.

Fourth, the Russian government under Putin has been keen to develop military/technical cooperation in areas of perceived comparative advantage. Europe's lack of a strategic airlift capability has long been noted; Russia has offered its resources to fill the gap. European states have decided to develop a specifically European capability, however: the A-400M aircraft is slated to come online by 2007. Moscow has proposed that the EU draw on Russia's satellite imaging capabilities to bolster the ESDP. Indeed, the EU Satellite Centre has purchased Russian satellite images in the past, but no special relationship has been established.

Finally, the EU and Russia cooperate on questions of nuclear safety and disarmament. Both parties maintain a similar position on the need to reinforce multilateral arms control and disarmament agreements, such as the Nuclear Non-Proliferation Treaty. More specifically, in December 1999, the EU approved a joint action establishing a Cooperation Programme for Non-Proliferation and Disarmament in the Russian Federation. The programme supports the development of a culture of nuclear safety and the creation of appropriate monitoring agencies in Russia. Since the June 2002 G-8 Summit in Kananaskis, Canada, EU programmes have become part of a wider effort to support the dismantling and securing of Russia's nuclear, biological and chemical weapons, agents, materials and infrastructure. Twenty billion dollars has been pledged to the G-8-led Global Partnership over the next ten years, of which the EU has promised to donate €1bn.[29]

In sum, Brussels and Moscow have cleared a certain amount of ground and laid out a course for the future. Nonetheless, the dialogue remains nascent and largely declaratory. Serious challenges hinder more meaningful progress.

Challenges

At the most basic level, Russia and the EU are different kinds of actors.[30] Russia is a sovereign state, with a political, economic and military system that it is seeking to consolidate, an elected leadership that is dedicated to advancing the interests of the state, and institutions that coordinate the means to achieve desired ends. The EU is nothing of the sort. It has divided institutions, unclear sovereignty, a weak sense of common interest, and few institutions in the political arena that are able to meet independently the declared aims of the Union. Europe is as much a union of interests as a community with shared values. Moscow sees the blending of values and interests in EU policy and rhetoric as interference in Russian affairs. As a result, EU statements about the Chechen conflict have only provoked irritation in Moscow, as have European declarations about the need for the fair application of the rule of law during the Yukos affair.

The EU and Russia also hold different views on EU security policy. For Moscow, the ESDP should advance Russia's interests by providing a European security model that grants Moscow an equal say in all security issues, and, more broadly, serves as an instrument to create a greater Europe. The EU sees the ESDP in a very different way. For the EU, the ESDP is not a motor to spur the creation of a common European security space, but, rather, a limited EU foreign-policy instrument.

Consequently, the modalities governing Russian involvement in ESDP operations fall short of Russian demands. At an optimum, Moscow seeks equality with EU member states at every level of decision-making – that is, a joint EU–Russia assessment of a situation and agreement on whether it constitutes a crisis (Russia did not view events in Kosovo in the same way as the North Atlantic Treaty Organisation (NATO), for example), followed by joint planning and joint command and control. For the EU, however, non-EU states may participate in an ESDP operation if they desire to do so, and the EU believes that their participation is necessary. Yet external involvement allows for just that, involvement, nothing more, certainly not full participation in decision-making. Even if a non-EU party does provide significant forces to an ESDP operation, that state is still not invited to help draft the concept of operations.

The conditions for Russian involvement in EU operations are less accommodating than those for NATO missions. Linked to this is the EU's vague stance on whether it will seek a UN mandate for all of its operations. The EU's desire potentially not to seek the sanction of the UN worries Russia, which wants to avoid a repetition of the Kosovo case, when a regional organisation used force without the approval of the UN. Putin's government is also concerned about the growing geographical scope of EU operations, specifically, that the EU is considering establishing operations within a 4,000km radius of Brussels, possibly up to Russia's borders in the former Soviet Union. Russia's concern here is that the ESDP will follow the path of the OSCE, narrowing its focus to centre on Russia. Russia seeks to be a subject of the ESDP, not its object.

Moreover, in security terms, neither the EU nor Russia has yet to experience an immediate and pressing need for the other. Both are still caught up in their own internal transformation projects.[31] Disparate priorities reduce the urgency to develop deeper ties.

Factors specific to the EU and Russia have also hampered the security dialogue. Russian policy is heavily presidential. The vast bureaucracies of the Ministry of Foreign Affairs and the 'power' ministries standing behind Putin are conservative and often obstructionist. Meanwhile, in Brussels, the dispersal of decision-making power between different institutions affects the EU's ability to interact strategically with Moscow, projecting the internal composition of the EU on to its relationship with Russia. Indeed, the biannual summits are more a function of the EU presidency which rotates to a different member state every six months than the needs of the partnership.

Finally, and partly as a result of the factors discussed above, the political dialogue has tended to lurch from one crisis to another. The style of Russian diplomacy in relation to the EU bears much responsibility for creating continual crises. The sequence of events surrounding the matter of transit to and from Kaliningrad in 2002 and the issue of the automatic extension of the PCA to the new EU member states in May 2004 demonstrates Moscow's tendency to raise the stakes rhetorically on questions of discord with the EU. Moscow is trying to maximise its eventual gains in negotiations with the Union by dividing EU member states into two camps: those that prefer to compromise with Russia and those that are less accommodating. To be fair, the EU is a very difficult organisation with which to negotiate, with different sources of authority and with member states with varied interests. At times, shouting may indeed be the only way to be heard. However, the results have not been entirely inspiring for Russia either on the issue of Kaliningrad or EU enlargement.

Conclusion

The conflict in Moldova provided an important indirect testing ground for EU–Russia relations in 2003.[32] In May 2003, the European Council initiated a discussion on the possibility of EU involvement in a peace consolidation mission in Moldova – which lies on the periphery of both the EU and Russia – replacing the current Russian-led peacekeeping operation and underpinning a settlement between the Moldovan government and the separatist Transdniestrian authorities. In response, Russian Ministry of Foreign Affairs' spokesperson Aleksandr Yakovlenko declared on 21 July 2003 that: 'One should [...] avoid any statements or initiatives which complicate the already very difficult negotiations and prematurely distract the attention of their participants from the most vital substantive issues of settlement and lastly that are taken without a prior diplomatic discussion with the use of the well-oiled negotiating mechanisms.'[33] Facing the recalcitrance of Russia, and, therefore, of Transdniestria, the EU retreated, even if it remains poised to become engaged in a post-settlement security arrangement.

Russia also learned the lesson that unilateral initiatives can fail. On 16 November, to the great surprise of the EU, the OSCE and the US, Dmitry Kozak, then Deputy Head of the Russian Presidential Administration, presented a draft memorandum on a division of competencies between Moldova's central authorities and the Transdniestrian leadership. The memorandum called for the creation of a new Federal Republic of Moldova that, in practice, would have attributed so many powers to the federal subject – Transdniestria – that, in effect, Moldova would have become a confederation. Under intense domestic pressure, Moldovan President Vladimir Voronin decided not to sign the memorandum, much to the ire of Moscow (reportedly Putin's plane had been readied for a visit to Chisinau for a signature ceremony). The OSCE ministerial meeting in Maastricht, Netherlands, in early December confirmed the collapse of the Russian plan. Almost all of the OSCE participating states called for a return to the multilateral negotiating format and the deployment of a genuinely multinational peace-support mission to secure any settlement that might be reached.

More than ten years after the collapse of the Soviet Union, the EU and Russia have finally started to develop conscious and considered policies towards each other. Within the EU, the Wider Europe communication represented a first attempt to clarify a new Eastern border policy. But this is not enough to consolidate relations with Russia, leading the European Council to review its policy and to present new policy guidelines. A first test of the new border relationship emerged as a result of the issue of transit to and from Kaliningrad; for the moment, an effective compromise has been found. In practical terms, Moldova represents another testing ground for new 'border' relations. Moldova is an enduring 'frontier' in the region, separating Russia and the EU, where the lines of power are unclear. It is characterised by overlapping spheres of influence and different interests.

EU enlargement has changed the geography of Europe, bringing the EU and Russia much closer to one another and raising a host of new questions in regard to their relationship. Enlargement has also created a new EU for Russia: some of the new members have difficult relations with Moscow and most have adopted tougher policies towards Moscow compared to the old EU member states. As a result, there is likely to be a period of pushing and shoving in the dark, as new relations are defined, particularly in the new border region.

Notes

1 Heather Grabbe draws an imperial analogy in her overview of EU enlargement policies, 'The Challenges of EU Enlargement', in Lieven, A. and Trenin, D. (eds), *Ambivalent Neighbors: The EU, NATO and the Price of Membership* (Washington, DC: The Brookings Institution, 2003), pp. 67–89.

2 Communication from the European Commission to the European Council and the European Parliament, *Wider Europe – Neighbourhood: A New Framework for Relations with our Eastern and Southern Neighbours*, COM (2003) 104, Brussels, 11 March 2003.

3 See, for example, Pelczynka-Natecz, K., Dukba, A., Poti, L. and Vatapek, V., *The Eastern Policy of the EU: The Visegrad Countries' Perspective* (Warsaw: Centre for Eastern Studies, February 2003); Gromadzki, G. and Boralynski, J., *The Half-Open Door: The Eastern Border of the Enlarged EU*, Policy Papers 'On the Future of Europe', Policy Paper 2 (Warsaw: Stefan Batory Foundation, March 2001); Gromadzki, G. et al., *The Enlarged EU and Ukraine – New Relations* (Warsaw: Stefan Batory Foundation with the Centre for European Policy Studies (CEPS), 2003); Naumczuk, A. et al., *The Forgotten Neighbour – Belarus in the Context of EU Enlargement to the East*, Policy Papers 'On the Future of Europe', Policy Paper 4 (Warsaw: Stefan Batory Foundation, September 2001); and *New Neighbourhood – New Association: Ukraine and the EU at the Beginning of the 21st Century*, Policy Papers 'On the Future of Europe', Policy Paper 6 (Warsaw: Stefan Batory Foundation, March 2002).

4 *A Secure Europe in a Better World, European Security Strategy*, available online at www.iss-eu.org/solana/solanae.pdf.

5 Of course, the EU has shared a border with Russia for a number of years, following the accession of Finland to the EU in 1995. The point here is that the 2004 wave of enlargement is on a qualitatively different scale, and raises a host of new questions.

6 Much of the following discussion of the PCA is taken from *Russia Faces Europe* by this author, Chaillot Paper No. 60 (Paris: European Union Institute for Security Studies, May 2003).

7 See www.europa.eu.int/comm/external_relations/ceeca/pca/pca_russia.pdf.

8 Braithwaite, R., *Russia in Europe* (London: Centre for European Reform, 1999), p. 33.

9 *European Community–Russian Federation: Trade and Trade-related Matters/ Interim Agreement*, Press: 224 Nr: 9010/95, 17 July 1995.

10 'Common Strategy of the EU on Russia of 4 June 1999', *Official Journal of the European Communities*, 1999/414/CFSP, European Union's Publication Office, 24 June 1999.

11 See the discussion in Haukkala, H., *The Making of the EU Common Strategy on Russia*, Working Paper 28 (Helsinki: Finnish Institute of International Affairs, 2000).

12 'EU–Russia: Cooperation Council, First Meeting, CFSP, Presidency Statement', Press: 15 Nr: 05273/98, 27 January 1998.

13 On early Russian policy, see Leshukov, I., *Beyond Satisfaction: Russia's Perceptions on European Integration* (Bonn: Center for European Integration Studies, 1999).

14 Available on the website of the delegation of the European Commission in Russia, www.eur.ru/eng/neweur/user_eng.php?func=apage&id=53.

15 Interviews by the author with officials in the European Commission and the Secretariat of the European Council, Brussels, April 2003.

16 General Affairs and External Relations Council, doc.14078/02, 18 November 2002.

17 At the insistence of the President of the European Commission, Romano Prodi, it would seem.

18 *Wider Europe – Neighbourhood*, op. cit.

19 Interview by the author with an official in the European Commission, Brussels, April 2003.

20 For a more general and complete analysis of the communication, see Lynch, D., 'The New Eastern Dimension of the Enlarged EU', in 'Wider Europe', Chaillot Paper, (Paris: European Union Institute for Security Studies, 2004).

21 See *The Common European Economic Space: The Concept Paper*, Annex One to the Joint Statement, agreed at the Rome Summit, 7 November 2003.

22 Available at http://europa.eu.int/comm/external_relations/russia/summit11_03/1concl.pdf (accessed on 16 December 2003).

23 *Communication from the Commission to the Council and the European Parliament on Relations with Russia*, COM (2004) 106, 9 February 2004.

24 See the author's discussion in 'Russia's Strategic Partnership with Europe', *Washington Quarterly*, 27(2), Spring 2004, pp. 99–118.

25 *Presidency Report on ESDP*, 10160/2/02 REV 2 ESDP 188, Annex IV, Arrangements for Consultation and Cooperation Between the EU and Russia on Crisis Management, Brussels, 22 June 2002.

26 *Statement on International Terrorism*, EU–Russia Summit Press Release 342Nr 12423/01, Brussels, 3 October 2001.

27 *Joint Statement on the Fight Against Terrorism*, EU–Russia Summit, Brussels, 11 November 2002.

28 *European Union Action Plan on Common Action for the Russian Federation on Combating Organised Crime*, Report No. 2000/C 106/02, Official Journal

C 106, 13 April 2000, pp. 0005–0012.

29 For more on EU programmes in this area, see Höhl, K., Müller, H. and Schaper, A., 'European Union', in Einhorn, R.J. and Flournoy, M.A., *Protecting Against the Spread of Nuclear, Biological and Chemical Weapons: An Action Agenda for the Global Partnership, Volume 3: International Responses*, CSIS Report (Washington, DC: Center for Strategic and International Studies, January 2003).

30 See also the discussion by Vahl, M., *Just Good Friends? The EU–Russia 'Strategic Partnership' and the Northern Dimension*, CEPS Working Document No. 166, Brussels, March 2001.

31 This point is made by Danilov, D., *The EU's Rapid Reaction Capability*, CEPS and the International Institute for Strategic Studies (IISS), European Security Forum (ESF) Working Paper No. 4, Brussels, November 2001.

32 For an exploration of a possible EU operation in Moldova, see Lynch, D., *Russia Faces Europe*.

33 See the report by the Information and Press Department, Ministry of Foreign Affairs, Moscow, 21 July 2003, available at www.mid.ru (accessed on 17 December 2003).

2. The Northern Dimension of EU Foreign Policy

Hiski Haukkala

The end of the Cold War has opened up a new geopolitical landscape in northern Europe. The old question of a chronic conflict between the Soviet Union and the Atlantic Alliance, with two neutral states – Finland and Sweden – sandwiched in between, has been swept aside. The Soviet Union has dissolved, while the European Union (EU)'s presence in the region has expanded. This process has had major implications, both for the Union itself and for northern European countries and other local actors.

For the EU, it has meant increased exposure to northern Europe in general, and to the Russian Federation in particular. For the states in northern Europe, the new situation has brought new challenges, as they have been called upon to cooperate with, and seek influence over, the EU, an entity that previously enjoyed only a marginal presence in the region.[1]

The challenge has been perhaps severest for Russia, a country still grappling with the forces of disintegration, and seeking to forge a new identity while coming to terms with external pressures for increased cooperation and openness in the north.

It is against this background that the emergence of a Northern Dimension (ND) in the EU's agenda must be examined. Since 1995, the EU has, for the first time, enjoyed direct physical contact with Russia in the form of the 1,300-kilometre Finnish–Russian border. With the 2004 enlargement, this exposure has grown further. The accession of Estonia, Lithuania and Poland has doubled the length of the border that the EU shares with Russia, and also resulted in part of the Federation – Kaliningrad *oblast* – becoming an enclave within the enlarged EU.

Enlargement will increase the importance of the EU's relations with Russia. It will also raise challenges for the EU's regional component – the ND. Moreover, with the advent of new Central and Eastern European members, new 'dimensions' may emerge. Poland, for example, has talked of the need for an 'eastern dimension'. Regardless of whether the EU decides to adopt new dimensions, or whether a more overarching neighbourhood policy is pursued, the question of managing its outer boundaries will remain salient in coming years.

The ND can be seen as the most innovative policy the EU has devised for the management of its external boundary. But it has had a mixed record. On the one hand, it has raised awareness about northern issues within the EU, and generated some new, although fairly modest, funds.[2] On the other, the actual results of the initiative have been disappointing, especially when compared to its initial ambitious objectives.[3] The challenge of 'dimensionalism' has proved too difficult for the Union, and in the post-enlargement era is likely to become more difficult still.[4] With the advent of new neighbours, there is a need for new policies that are potentially much more challenging. For example, answering Ukraine's calls for closer ties in a manner that is acceptable to both parties, and engaging isolationist and authoritarian Belarus, are likely to be more difficult for the EU than administering the current 'strategic partnership' with Russia. Circumstances will call for new approaches to the EU's new neighbours, but will also force the EU to define its relations with Russia more clearly. Simply put, the question that the EU must answer is whether Russia will be allowed to retain its place as the strategic partner par excellence – and what role that might entail in the future – or will Russia be put into the same basket as the rest of the EU's neighbours?

The Northern Dimension

In September 1997, Finnish Prime Minister Paavo Lipponen launched the ND initiative. In a speech in Rovaniemi in Lapland, Lipponen argued that, with the accession to the EU of Sweden and Finland in 1995, the EU had acquired a 'northern dimension'. This presented the Union with a double challenge: first, how to prevent the emergence of new dividing lines and to handle the multitude of 'soft' security threats, especially emanating from north-western Russia; and second, how to benefit from the vast economic opportunities that the region provided, especially in energy (oil and natural gas) and forestry.[5]

Lipponen pointed out that the EU did not have a policy on tackling these issues, and suggested that it should adopt one. Such a policy would tie together the EU and northern European countries (Estonia, Iceland, Latvia, Lithuania, Norway, Poland and Russia) as partners in devising and implementing a coherent approach to the region. But the ND would not be a new EU policy with its own budget line. Rather, it would draw on the policies and financial instruments that already existed in the region. In essence, it would seek to act as an 'organising principle' for existing cooperation in the north. This made sense, given that even in 1997 there was no shortage of regionally based cooperation in northern Europe.[6]

The initiative was quick to gather political momentum, and was officially accepted as part of the EU's external relations in 1998. This was done on the basis of a Commission communication which, like Lipponen's original speech, described the ND largely in terms of what it was not: it was not a new institution requiring new money, nor was it a new form of regionally based cooperation in northern Europe.[7] In May 1999, the General Affairs Council (GAC) set guidelines for the initiative's further development. According to the GAC, the 'value added' aspect of the initiative would come solely from better coordination and complementarity between Community and member state actions in northern Europe.[8] The partner countries were invited to comment on the content of the initiative in November 1999, when the first ND foreign ministers' conference took place. The conference, held in Helsinki, reaffirmed the course of action chosen by the GAC and endorsed the idea that the Commission should be asked to draw up an ND action plan.[9]

The Feira European Council adopted the ND action plan for 2000–03 in June 2000. The document spelt out that the ND's main value is to be derived from 'reinforced coordination and complementarity in EU and Member States' programmes and enhanced collaboration between the countries in Northern Europe', and that it is 'an on-going process without a specific budgetary appropriation'.[10] The document also enumerated the relevant sectors of cross-border cooperation, ranging from infrastructure and the environment to public health and justice and home affairs.[11] The list was exhaustive, but the action plan failed to add significant new content in terms of concrete actions to be taken during the first four-year term. The shortcomings in the document have become even more visible in practice: the lack of clear priorities, unclear relationship between the Commission and the sub-regional players and of adequate funding have all been highlighted during the first action plan.[12]

Some of these shortcomings could be addressed in the second plan (2004–06), which was adopted by the Brussels European Council in October 2003.[13] This seeks to improve the focus by identifying five sectors – economy and infrastructure, social issues (including education, training and public health), environment, nuclear safety and natural resources, justice and home affairs, and cross-border cooperation – where clearer objectives and steps are needed.[14] The document also contains a new conceptual innovation, as subsidiarity is mentioned for the first time in this context.[15] Although this can be seen as a sign of the Commission's growing appreciation of the role of partner countries and sub-regional councils, it may also be a move to shift the burden of the ND's implementation and financing to the regional level, and subsequently losing its problematical image of being the prime engine in the development of the policy. This would spell trouble for the entire region-building project in the north, as it could result in a decrease in overall EU interest and funding in the region. This would put the north-western regions of Russia particularly in a precarious position, as they are largely dependent on Western funding for cross-border cooperation with the EU.[16]

The Commission's attempts at burden sharing are understandable: the ND has proved to be a difficult policy to handle, for two reasons. First, the initiative has called for an unprecedented amount of coordination between previously separate pillars and programmes within the Union. This has not been an easy task as the persistent problems in combining funding from, for example, the Tacis and Interreg programmes have shown.[17] Second, the ND's successful implementation requires a multi-level approach, in which actors external to the Union must play a significant role.[18] This has resulted in both internal and external complications. Internally, implementing the ND model in full would require that the partner countries as well as the regional councils were given a role in developing and agreeing the content of EU policies and strategies. But not all in the EU have approved of discussing policies with third parties before a unified EU stance has been reached.[19] Externally, the ND requires that the partners and a host of sub-regional actors are willing to be subordinated to the aims of the ND. But this would mean that they become to all intents and purposes mere sub-contractors of EU policy that has been adopted outside the region. In most cases, and especially in Russia, this has been out of the question.

This interpretation has been contradicted by Sicard Filtenborg, Stefan Gänzle and Elisabeth Johansson, who have argued that the ND could be seen as an 'innovative network governance strategy', whereby the EU draws on existing external resources to strengthen its own problem-solving capacity in the region.[20] The experience so far, however, seems to point to a different conclusion: the EU has not been able to draw on the other actors' resources, nor has its problem-solving capacity been noticeably strengthened.[21] Despite the steady flow of action plans, inventories and annual reports, the EU has not been able to subordinate local players to its will. The Commission is clearly not aware even of the scope of activities that the other players are carrying out in the region. This is reflected, for example, in the Commission's working document on the second action plan, which states that the annual reports, meant to be one of the main instruments for ensuring the coherence of individual actions in the north, have been problematic.[22] Instead of getting access to the required information, the Commission is faced with competition from these local actors. This can easily lead to sub-optimal results, unnecessary duplication and wasted resources.[23]

The EU's own inaction has been another part of the problem. The Commission has taken a relatively passive role in the work of the regional councils. This is largely explained by the lack of clear legal rules in the EU, which would authorise and regulate the Commission's role in this area.[24] As a consequence, the potential of the ND in coordinating and encouraging cross-border cooperation has been under-exploited. To be fair, the main bulk of funding for cross-border cooperation in the north comes from EU sources. For example, the Tacis cross-border cooperation programme allocated €112 million to north-western Russia between 1996 and 2003. In addition, many ND projects have been financed through other Tacis programmes, notably the national programme for Russia. Five programmes under the Interreg III initiative allocate another half a billion euros to cross-border inter-regional cooperation in northern Europe.[25]

Russia – the main and soon virtually the only partner – has been another source of problems for the ND. Russia has not devised a coherent policy towards the ND and has not at any point articulated a clear set of priorities and objectives on the issue.[26] This has not, however, prevented the central government in Moscow from voicing its general dissatisfaction with the content of the initiative. Moscow has frequently complained that its priorities are flawed, with too much emphasis on soft security threats and not enough money being devoted to developing Russian infrastructure and industries, issues that for obvious reasons are not high on the EU's agenda.[27]

But there is also a deeper problem. The EU's emphasis on fostering 'positive mutual interdependence' and attempts at subordinating local activities under the ND framework are generally unwelcome in Russia. Instead of accepting limits to its autonomy by embracing interdependence with the EU, Russia seeks to preserve and maximise its sovereignty and freedom to manoeuvre.[28] The very logic of the ND is alien to Russian thinking about what kind of relationship is feasible with the EU.[29]

The weak role of Russia's north-western regions has also caused complications. The effect that Russian regionalism has had on the ND must be examined against the backdrop of the internal struggle between the centre and the regions in Russia. The tumultuous events of the 1990s – when the very existence of the Federation seemed to be at risk – gave the regions a great degree of independence. As a consequence, the very concept of regionalism has a negative ring to it in Moscow, where it is seen as uncontrolled and unwanted devolution due to the erosion of central power. There is a fear that regionalism could make secessionist conflicts more likely, especially on the outskirts of the Federation.[30] Russian President Vladimir Putin has emphasised the territorial integrity of the Federation, and strengthened the power of the centre over the regions.[31] This has resulted in the regions often lacking the autonomy and resources to make a meaningful contribution to the ND.[32]

Despite Putin's efforts at internal consolidation, the final outcome of these reforms remains unclear. While regional leaders have nominally agreed to these changes, there is a gap between how the law is written and how it is implemented – or rather not implemented – on the regional level.[33] This does not necessarily yield positive results for the ND, as it does not empower the regions to take part in cooperation. Rather, it betrays the lack of rule of law that is endemic to the Russian system. This failing constitutes a source of chronic problems in the wider EU–Russia relationship as well.

There are other problems and obstacles on the regional level that have to be overcome. Some of them are a direct result of the backwardness that cooperation is supposed to surmount, such as the lack of basic infrastructure on the Russian side. These are deep asymmetries and structural problems, and are likely to hinder cooperation well into the future. In addition, historical animosities, an abundance of bureaucracy and a chronic lack of reciprocal funding on the Russian side and differences in mindsets on both sides of the border have also made cooperation difficult.[34] In many cases, cooperation is dependent on funding provided by EU partners and, as a consequence, often more closely resembles development or even humanitarian aid than cooperation between equal partners.[35]

All this has put the EU in a precarious position with regard to its ND. The unclear situation in Russia has both hindered and cautioned against further engagement on the regional level. This has led the EU to adopt an incremental approach. There are three basic features: first, cooperation has been de-politicised by avoiding difficult and divisive issues with Russia, and resides instead in the realms of 'low politics' (social and economic rather than security policies) and technical assistance. Second, cooperation is being strengthened at the same pace as EU enlargement towards Russia, so it seems to be reactive rather than proactive: a response to new challenges and growing exposure to a turbulent Russia. Third, instead of seeking direct ties with Russia's regions, the EU encourages individual regions to take a lead in fostering cooperation, especially with the north-western parts of the country. This approach in fact forms an important part of depoliticising the EU's role in Russian regionalism.[36]

In summary, the actual impact that the ND has had on cross-border cooperation between the EU and Russia is hard to assess. The policy itself has been amorphous, and it has at times been hard to grasp from the documents and speeches available what it has all been about. The fact that the ND is a loose umbrella concept has meant that it has been practically impossible to distinguish its impact from other region-building efforts in the north. The ND's largest outcome so far seems paradoxically to be the lack of impact. To be precise, the ND has been useful in highlighting the problems that the EU and Russia encounter in fostering cross-border cooperation, the internal problems the EU has in combining different policies and financial instruments, the relative poverty of Russia's regions, which hampers them from taking full part in the cooperation and often reduces it to mere humanitarian aid, as well as the residual suspicions on both sides of the fence concerning the underlying motives of the partner. Despite its original promise, and notwithstanding the vast potential of, and dire need for, cross-border cooperation in the north, the actual results have been slow in coming.

The 'Eastern Dimension'

The Northern Dimension is by no means the only regional dimension that will have a bearing on the EU's relationship with Russia. The still nascent 'Eastern Dimension' (ED) is another instance where Russia can be expected to play an important role. The term was introduced by Poland in March 1998 when, in the initiating statement for enlargement negotiations, it noted its willingness to participate in the development of the policy. To date, Warsaw has produced two documents on the topic.[37] Although Poland has been the prime mover, the UK and Sweden in particular have also shaped the EU's new eastern policy. In spring 2002, British Foreign Secretary Jack Straw wrote to Commission President Romano Prodi, providing the impetus for a debate on the so-called 'Wider Europe' policy towards the EU's post-enlargement eastern neighbours (Belarus, Moldova and Ukraine). Straw's letter was followed by a similar intervention by the late Swedish Foreign Minister Anna Lindh. The Swedish vision entailed a much broader reach, suggesting a neighbourhood policy 'from Russia to Morocco'.

It seems likely that the Swedish vision will prevail. Therefore, instead of adopting a distinctive ED as such, it seems clear that all the neighbours, both old and new, will be subsumed under the rubric of 'Wider Europe' or the 'European Neighbourhood Policy' (ENP) being developed by the Commission. In March 2003, the Commission produced a communication stating that the new policy is meant for countries that do not currently enjoy the prospect of EU membership.[38] Instead, the EU offers enhanced relations based on shared values. According to the communication, the aim is closer integration between the EU and its neighbours. The mechanism is simple: in return for effective implementation of reforms (including aligning national legislation with the EU *acquis*), the EU will grant closer economic integration with the prospect of realising the so-called Four Freedoms of movement (persons, goods, services and capital) within the 'Wider Europe', which would include the southern shores of the Mediterranean, the north-western parts of Russia, and everything in between.

The development of ENP has not been without its problems. In Ukraine and Moldova the initial reaction to the Commission's proposals was less than enthusiastic.[39] Ukraine in particular saw it as poor consolation for the lack of clear prospects of membership. Uncertainty over the EU's ironclad commitments on the Four Freedoms made Kiev disconcerted. The negotiations on the so-called Neighbourhood Action Plans with the EU's neighbours during spring 2004 ran into difficulties too, but for an internal reason: the Council called a temporary halt to the negotiation process because it felt it was not receiving sufficient information from the Commission, and thus did not have enough control over the process.[40] Although the negotiations were quickly resumed, this member state activism shows that the ENP is a fairly contested policy in the EU.

A special relationship with Russia

Russia is not included in ENP. This decision reflects recognition by the EU that Russia – although geographically part of the same post-Soviet space – is nevertheless different from the other neighbours. The idea adopted at the St Petersburg EU–Russia summit in May 2003 of creating a set of 'common spaces' between the EU and Russia, ranging from the economy to external security and higher education, suggests that the EU is indeed interested in preserving Russia's special role in post-enlargement Europe.[41] By acknowledging Russia's interpretation of its place in Europe, the EU could find it easier to cooperate with the country. It could also facilitate the inclusion of Russia in devising a joint policy for the new eastern neighbours, which has thus far proved to be unsuccessful. In this sense, a separate ED seems justified as a natural way of affording Russia a constructive role in policy towards the three new eastern neighbours, Belarus, Moldova and Ukraine.[42]

A word of caution: it is true that perhaps the only way forward for the EU to promote change in countries like Belarus and Ukraine will come from seeking more robust joint actions with Moscow. This would require that the EU cultivate a special relationship with Russia in the future, which in turn requires that the EU must also take note of Russian concerns. But at the same time the EU should avoid lending too much credibility to Russia's claims of supremacy in the post-Soviet space. Russia has not in the past shied away from declaring the Commonwealth of Independent States (CIS) its special zone of influence. For example, Russia's Medium-Term EU Strategy states that partnership with the EU should help it to consolidate its place as the leading power in the CIS.[43] In the post-enlargement era, the EU should be aware of this tendency in Russian foreign policy, as it is easy to lose credibility in the eyes of the other eastern neighbours, especially Ukraine, if Russia is seen as being given a free hand in the region.

Conclusions

The EU's experience with the ND is mixed. Although it has opened up new possibilities for cooperation and has broadened the scope of EU–Russia relations, its main achievement has been highlighting the problems that the EU faces in its external relations in general, and its relationship with Russia in particular.

Internally, the ND has suffered from bottlenecks in the EU's external relations machinery. Being a cross-pillar policy where 'instruments stem from the first, its objectives from the second, and its problems from the third', it is no surprise that it has encountered problems of internal coherence and coordination.[44] The role of partner countries and sub-regional actors has also proved to be a complication. But these problems could be alleviated in the future, when the New Neighbourhood Instrument (NNI) is adopted from 2007. The new financial instrument would combine Interreg, Phare, Tacis, Cards (Community Assistance for Reconstruction Development and Stabilisation in the Western Balkans) and Meda (Mediterranean Development Assistance) into a single fund.[45] This does, however, leave open the question of how the ND will fare in the overall competition for money that a new larger combined funding instrument will generate. It could be that it will not fare well, as the other 'dimensions' in the east and the south will present the EU with more pressing problems.

Externally, the ND has highlighted that the EU and Russia do not perceive the role and importance of their 'strategic partnership' in the same way. While the EU stresses networking and the incremental harmonisation and integration of economies, Russia emphasises sovereignty and seeks to use the relationship as an instrument for achieving other goals, such as the restoration of great power status and facilitating the emergence of a multipolar world.[46] These differences have been present in the case of the ND. The EU's aims of encouraging better coordination and increased synergies within existing funds and instruments have been met by Russia's hopes of securing new funding for major infrastructure projects.[47] Russia and its regions have also looked to the ND to offer 'a constructive way' of engaging with European processes.[48] In the Russian reading, this engagement has included securing greater influence on those EU policies that will have an effect on the country. But Russia has found to its growing displeasure that neither money nor influence seems to be forthcoming. Although Russia's original reactions to the ND were positive, the tone has changed as Moscow has come to realise that its original enthusiasm was based on a misreading of the EU's intentions.

On a regional level, the lack of political autonomy and financial and administrative resources prevents Russia's north-western regions from making a fruitful contribution to the ND. This has put the EU in a difficult position, since the problem lies with the internal politics of Russia, where the Union has, of course, only negligible influence and even less willingness to use what influence it has. In addition, Russia's attitude towards cross-border cooperation does not help. On the one hand, Moscow is encouraging the creation of cross-border links as a way of facilitating foreign trade and investment. This, together with the direct economic aid provided by partners to the west, is seen as beneficial to Moscow because it eases the financial burden on the centre of economic development for the poor fringes of Russia.[49] Simultaneously, however, the economic benefits of cross-border cooperation are seen as problematic because of their potential to increase economic disparities within the Federation. This is seen as a possible threat to the Federation's still-fragile territorial integrity.[50]

The situation could come to a head in the near future. Eastern enlargement will result in growing contact between the EU and Russia. If the Russian regions fail to make positive use of the new opening, the growing economic disparities between the EU and Russia could place further strains on the unity of the Federation. The challenge for the EU is to show Russia that it does not have anything to fear from engaging in cross-border cooperation. In fact, the opposite is true. The most important test case in coming years will be Kaliningrad. Paradoxically for Moscow, its reluctance and inability to engage fully in fruitful cooperation will only make the realisation of Russia's worst fears more likely. For example, the growing difference in living standards between Kaliningrad and the rest of the Federation may make the idea of secession more appealing for Kaliningraders, as well as for those in other regions bordering the EU.

Eastern enlargement is likely to bring other changes to the EU's relationship with Russia. The increase in mutual exposure and economic interdependence is the most obvious. But there may also be changes in the very nature of the 'strategic partnership'. Russia seems to be worried that the accession of the former Soviet satellites could bring a more existential threat to the future of the relationship, as the EU newcomers might seek a toughening of the EU's Russia policy. The Russians could be right in their fears. For example, the former foreign minister of Estonia, Toomas Hendrik Ilves, has warned that the new members will not share the 'naïve, awestruck or fearful' perceptions of Russia that are deemed to hold sway in the EU. Instead, they will push for more critical evaluations of Russia, especially in questions of financial assistance. Russia can expect to move down the EU's agenda, as the 'Russia constituency' becomes weaker in the enlarged EU.[51] Although it might be unrealistic to expect that the relatively inexperienced and lightweight new members would start seriously upsetting relations, Ilves' words contain an element of truth.[52]

There will also be other changes. After EU enlargement, there will be calls for new external policies or 'dimensions' from the EU. Russia is likely to find most desirable a form of neighbourhood policy where it is allowed to retain its special relationship with the EU. If, however, Russia is grouped together with the rest of 'Wider Europe', the EU will encounter a set of new problems. Clear targets, benchmarks and differentiated conditionality are all things that Russia deeply detests, just as it sees itself – with good reason – as being a case apart from the rest. Therefore, there are special sensitivities that the EU must take into consideration when adopting common policies for its new neighbours. Russia is not part of the same problematique, but, and if approached constructively, is an essential player in solving the problem that the EU will face with its new eastern neighbours in the post-enlargement era.

Notes

[1] Denmark has of course been a member since 1973.

[2] The prime example is the so-called Northern Dimension Environmental Partnership (NDEP), with a budget of €200 million.

[3] See Oksana Antonenko and Kathryn Pinnick, 'Cross-Border Cooperation between Russia's North-west and Its Neighbours', *North-west Russia in the Baltic Sea Region* (London: IISS Russian Regional Perspectives Journal for Foreign and Security Policy, Issue 1, 2002), p. 11; Hiski Haukkala, 'The Northern Dimension: A Presence and Four Liabilities', in Roland Dannreuther (ed.), *The European Union Foreign and Security Policy: Towards a Neighbourhood Strategy* (London, New York: Routledge, 2004); and Hanna Ojanen, 'The EU and Its "Northern Dimension": An Actor in Search of a Policy, or a Policy in Search of an Actor?', *European Foreign Affairs Review*, vol. 5, no. 3, 2000, pp. 370–71. See also the chapter by Derek Averre and Oleg Reut in this volume, pp. 155-172.

[4] Here, the term 'post-enlargement' refers to the EU's eastern enlargement alone. The effects of the forthcoming NATO enlargement, although significant, are not included.

[5] Paavo Lipponen, 'The European Union Needs a Policy for the Northern Dimension', speech delivered at the conference 'Barents Region Today', Rovaniemi, 15 September 1997. The scope of 'soft' security challenges in the north has been discussed in Christer Pursiainen, 'Soft Security Problems of North-west Russia', in Holger Moroff (ed.), *European Soft Security Policies: The Northern Dimension* (Helsinki and Berlin: Finnish Institute of International Affairs and Institut für Europäische Politik, 2002).

[6] The three most important regional councils in the north are the Council of the Baltic Sea States (CBSS), the Barents Euro-Arctic Council (BEAC) and the Arctic Council (AC). For more about them and other forms of sub-regional cooperation in the north, see Kathryn Pinnick's contribution in this volume, pp. 225-242.

[7] *A Northern Dimension for the Policies of the European Union*, COM (1998) 589 (25 November 1998), at www.europa.eu.int/comm/external_relations/north_dim/doc/com1998_0589en.pdf.

[8] *Conclusions of the 2186th Council Meeting – General Affairs – Brussels, 31 May 1999*, PRES/99/171.

[9] *Conclusions of the Chair, Foreign Ministers' Conference on the Northern Dimension, Helsinki, 11–12 November 1999*; at www.europa.eu.int/comm/external_relations/north_dim/conf/formin1/index.htm. For the proceedings of the conference, see *Foreign Ministers' Conference*

on the Northern Dimension: A Compilation of Speeches (Helsinki: Unit for the Northern Dimension in the Ministry for Foreign Affairs of Finland, 2000).

10 *Action Plan for the Northern Dimension with External and Cross-border Policies of the European Union 2000–2003*, 9401/00 (14 June 2000), I.1, I.6; at www.europa.eu.int/comm/exter nal_relations/north_dim/ndap/ 06_00_en.pdf.

11 In all, the action plan covers energy, transport, telecommunication/information society, environment and natural resources, nuclear safety, public health, trade, business cooperation and investment promotion, human resources development and research, justice and home affairs and regional and cross-border cooperation; there is also a special reference to Kaliningrad.

12 Holger Moroff, 'The EU's Northern Soft Security Policy: Emergence and Effectiveness', in *European Soft Security Policies*, pp. 206–219.

13 *The Second Northern Dimension Action Plan, 2004-06;* at http://www.europa.eu.int/com m/external_relations/north_dim /ndap/ap2.pdf.

14 It is too early to assess the significance of this innovation. At first sight, however, it would seem that the Commission has only coupled previously separate sectors into larger ones without improving the list of

priorities as such.

15 *The Second Northern Dimension Action Plan*, p. 2.

16 Natan M. Shklyar, 'Russian Regions in Subregional Cooperation', in Renata Dwan and Oleksands Pavliuk (eds), *Building Security in the New States of Eurasia: Subregional Cooperation in the Former Soviet Space* (Armonk, NJ and New York: East–West Institute and M. E. Sharpe, 2000), p. 110.

17 For more about these problems, see Moroff, 'The EU's Northern Soft Security Policy', pp. 167–169.

18 For more on multi-level implementation of the Northern Dimension, see Nicola Catellani, 'The Multilevel Implementation of the Northern Dimension', in Hanna Ojanen (ed.), *The Northern Dimension: Fuel for the EU?* (Helsinki and Berlin: Finnish Institute of International Affairs and Institut für Europäische Politik, 2001).

19 Ojanen, 'The EU and Its "Northern Dimension"', p. 373.

20 Mette Sicard Filtenborg, Stefan Gänzle and Elisabeth Johansson, 'An Alternative Theoretical Approach to EU Foreign Policy: "Network Governance" and the Case of the Northern Dimension Initiative', *Cooperation and Conflict*, vol. 37, no. 4, 2002, p. 393.

21 See Antonenko and Pinnick, 'Cross-Border Cooperation'; Haukkala, 'The Northern Dimension: A Presence and Four

Liabilities'; and Moroff, 'The EU's Northern Soft Security Policy'.

22 *The Second Northern Dimension Action Plan, 2004–06*, p. 16.

23 Åge Mariussen, Hallgeir Aalbu and Mats Brandt, *Regional Organisations in the North*, Studies on Foreign Policy Issues 5 (Oslo: Royal Norwegian Ministry of Foreign Affairs, 2000).

24 Anne Myrjord, 'Governance Beyond the Union: EU Boundaries in the Barents Euro-Arctic Region', *European Foreign Affairs Review*, vol. 8, no. 2, 2003, pp. 243–244.

25 *2002 Annual Progress Report on the Implementation of the Northern Dimension Action Plan*. A Commission Staff Working Paper, SEC (2002) 1296 (26 November 2002), pp. 32–35; at www.europa.eu.int/comm/ external_relations/north_dim/d oc/progrep02.pdf.

26 Antonenko and Pinnick, 'Cross-Border Cooperation', p. 8.

27 See speech by Viktor Khristenko at the International Forum for the Northern Dimension, Lappeenranta, 22 October 2001; at www.arcticcentre.urova.fi/ pohjoinen_ulottuvuus/lapr_docs /O_Hristenko_EN.pdf. For a fuller account of Russian expectations vis-à-vis the ND, see Igor Ivanov, 'Co-operation between the EU and Russia in the European North', in *Foreign Ministers' Conference on the Northern Dimension*.

28 Dov Lynch, *Russia Faces Europe*, Chaillot Paper 60 (Paris: EU Institute for Security Studies, May 2003), pp. 14 and 58.

29 For more about this issue, see Hiski Haukkala, 'The EU and Russia: A Problematic "Strategic Partnership"', in Dov Lynch (ed.), *EU–Russian Security Dimensions*, Occasional Paper 46 (Paris: EU Institute for Security Studies, August 2003); Lynch, *Russia Faces Europe*; and Marius Vahl, *Just Good Friends? The EU–Russian 'Strategic Partnership' and the Northern Dimension*, CEPS Working Document 166, March 2001.

30 Tair Tairov, 'Turbulence in Russia and Border Cooperation', in Lassi Heininen and Gunnar Lassinantti (eds), *Security in the European North: From 'Hard' to 'Soft'* (Rovaniemi and Stockholm: Arctic Center, University of Rovaniemi and Olof Palme Center, 1999), pp. 172–173.

31 These reforms have been discussed in, for example, Peter Reddaway, 'Will Putin Be Able to Consolidate Power?', *Post-Soviet Affairs*, vol. 17, no. 1, 2001, pp. 23–44; and Robert Sharlet, 'Putin and the Politics of Law in Russia', ibid., vol. 17, no. 3, 2001, pp. 195–234.

32 Antonenko and Pinnick, 'Cross-Border Cooperation', pp. 8–9.

33 Sharlet, 'Putin and the Politics of Law', p. 222.

34 C. Brown-Humes, 'Border Neighbours Build on

Finnish–Russian Links', *Financial Times*, 18 August 2001. See also Tarja Cronberg, 'Euregio Karelia: In Search of a Relevant Space for Action', in Lars Hedegaards and Bjarne Lindström (eds), *The NEBI Yearbook 2003: North European and Baltic Sea Integration* (Berlin: Springer, 2003).

35 Hiski Haukkala, 'Every Man for Himself? Russian Regionalism in a European Context', in Markku Kivinen and Katri Pynnöniemi (eds), *Beyond the Garden Ring: Dimensions of Russian Regionalism* (Helsinki: Kikimora Publications, 2002), p. 134.

36 Ibid., pp. 139–140.

37 *The Eastern Policy of the European Union in the Run-up to the EU's Enlargement To Include the Countries of Central and Eastern Europe – Poland's Viewpoint* (Warsaw: Ministry of Foreign Affairs, 2001); and *Eastern Dimension Non-paper* (Warsaw: Ministry of Foreign Affairs, January 2003). These documents have been analysed in Hiski Haukkala, *Towards a Union of Dimensions: The Effects of Eastern Enlargement on the Northern Dimension*, FIIA Report 2/2002 (Helsinki: Finnish Institute of International Affairs, 2002); and Hiski Haukkala, 'New Forms of EU Neighbourhood Policy: The Case of the "Eastern Dimension"', in *Yearbook of Finnish Foreign Policy 2003* (Helsinki: Finnish Institute of International Affairs, 2003).

38 *Wider Europe – Neighbourhood: A New Framework for Relations with Our Eastern and Southern Neighbours*, COM(2003) 104 final, 11 March 2003, at www.europa.eu.int/comm/exter nal_relations/we/doc/com03_1 04_en.pdf.

39 Belarus was not offered the package because the EU has had sanctions in force since 1997.

40 'Negotiations to resume with EU neighbours', *euobserver.com*, 2 April 2004; at www.euobserver.com/index.pht ml?sid=24&aid=15051.

41 See *Joint Statement of the EU–Russia Summit, St Petersburg, 31 May 2003*; at www.europa.eu.int/comm/exter nal_relations/russia/sum05_03/ js.htm.

42 Haukkala, *Towards a Union of Dimensions*, p. 35.

43 *Medium-term Strategy for Development of Relations Between the Russian Federation and the European Union (2000–2010)*, 1.8 (unofficial English translation); at www.europa.eu.int/comm/ external_relations/russia/russia n_medium_term_strategy/index .htm.

44 Ojanen, 'The EU and Its "Northern Dimension"', p. 374.

45 See *Paving the Way for a New Neighbourhood Instrument*, COM(2003) 393 final, 1 July 2003; at www.europa.eu.int/comm/exter nal_relations/we/doc/com03_3 93_en.pdf.

46 See Haukkala, 'The EU and Russia: A Problematic "Strategic

Partnership"'; Lynch, *Russia Faces Europe;* and Vahl, *Just Good Friends?*

[47] Pekka Sutela, *The Northern Dimension: Interdependence, Specialization and Some Popular Misconceptions,* BOFIT Online No. 2/1999; at www.bof.fi/bofit/fin/7online/abs/pdf/bon0299.pdf, p. 4.

[48] Shklyar, 'Russian Regions', p. 90.

[49] Ibid., pp. 112–113.

[50] Pavel K. Baev, 'Russian Policies and Non-Policies Toward Subregional Projects Around Its Borders', in Dwan and Pavliuk (eds), *Building Security in the New States of Eurasia,* pp. 139–141.

[51] Toomas Hendrik Ilves, 'The Grand Enlargement and the Great Wall of Europe', in Andres Kasekamp (ed.), *The Estonian Foreign Policy Yearbook 2003* (Tallinn: Estonian Foreign Policy Institute, 2003), p. 195.

[52] Ilves is by no means alone. At a conference on the Common Foreign and Security Policy (CFSP) post-enlargement, organised by the Diplomatic Academy in Vienna in March 2003, many scholars from the accession countries made the point that, when it came to Russia's international obligations, the EU was 'too permissive'. Russia's policy on Chechnya was mentioned as one example where the EU should pursue a tougher line.

3. Russia's European Problem: Eastward Enlargement of the EU and Moscow's Policy, 1993–2003

Timofei Bordachev

Although preparations for the eastward enlargement of the European Union (EU) officially began as early as 1993, those who then held power in Russia did not attach much importance to it. In effect, no response was forthcoming from Moscow until the end of summer 1999, by which time the matter had already been settled in the EU and the technical parameters, including the adherence of the candidate countries to the community *acquis* and Schengen legislation, had been agreed.

It is, therefore, unsurprising that, of all of the issues related to enlargement, the most important to Russian politicians and diplomats has been the issue of land access for Russian citizens to the Kaliningrad *oblast*, following changes made by Lithuania to the visa regime while adopting Schengen legislation. Other issues, such as changes to Russia's foreign trade arrangements with the EU accession countries or the prospects for cross-border cooperation, remained on the periphery of Russian foreign-policy discourse.

The reason for this state of affairs lies both in the way that the Russian élite has traditionally perceived the EU and in the idiosyncrasies of the entire process of European integration – of which enlargement has become a part – that prevent third countries from organising a timely and adequate response to it. In the EU itself, fundamental questions concerning enlargement were under discussion for a long time, despite the fact that the so-called Copenhagen criteria for membership were approved as far back as 1993. Moreover, the slow pace of the enlargement debate and open discussion among EU nations of the major enlargement-related problems left Russia with the impression that it would still be a long time before any practical steps were taken.

It should also be noted that, unlike Brussels, Moscow does not regard the problem of uneven development in the border regions of Russia and the EU as a 'soft' security issue. Whereas in EU states and the 'capital of Europe' the focus of the discourse on the concepts of 'direct neighbourhood' or, after 2003, 'Wider Europe' is on overcoming the threats that a successful Europe might face from its less fortunate neighbours, this has never really been an issue for Russia, where the matter of the accession of new member states to the EU is most serious only in connection with visa issues and the change in the trade regime.

Terra Incognita: the EU and Russian foreign policy in the 1990s

Despite their largely pastoral outward appearance, throughout the 1990s, Russian–European relations were characterised by a series of fundamental disagreements that affected Russia's perception of EU enlargement. The most significant was the opposing views of the parties in regard to who constituted Russia's main partner in Europe. Moscow and the European capitals had different answers to this question, which impacted on day-to-day relations and was a major contributing factor to their noticeable breakdown in 1999. At that time, nearly all of the EU countries backed the North Atlantic Treaty Organisation (NATO)'s operation in former Yugoslavia (which Russia opposed) and later strongly condemned the Kremlin's assault on Chechnya.

A number of European authors believe that Russia failed to develop a coherent single policy on the EU in the 1990s.[1] Russia has always maintained relations with France, Germany, Italy, the UK and other European countries, and these have dominated its relationship with the EU. From the beginning of the 1990s, European integration also assumed a foreign-policy dimension, intended to address the imbalance between the EU's considerable economic weight and its humble contribution to international affairs. Nonetheless, as some Russian observers even admit today, Moscow has always viewed the EU as being on a par with other international organisations – the Council of Europe, NATO and the United Nations (UN) – in which national governments play a deciding role in all issues.[2]

Russian foreign policy inherited this particular attitude to the EU from the Soviet Union (USSR), which essentially refused to do business with the European Community as a supranational organisation until the late 1980s and regarded it on a superficial level as an economic appendage to NATO. In 1988, a declaration of mutual recognition was signed between the Council for Mutual Economic Assistance (the Soviet-dominated trade bloc of socialist economies) and the European Community, but until then the USSR had only maintained bilateral relations with EU member states. The first agreement on trade and cooperation between the EU and the USSR was signed in 1989 and a Partnership and Cooperation Agreement (PCA) in 1994 but it was not until six years after the Soviet Union's collapse that the PCA came into force between the EU and Russia in 1997. Moscow's reserved attitude towards cooperation with the EU is also reflected in the very limited written record of bilateral relations, which, until 1999, consisted of only three documents adopted in the EU and one PCA signed by Russia.[3]

The Europeans believe that Russia's flawed view of the EU is linked to one of the most significant characteristics of Moscow's European policy practice of the 1990s: the prevailing bilateral approach. For the duration of the 1990s, Russia strove to establish constructive ties with the leading European powers. A great deal of its diplomatic activity on the European front failed to bring about a rapprochement with the EU. This was primarily due to the fact that all of the EU countries' foreign economic activity had already (by the late 1970s) come under the jurisdiction of supranational bodies in Brussels, which Russia overlooked as before.

It is possible to identify at least three reasons for this situation. First, intense contacts were fostered with the leaders of the European states in the spirit of the personal diplomacy of the 1990s, which corresponded with the individual leanings of the head of state and were partly intended to compensate for the lack of competitiveness of the Russian economy.[4] Such a policy could not be applied to relations with the EU. It is hard to imagine an informal meeting between the Russian president and the representatives of the EU 'Troika', let alone the 20 members of the European Commission. Second, focusing attention on the European 'superpowers' coincided with the doctrine of establishing triangular geopolitical combinations, which was the chief obsession of Russian foreign policy in the 1990s. Finally, from the point of view of the workings of the bureaucratic machine, the Russian Ministry of Foreign Affairs was far more accustomed to dealing with European countries on a bilateral basis, as reflected by its internal structure, which to this day does not have a department devoted exclusively to the EU.

However, the main reason for the predominance of the bilateral approach in Russia's European policy was the fact that the phenomenon of European integration does not fit with the traditional points of reference of Russian foreign policy. As many Russian and foreign authors note, for Russia, the 1990s became a time of harking back to the principles of nineteenth-century diplomacy rather than searching for new solutions.[5] Although there are numerous reasons for this, the most significant was the prevalence of the principles of political realism in Russian foreign policy.[6] The notion of international relations as a state of chaos in which each country simply pursues its own interests contradicted the liberal institutionalist views that not only dominated Western foreign-policy thinking in the 1990s, but that had also long since become the ideological basis for the process of European integration. Whereas in the case of the US, the idiosyncrasies of the world views held by representatives of US President Bill Clinton's administration most likely played a significant part in foreign policymaking and it was foreseeable that the paradigm of American foreign policy would change once the Democrats left the White House, in the 'Old World', Russia encountered a model of relations between the countries of the region that was fundamentally at odds with realpolitik. Russia's attempts to formulate European policy with an emphasis on the self-centred interests of the EU's leading powers were predestined to failure.

Consequently, throughout the 1990s, Russia regarded the EU as an intergovernmental regional association in which the supranational element played little part and the European 'superpowers' took all of the key decisions independently – in accordance with the current demands of intrinsically chaotic international relations. Needless to say, Moscow's stance was a source of active displeasure to Brussels and the European capitals and was countered by their efforts to act in apparent defiance of it by taking all of the most important decisions on Russian matters collectively. Here one can see a fundamental contradiction that not only prevented progress in bilateral relations, but also hindered fulfilment of the terms of agreements already in place.

A clear example of the difference of opinion can be found in the tone and substance of the following conceptual documents adopted by Russia and the EU in 1999: the EU's Common Strategy on Russia; and the Medium-Term Strategy for the Development of Relations between the Russian Federation and the European Union (2000–10).

It would be no exaggeration to say that Moscow misconstrued the EU's Common Strategy. In the first place, it was perceived as a sign of the EU's aspiration to develop some kind of special relationship with Russia. Even experienced Russian commentators and diplomats emphasised the significance that Russia was the first country with which the EU signed one of these new strategy documents for individual countries.[7] Meanwhile, other assessments of the document vary from the restrained to the openly sceptical. As a rule, these are the opinions of European experts and, at best, they underline the strategy's incompatibility with Russia's priorities and expectations.[8]

The Medium-Term Strategy for the Development of Relations between the Russian Federation and the European Union, presented in late 1999, is a largely declarative document intended to express Moscow's interest in a strategic partnership with the EU. Some observers attribute the very fact that it was adopted to the need to enhance the role played by then Russian Prime Minister Vladimir Putin at a meeting of EU leaders in Helsinki, Finland, on 22 October 1999.[9]

The basic provisions of the document included an initiative to build a strategic partnership between Russia and the EU and an appeal to the European Union to facilitate Russia's accession to the World Trade Organisation (WTO), to increase assistance programmes and to revoke anti-dumping measures against Russian goods. The ritual passage about the need for cooperation in the security sphere had the greatest negative impact. The mention of a need to 'counterbalance NATO-centrism in Europe' immediately prompted an angry response from the majority of European observers and, as a relatively meaningless remnant of 1990s foreign-policy thinking, even overshadowed the constructive element of the Russian proposals. Whatever the case, the content of all the official documents and the consequences of their adoption demonstrated that Russia lacked a clear idea of whom it was dealing with in Europe.

Moreover, the aims set out in the two documents are completely different. The EU describes its strategic goal as the construction in Russia of 'a stable, open and pluralistic democracy [...] governed by the rule of law and underpinning a prosperous market economy benefiting alike all the people of Russia and of the European Union'.[10] In Moscow's opinion, a strategic partnership with the EU 'can manifest itself in joint efforts to establish an effective system of collective security in Europe on the basis of equality without dividing lines, including through the development and implementation of the Charter for European Security…'.[11]

Whereas the EU made its main objective to change the internal situation in Russia with an emphasis on the need for progress in the human-rights field and the creation of civil institutions, Moscow called on the EU for cooperation on 'equal terms' in a broader international context. The aims of the parties again proved completely at odds, thereby effectively bringing the potentially positive effect of the two new documents to naught.

Hence, the main problem in Russian–European relations in the period 1993–2003 was that Russia was unable properly to identify a partner in Europe and to draw up its foreign-policy measures accordingly. This failure to understand the role and potential of the EU as a single international player, at least as far as the fundamental issues of enlargement were concerned, inevitably resulted in a heedless and even dismissive attitude towards the matter of the EU's physical advance towards Russia's borders.

The process of NATO enlargement, which was discussed from 1994, following a summit in Brussels, played an important part in shaping the dismissive attitude taken towards EU enlargement by the Russian élite and authorities. If one looks at the main foreign-policy declarations and documents adopted by Russia in the 1990s with respect to European security issues, one is struck by the pronounced difference in Moscow's views of the role, essence and potential of the two largest institutions in the Western world, namely the NATO bloc (with the US as its backbone) and the European Union. The former is depicted as a Cold War relic, a completely meaningless and potentially aggressive military instrument, the very existence of which is supported by the 'hawks' in Washington and the bureaucrats in its Brussels headquarters who are afraid of losing their jobs. Conversely, the EU is perpetually viewed as a constructive element that facilitates the region's economic development and represents an important partner for Russia.[12]

No attention was paid to the fact that, of the EU's 15 member states in 1995, 11 (the largest and most significant of which included France, Germany, Italy, Spain and the UK) were members of NATO and acted in full accord with the US. Despite the fact that disagreements periodically flared up between Moscow and Washington and that the leading EU countries invariably stressed their adherence to the principles of transatlantic solidarity, Russian foreign policy never identified the US with its Western European allies.

Moscow's attitude towards the two parallel processes of eastward enlargement of these Western institutions likewise differed. NATO enlargement was always treated as a factor that would undermine European security, whereas the possibility of the countries of Central and Eastern Europe acceding to the EU was seen as more of a positive phenomenon by Russia, even though all of the candidate countries also aspired to become members of NATO. Furthermore, during the 1990s, the EU did not disguise its intention to increase its military potential in part with the help of American resources and in no way in opposition to the US.[13]

Facing EU enlargement

As noted above, for the Russian political élite, the subject of EU enlargement remained hidden behind the smokescreen of the tense debate surrounding NATO expansion right up until 1999. Accordingly, issues related to the prospect of the EU approaching Russia's borders were not the focus of public attention and were given little coverage in the Russian media, and if they were mentioned it was in positive and protective tones. EU representatives also did a great deal to nurture this attitude, assuring Moscow at all levels of the exclusively positive effects of broadening Russian–European relations.[14]

The view that the Russian political élite takes of EU enlargement is consistent with the different opinions towards the West held by representatives of the right (liberal pro-market) and left (communist expansionist) sides of the political spectrum. Russia's liberal Westernisers have traditionally regarded the EU as the source of the transformation of Russia itself and welcomed the growth of European institutions (except

NATO) and Russia's participation in them. Russia's accession to the Council of Europe in February 1996 represented a great success for this wing of the Russian élite. Notably, this spirit of goodwill did not extend to NATO. Since the very beginning of the public campaign against the Alliance's eastward enlargement (in 1993), even Russia's liberal Westernisers have been compelled in effect to express solidarity with their communist-*derzhavniki* (advocates of Russia as a Great Power) opponents and generally to support the line taken by the Kremlin and the Russian Ministry of Foreign Affairs. In all likelihood, this is due both to the Russian public's demand for anti-NATO rhetoric (in complete contradistinction to its attitude to the European issue) and the sincere belief that, without the prospect of Russian membership, NATO enlargement would cause the security situation in Europe to change.

The representatives of the left wing of the Russian political spectrum took a more unequivocal stance. The communists and their allies were opposed equally to the enlargement of NATO and of the EU. In their eyes, both institutions are instruments for managing the power of world capital in order to 'establish the global supremacy of the developed capitalist countries with the help of a "new world order"'.[15] In this context, NATO represents the policy's military instrument, while the EU is its economic accompaniment. This is not significantly different to the Soviet attitude towards European integration, which was regarded as the economic extension of the military bloc of countries of the capitalist West. Nonetheless, leaders of the nominal 'left–wing' publicly expressed their opinions about the EU in much softer tones than those in which they talked about the US and NATO.

The situation only changed qualitatively in 2002, when the vociferous debate on the problem of the overland transit of Russian citizens to Kaliningrad *oblast* began in Russia. In this particular instance, almost all of Russia's politicians advocated the idea of visa-free entry to the *oblast* for Russians,[16] although they proposed different technical solutions to the problem, which were often unrealistic and speculative.[17] Putin was the first to articulate the need to have a visa-free transit regime, reasserting it at the Moscow summit in May 2002 with the support of representatives from across the Russian political spectrum.

Russia's delayed reaction to the challenges of EU enlargement was caused by a general lack of inquiry into the topic by the federal authorities and the political élite. As noted above, for the duration of the 1990s, the European issue was not among the subjects of interest to the Russian political élite or media; expert opinion on the issue remained limited and practically uncalled for.

The formulation of a coherent Russian position, at least in the form of a document, was also hindered by the fact that the Russian Ministry of

Foreign Affairs was not administratively prepared for the EU challenge. As highlighted earlier, it still has no office that deals with the EU. Other Russian ministries are likewise devoid of such departments. Furthermore, the countries of Central and Eastern Europe are not priorities in Russian foreign policy and the process of their accession to the EU was not of great interest to either members of the Russian élite or civil servants. In addition, bilateral relations between Russia and the Baltic States remain complicated.

The process of EU enlargement and the prospect of Latvia, Lithuania and Estonia joining the Union had very little impact on the settlement of border issues with Russia right up until the point at which the enlargement process passed into the technical phase. On the one hand, Moscow remained convinced for quite some time that the outstanding issue of their borders with Russia would hinder the Baltic States from joining the EU and NATO. With this in mind, some Russian politicians suggested that, by artificially prolonging the matter through talks, Moscow would gain leverage in regard to the problem of Russian-speaking minorities in the Baltic States. On the other hand, however, reality showed that the Baltic States were not going to be prevented from entering the EU by the unfinished process of concluding border agreements with Russia. Meanwhile, the enlargement process itself and, in particular, Lithuania's preparations to join the EU and the lively development of the Kaliningrad transit issue resulted in a genuine breakthrough in Russian–Lithuanian relations. Proof of this was Russia's ratification of a re-admission agreement with Lithuania in May 2003.

Russia in the 'ring of friends'
In March 2003, the European Commission presented a communication entitled *Wider Europe – Neighbourhood: A New Framework for Relations with our Eastern and Southern Neighbours* for consideration by EU heads of state. The document in question was the result of a joint initiative by the EU Commissioner for External Relations, Chris Patten, and the EU High Representative for Common Foreign and Security Policy, Javier Solana, and was supposed to stipulate the basic outline and strategic parameters for expanding EU policy in relation to those neighbouring countries that are not regarded as candidates for accession.

An examination of the European Commission's proposals shows that, even before completing the process of its own enlargement, the EU set about establishing a circle of allies closest to its borders that, although formally independent, will nonetheless have to assimilate the lion's share of European rules and legal standards. It is no secret that the more detailed development of the 'ring-of-friends' idea (first proposed by the President of the European Commission, Romano Prodi) also presupposes tangible conditions for such friendship. These include the fulfilment of a series of EU requirements and the reformation of the national economies and political systems of partner countries on the basis of these demands. By way of reward, the especially worthy will be granted access to the EU common market and the opportunity to enjoy fundamental European freedoms of movement (of goods, services, persons and capital).

The list of the EU's friends includes the countries of the southern Mediterranean and the western newly independent states (WNIS), as well as Russia. There is no denying that, even though the Commission document emphasised the special role of relations with Russia, the very nature of the issue justifiably prompted doubts in Moscow. One should not forget that, although Russia might indeed occupy a very important place in the ring of friends, it does so along with a number of other countries, including North African and Middle Eastern states. The countries of the southern and eastern Mediterranean could be the source of far greater threats to the EU in the security sphere than Russia. Hence, one can already predict that the scale of European involvement will be greater in those areas. Moreover, unlike Russia, the North African countries have a long history of subordination to some EU states and it will be much easier for them to adapt to the model of 'New Neighbourhood' proposed by Brussels.

For its part, Moscow has advanced the idea of building up a strategic partnership between Russia and the EU in the climate of a multi-polar world. In Russia's opinion, such a partnership could entail working together in the international security arena, increasing the export of Russian energy resources to Europe and stimulating the investment process. However, the EU has not yet reached the state of internal unity necessary for a responsible foreign policy. As a result, most attempts to establish a military and political dialogue with Moscow are limited to tactical cooperation between Russia and certain influential EU countries. Furthermore, the poor compatibility of the political and economic systems of Russia and Europe make it difficult to lay the economic foundations for such a strategic partnership. The striving to put forward a model of 'special partnership', which was not included in the concept of Wider Europe, led Moscow to propose the concept of 'common spaces' at the EU–Russia Summit in St Petersburg in May 2003. Moscow suggested establishing four common spaces between Russia and Europe: a common economic space; a common justice and home affairs space; a common security space; and a common education space. This way of constructing bilateral relations can potentially make a distinction between Russia and other 'new neighbours' of the enlarged EU. Russia did not welcome the Wider Europe communication and wanted to introduce a slightly different agenda that has nothing in common with the anticipated EU Action Plans for Algeria and Ukraine, inter alia.

Troubles on the eve of enlargement

EU–Russia relations faced a new crisis at the end of 2003. First, Putin sharply criticised the European Commission for its uncompromising position during talks on Russia's accession to the WTO and accused the Brussels-based bureaucracy of 'attempting to twist Russia's arm'. Following this, there was a diplomatic conflict over settlement of the Transdniestria problem in Moldova. The Europeans, for the first time, sent a clear signal to Russia that Moscow could no longer have free rein to engage in independent action within the post-Soviet space. Then, as if any doubt remained that EU–Russia relations had entered a complicated period, Russia took a tough stance on the extension of the PCA to the new EU member states. The European Commission and the European Parliament responded by issuing highly critical statements about Russia.

Although the PCA question was resolved diplomatically on the eve of EU enlargement, several serious areas of discord remain between the parties. First, they differ on the energy issue. In the second half of 2003, it became obvious that the Russian government intends to maintain strategic control over raw materials and to use Russian energy exports to apply leverage in the foreign-policy realm. The promising project to establish an energy dialogue with Russia – including discussion of European plans to invest in gas and oil production in Russia – has stalled.

Second, the EU and Russia have been increasingly divided by problems associated with the post-Soviet space. Moscow's initiatives to encourage economic integration between the members of the Commonwealth of Independent States (CIS), and its strategy for local conflict resolution, have not been looked upon favourably by the EU. Conversely, the EU is keen to intensify its own policy in relation to the western newly independent states (WNIS), such as Belarus and Moldova, and the countries of the South Caucasus, since, subsequent to EU enlargement, these regions have become the Union's immediate neighbours. Simultaneously, the leaders of many post-Soviet states are showing much interest in the European project – a factor that greatly increases the rivalry between Russia and the European Union. Just one example: the EU is putting increasing pressure on the Moldovan leadership to accept its plan to resolve the conflict in Transdniestria without the active participation of Russia.

Third, the new EU member states from Central and Eastern Europe might bring their traditionally strong anti-Russian sentiments into the EU policymaking arena. Some of the new EU members will probably attempt to reap financial and political dividends on the basis of their status as 'pseudo-frontline' territories; it is predicted that they will embellish their concerns about bordering an allegedly unfriendly state. Furthermore, the new EU members may attempt to act as 'arbiters' in the WNIS and South Caucasus. This is sure to provoke Moscow.

Fourth, there is not enough diplomacy going on. On the one hand, Brussels has been surprised that Moscow is seeking to minimise its economic losses as a result of EU enlargement. On the other hand, Brussels sees flaws in Russia's negotiating stance. The EU is annoyed by Moscow's persistent attempts to link problems that are not directly related. Consequently, even relatively simple questions remain unresolved and the potential for escalation rises accordingly. Furthermore, the West knows from experience that Moscow is prone to making stern statements that it will not accept EU conditions, only to give in eventually and to present a limited and realistic set of demands. Brussels viewed the 14-point list of demands that Moscow released in early 2004 as a purely 'technical list'; Brussels will not countenance compensation to a state outside the EU (especially a non-member of the WTO) for the consequences of purely internal decisions. Besides, Russia has already set a precedent by consenting to the automatic extension of the PCA to new EU member states in 1995 (when Austria, Finland and Sweden joined the Union).

Fifth, the primary integration projects – the establishment of an energy dialogue and four common spaces – are at a standstill. Negotiations on Russia's accession to the WTO have been difficult partly due to extremely high initial expectations, and partly because Russia has proven unprepared to fulfil its obligations. A glaring example is Moscow's stated intention to bring its domestic laws into line with European law unilaterally, which was agreed upon in Article 55 of the PCA (in 1994), but upon which, in practice, there has been no progress. Perhaps Russia should not have made those commitments, but, in the EU's opinion, Russia cannot refuse to fulfil them without officially withdrawing its original promises to comply. The same is true with respect to the 1997 Kyoto Protocol to the 1992 United Nations Framework Convention on Climate Change, the opening up of the Russian banking and insurance services market, and other matters on which Russia is perceived to have made promises.[18] It seems to the EU that Russia refuses to take into account the interests of the EU, its member states and economic agents. For example: Moscow is in no hurry to alleviate European concerns over the environment or maritime safety; Russia does not provide its constituent regions with sufficient freedom to engage in foreign economic activity (which European businesses are pressing for, since they do not want to engage exclusively with Moscow); and Russia has made visa application procedures more stringent for visitors from the EU.

Finally, the EU's relations with Russia are influenced by dynamics and opinions within the Union. At the November 2003 EU–Russia Summit, Italian Prime Minister Silvio Berlusconi appeared to condone the Russian government's stance on Chechnya and the arrest of businessman Mikhail

Khodorkovsky, in contravention of the EU's stated position. In their attempts to address the internal crisis within the EU, the Europeans have sought to appear efficient, and this is true in regard to relations with Russia. The lack of a resolution of the situation in Chechnya and Russia's thorny political processes provide European intellectuals and politicians with an opportunity to show their worth in defending democratic norms and human rights. The 'Old World' does not seem to get tired of criticising Russia; there are incessant calls to take a harder line and even to impose sanctions against the country. But if the EU fails to shape its relations with Russia in a favourable or, at least, an acceptable way, the Union will resemble nothing more than an economic community with a few policing functions. In such a situation, all discussion about the EU's global role will be just idle talk.

It is obvious that each side has its share of responsibility. Russia appears unprepared to meet the obligations that it assumed under the PCA. Moscow has failed to establish an appropriate system of interaction with the EU. Likewise, the EU has proved incapable of building a relationship with Russia under which the country is treated as an equal strategic partner. Russia consistently seeks independent solutions to its own foreign-policy challenges and in accordance with its own national interest. Putin's Russia of the past four years does not conform to the existing concept of Europeanisation, according to which Moscow should gradually adopt the principles proposed by the EU for domestic and foreign policy. Russia is not willing to adjust its policies to the demands of the EU. In some fields – for instance, with regard to ratification of the Kyoto Protocol – Russia's modernisation goals run counter to the terms of cooperation put forward by the EU.

After enlargement: opportunities for cooperation

Thus, it seems unlikely that rapprochement between Russia and the enlarged EU on the basis of the projects for Wider Europe or strategic partnership is possible. In the short term (the next 10–15 years) we may, in all likelihood, be looking primarily at the development of small-scale forms of cooperation, including the cross-border cooperation programmes connected with the challenges of enlargement and the almost inevitable increase of EU participation in the affairs of the Kaliningrad *oblast*. The EU Commission's proposal gradually to consolidate all European technical assistance programmes (such as Phare and Tacis) and to create a new neighbourhood funding instrument in their place represents a very promising initiative.[19] According to plans, the new superfund should be geared towards reducing inequality in the development of the regions on either side of the external borders of the expanded EU.[20]

Currently, the level of socio-economic development in the border regions of the new EU member states is not only lower than the European average, but also lower than the national average for these states. It is already feared that these internal disparities will increase significantly after accession, which could result in people moving from north-east Poland and the eastern regions of Latvia and Estonia to the West in search of better work opportunities. In Russia, too, the regions bordering the EU are below the national level of development (Leningrad *oblast* may be the only exception).

At this stage, the EU's main aim is to reduce the immediate threats to security emanating from its neighbours' border territories. In future, however, cooperation through the New Neighbourhood initiative could be used to bring about the genuine mutual enhancement of the economies of the border regions of Russia and the EU. The greatest value of the initiative lies in the potential for investment in projects that can be implemented on both sides of the border on the basis of a joint budget.

A number of criticisms have already been levelled at the implementation of the Northern Dimension initiative, which was first proposed in the EU by the representatives of Finland and Sweden in 1998. Nonetheless, the Northern Dimension is the only Russian–European project that is truly functional at a grassroots level. Moreover, once the Baltic countries have joined the EU, the main emphasis of the Northern Dimension will shift towards the Russian border regions, namely the Republic of Karelia and the Leningrad, Murmansk and Pskov *oblasts*.

The existence of the Kaliningrad exclave has become another of the challenges presented by EU enlargement that is of exceptional importance to Moscow. Even after the apparent settlement of the all-important issue of land access for Russian citizens, there is a real possibility that the more important issues of the *oblast's* social and economic development will remain forgotten. This, in turn, could give rise to unpredictable political processes in Kaliningrad *oblast* itself. At present, the bulk of European investment is directed towards ensuring the environmental safety of the region and combating public health issues. However, positive changes could also be made in this regard. First and foremost, these should entail broadening the scope of European investment projects to include areas such as developing human resources and supporting small- and medium-sized businesses.

It is here, in small-scale, even down-to-earth forms of cooperation – the independent influx of European companies to Russia and the development of cross-border projects designed to enhance specialised areas of activity on both sides of the border and to boost contacts in the field of education – that the answer to Russian–European incompatibility lies. Over the next 15–20 years, Russian–European relations may be based not on integration but on the objective complementarities of certain sectors of their economies, as well as on openness in those areas that do not touch on the basic working principles of the political and economic systems. The greatest achievement of this model of co-existence will be the gradual growth in, and diversification of, EU–Russia trade, not to mention an increase in human contact. Besides providing the answer to a whole number of enlargement challenges, this could also facilitate internal stabilisation within Russia and lay the foundations for more robust political relations with a united Europe.

Notes

1. Kempe, I., *Direct Neighbourhood Relations between the Enlarged EU and the Russian Federation, Ukraine, Belarus and Moldova* (Gütersloh: Bertelsmann Foundation Publishers, 1998).

2. Leshukov, I., 'Rossiya i evropeiskii soyuz: strategiya vzaimootnoshenii', in Trenin, D., *Rossiya i osnovnye instituty bezopasnosti v Evrope: vstupaya v XXI vek* (Russia and the Basic Security Institutions in Russia: the Path to the 21st Century) (Moscow: S&P Carnegie Moscow Center, 2000), pp. 23–38.

3. European Commission communication: 'The Future of Relations between the European Union and Russia' (1995); European Council general report: 'Strategy for EU–Russian Relations' (1995) and 'European Union Action Plan for Russia' (1996); at www.europa.eu.int/comm/external_relations/russia/russia_docs/index.htm.

4. On the idiosyncrasies of personalised Russian foreign policy, see Bogaturov, A., 'Pyat' sindromov Yeltsina i pyat' obrazov Putina', *Pro et Contra*, Vol. 6, No. 1–2, 2001, pp. 122–137.

5. See, for example, Fedorov, Y., 'Krizis vneshnei politiki Rossii: kontseptualny aspekt', *Pro et Contra*, Vol. 6, No. 1–2, 2001, pp. 31–49.

6. Primakov, E., 'Mezhdunarodnye otnosheniya nakanune XXI veka: problemy i perspektivy', *Mezhdunarodnaya Zhizn*, No. 10, 1996, pp. 3–14.

7. Danilov, D., 'Potentsialny soyuznik Moskvy', *Nezavisimaya Gazeta*, 3 December 1999; 'Rossiya na putyakh mirostroitelstva', *Nezavisimaya Gazeta*, 12 September 1999.

8. Gowan, D., *How the EU can Help Russia* (London: Centre for European Reform, 2001).

9. Leshukov, 'Rossiya i evropeiskii soyuz', p. 24.

10. In regard to the Common Strategy of the European Union on Russia, see www.eur.ru/eng/neweur/user_eng.php?func=rae_common_strategy.

11. In regard to the Medium-Term Strategy for the Development of Relations between the Russian Federation and the European Union (2000–10), see www.eur.ru/eng/neweur/user_eng.php?func=apage&id=53.

12. Pichugin, B.M., 'Rasshirenie ES na Vostok i ekonomicheskie interesy Rossii', *Doklady Instituta Evropy RAN*, No. 29, 1996; Maximychev, I.F., 'Ugrozy bezopasnosti Rossii, svyazannye s nachalom rasshireniya NATO (Vneshnepoliticheskie aspekty)', *Doklady Instituta Evropy RAN*, No. 42, 1998; Zhurkin, V.V., 'Evropeiskii soyuz: vneshnyaya politika, bezopasnost', oborona', *Doklady Instituta Evropy RAN*, No. 47, 1998; Danilov, D.A., 'Rossiya v Bolshoi Evrope: strategiya bezopasnosti', *Sovremennaya Evropa*, No. 2, 2000.

13 Schmidt, P., 'ESDI: "Separable but not separate"?', *NATO Review*, Vol. 48, No. 1, 2000, pp. 12–15; Heisbourg, F., 'European defence takes a leap forward', *NATO Review*, Vol. 48, No. 1, 2000, pp. 8–11.

14 Juppé, A., 'Budushchuyu Evropu ne stanut stroit' bez Rossii', interview with *Izvestiya*, 16 February 1996.

15 Abramov, Y.K. and Golovina, T.Y. (eds), *Politicheskie partii i dvizheniya Rossii* (Moscow: Press Ltd, 1998), p. 168; citing the Political Programme of the Communist Party of Russia.

16 'I believe that the inhabitants of the Kaliningrad *oblast* should all be granted Schengen passports so that … they have visa-free access to Poland and Lithuania today and should continue to have it once those countries have joined the European Union.' Boris Nemtsov, interview with NTV (shown on 'Geroi dnya'), 28 May 2002.

17 Deputies of the State Duma discussing the Kaliningrad issue, Telekanal RTR, 'Parlamentskii chas', 6 October 2002.

18 At the EU–Russia summit 21 May 2004 the EU stated it supported Russia's accession to the WTO; Russia promised to speed up its ratification of the Kyoto process and to open up the financial services sector to foreign competition.

19 'Wider Europe: Commission to strengthen cross-border cooperation with new neighbours', IP/03/922 – Brussels, 1 July 2003; at www.europa.eu.int/comm/exter nal_relations/we/intro/ip03_92 2.htm.

20 'Paving the way for a New Neighbourhood Instrument', see www.europa.eu.int/comm/exter nal_relations/we/doc/com03_3 93_en.pdf.

4. Russia and EU Enlargement: From Insecure Neighbour to a Common Space of Security, Justice and Home Affairs

Oksana Antonenko

The decision to enlarge the European Union (EU) through the admission of ten new members – eight states from Central and Eastern Europe (CEE), plus Cyprus and Malta – is seen as one of the most successful EU foreign-policy initiatives since the end of the Cold War. Regardless of the economic costs, political support for the enlargement process is based on the fact that it will bring more stability and security to former Eastern bloc countries and thus further consolidate the security benefits to those Western European nations that have already gained from integration. But, by granting membership to these states, the EU is entering into an even larger security commitment. By expanding up to the borders of Russia and some of the western newly independent states (WNIS),[1] the EU will have no choice but to pay more attention to, and to take more responsibility for, promoting the stability and security of these countries. According to the March 2003 European Commission communication *Wider Europe – Neighbourhood: A new Framework for Relations with our Eastern and Southern Neighbours* (hitherto referred to as Wider Europe), 'over the coming decade and beyond, the EU's capacity to provide security, stability and sustainable development to its citizens will no longer be distinguishable from its interest in close cooperation with its neighbours'.[2]

Both the EU and its new Eastern neighbours are conscious that, throughout the 1990s, relations with non-EU candidate states in the East, including Russia, were less of a priority than preparing CEE countries for membership. However, following the Copenhagen Summit of February 2003, which gave the 'green light' to enlargement, EU members started to develop a more focused strategy towards their Eastern neighbours.

Belarus, Moldova, and Ukraine are part of the EU's European Neighbourhood Policy (ENP) and the three South Caucasus states were also included in it in June 2004. Russia is not part of ENP but the EU and Russia are pursuing cooperation through the 'common spaces' framework adopted at the June 2003 EU–Russia summit. In terms of security, though, the EU has not developed a consistent strategy on how to protect its external borders from 'soft security' threats and how to avoid the building of a new dividing line on the EU's Eastern frontier.

Reshaping relations with Russia – the EU's largest neighbour and a source of many cross-border threats – remains one of the most difficult challenges confronting the EU. Due to the country's size and geography, as well as its weak economy, it is unlikely that it will be considered for EU membership in the foreseeable future. Yet Russia, as a major regional and global player, is seeking to develop a special relationship with the EU, which goes beyond the existing partnership and cooperation framework, and is striving for some form of integration.

From Wider Europe to 'common spaces' in the security field

On a strategic level, Russia views the concept of 'common spaces' as a positive alternative to the Wider Europe proposal, which later became the ENP. Unlike ENP, the common spaces initiative was proposed by Moscow and accepted, if only in principle, by the EU. The idea was finalised at the May 2003 EU–Russia Summit in St Petersburg. At the gathering, the two sides significantly expanded the list of areas where some integration (both outside of membership and explicitly not linked to the prospect of membership) could be pursued by the EU and Russia. Among the long-term objectives of security cooperation, the summit identified the creation of two distinct 'common spaces'. First is the common space of freedom, security and justice (the extension to Russia of EU internal security policies that sit in its Justice and Home Affairs (JHA) basket). Second is the common space of cooperation in the field of external security (linked to EU–Russia cooperation under the umbrellas of the EU's Common Foreign and Security Policy (CFSP) and its nascent European Security and Defence Policy (ESDP)).[3]

The difference between these two areas of security cooperation reflects the EU's own policy distinction between the CFSP and JHA and also remains true to the traditions of EU–Russia collaboration. In the past, the first area of EU–Russia cooperation was external security issues – regional and global. This initially involved ad hoc political dialogue (such as the Contact Group in the Balkans and the Quartet of powers engaged in the Middle East peace process) and was later institutionalised under the Partnership and Cooperation Agreement (PCA), taking the form of summits and regular ministerial meetings. Key topics include non-proliferation (Iran and North Korea), the fight against terrorism, the Middle East peace process, limited political dialogue on 'frozen' conflicts in Eurasia, and, most recently, discussions on developments in Afghanistan, Central Asia and Iraq. In addition, there has been limited practical cooperation on CFSP and ESDP matters: the EU provided assistance for safeguarding and disposing of stockpiles of nuclear and chemical weapons, which Russia inherited from the former Soviet Union. More recently, there has been cooperation in the military sphere, as the EU has sought to use Russian resources to fill temporary gaps in its defence capabilities, such as heavy-lift launchers and satellite imagery. Russia also took part, although only symbolically, in the EU policing mission conducted under the ESDP in Bosnia and Herzegovina in 2003.

For the most part, EU–Russia cooperation on external security issues is unlikely to be significantly affected by the enlargement process, with the exception perhaps of the EU's more assertive stance in regard to promoting the resolution of conflicts on its new borders. A testing point for this is the Transdniestrian conflict in Moldova. Russia still maintains a military presence in this post-Soviet state[4] and has influence over the political process both through its multilateral framework with the Organisation for Security and Co-operation in Europe (OSCE) and through its bilateral relations with the government in Moldova and the authorities in Transdniester. At the same time Russia made a commitment to withdraw its troops from Moldova (and Georgia) in accordance with the terms of an agreement reached at the 1999 OSCE Istanbul Summit. EU accession countries, such as the Baltic States and Poland, might push the EU to take a stronger position, demanding that Russia meets these obligations. Furthermore, they might press for greater political scrutiny of Russia's activities in the Commonwealth of Independent States (CIS). This could lead to friction in EU–Russia relations. However, the EU is unlikely to undertake military action or to police zones of insecurity in the CIS particularly without reaching agreement with Moscow. In 2003, the EU considered in principle the idea of deploying military forces if all of the parties to the Moldova–Transdniester conflict reached a political agreement. No final decision has been taken, though, due to reservations among some member states and due to the Russian Presidential Administration's unsuccessful unilateral attempt to push through a controversial peace proposal (a memorandum negotiated by Dmitry Kozak, then Deputy Head of the Presidential Administration). Moldovan President Vladimir Voronin rejected the proposal in November 2003.

Another area in which the EU and Russia can work together but to a lesser extent is in upgrading the ex-Soviet military hardware still in the possession of some of the new EU members. The equipment might be used to enhance EU capabilities in future operations. However, agreements on this equipment are likely to be made on a bilateral basis without EU involvement. In other areas, such as counter-terrorism cooperation, EU enlargement could lead to new reservations within the EU, given that many of its new members are known critics of Russia's war in Chechnya.

Thus, in practice, the idea of a common space of external security is likely to involve more dialogue and only limited practical cooperation between the EU and Russia in regard to third countries (such as the former Yugoslavia) and for the foreseeable future will exclude CIS members. The EU–Russia common space for external security does not involve greater strategic integration of the two parties' foreign- and security-policy goals and instruments. Moreover, the EU's procedures for participation of non-EU states in EU military operations are very complex and do not allow for joint operations.[5] The situation is that Russia can be asked by the EU to contribute forces but is unlikely to receive any special command arrangement like the one developed for SFOR and KFOR. At the same time, integration along these lines is currently taking place under the North Atlantic Treaty Organisation (NATO)–Russia Permanent Joint Council (PJC), which promotes common threat perceptions (through the development of a joint threat assessment), interoperability in areas like peacekeeping (in light of lessons learned from the Balkans) and symbolic military exercises and training,[6] and develops cooperation on military reform in Russia. Thus, PJC instruments, for example, under the Berlin Plus formula,[7] rather than separate EU–Russia arrangements, are likely to be employed if a political decision is taken at some point that calls for the EU and Russia to undertake a joint operation.

In contrast to the concept of a common space for external security, a common space of freedom, security and justice (or extending to Russia the principles and practices on which EU internal security policy is being constructed) implies more integration and practical cooperation. Integration in these areas will be directly and significantly affected by EU enlargement. From the EU's perspective, the objectives of cooperation in this area include encouraging normative changes in Russia's domestic security policies – such as respect for human rights, democratic values and the rule of law – and working together with Russia to minimise cross-border security threats, ranging from organised crime to border security to illegal migration and environmental hazards. This chapter examines the major internal and trans-border security threats, as seen from the EU and Russia, and assesses existing and anticipated policy responses.

In some cases, EU enlargement poses potential security threats, which are not traditionally covered by either the ESDP or the JHA field, but fall into the category of economic development. Within the European Union itself, there is widespread recognition of the correlation between security and development. This has already led to subsidies for the development of particularly economically deprived areas. From this viewpoint, the growing gap in regard to economic development along the EU–Russia border, as well as declining standards of healthcare, combined with the spread of infectious diseases (such as HIV and AIDS) in Russia, are bound to have human security implications for the EU. Hence, this chapter also assesses disparities in relation to development over the border, especially with reference to those border regions of Russia that are likely to be most affected by EU enlargement. This problem is also examined from the standpoint of it posing a potential security risk to the EU, as well as to Russia.

The limits of EU–Russia cooperation on JHA
Although EU officials and European leaders have declared repeatedly that Europe cannot be secure without a stable, prosperous and democratic Russia, the promotion of stability and security in Russia is not the main objective of the EU's security policies – be it under the umbrella of the ESDP or JHA. On the one hand, Russia is no longer viewed as the EU's main source of insecurity in the post-Cold War/post-11 September world. The majority of the EU's long-term security challenges emanate from other neighbouring regions, including the Balkans, North Africa, the southern Mediterranean (Israel and Syria), and the wider Middle East (Iran and Iraq). On the other hand, limited EU involvement in Russia's internal security problems to date could also be explained by the widespread perception that Russia's soft security problems are so vast that the EU simply does not have adequate resources or the political will to make a decisive contribution to their resolution. It should be remembered that the EU only started to develop stronger cooperative ties between member states in the field of justice and home affairs in 1993 when the Treaty of Europe (the Amsterdam Treaty) was signed. The EU itself appears uncertain on the scope of, and the timeframe for, integration in the area of JHA including the role of the European police office (Europol), capabilities for guarding its borders, and the creation of an EU intelligence service (dealing with crime and other internal threats).[8]

Last, but not least, Russia itself has been reluctant to accept outside involvement in its domestic security issues, even if external engagement concerned problems that have an impact beyond Russia's borders, such as illegal migration, organised crime and smuggling. Moscow's reluctance stemmed from the slow pace of reform of the country's security sector (or repeated re-organisation, as in the case of the Federal Migration Service[9]), Russia's financial problems (preventing the country from fulfilling its obligations to improve border infrastructure), lack of inter-agency coordination, and over-centralisation of JHA-related policymaking (which has left regional offices that handle migration and other matters without the power to interact internationally). At the same time, Russian politicians and officials have rebuffed the assertions of the EU that Russia was the major source of soft security threats to its Western neighbours and to the rest of the European Union, referring often to the fact that the so-called Russian mafia includes citizens from other CIS nations. Moreover, cooperation between the EU and Russia on internal security issues has always been complicated by Russia's policy on Chechnya; the EU and European capitals have been consistently critical of it and Russia has been opposed to international mediation or conditional assistance. Finally, the absence of an EU–Russia dialogue on internal security issues, including on such important topics as border security, migration and police collaboration, has been complemented by the lack of any substantial bilateral cooperation programmes between Russia and its Eastern neighbours which are now EU member states (although there have been a few bilateral meetings between Russian border officials and their Estonian, Finnish and Latvian counterparts on an informal ad hoc basis). One of the reasons for this is found in the legal vacuum that was created as a result of Russia's refusal to conclude and ratify border agreements with Estonia and Latvia or to conclude a re-admission agreement with those states and with Poland. A border treaty and re-admission agreement with Lithuania was only ratified by the Russian Duma on 21 May 2003, in the context of the 'Kaliningrad compromise' (the Lithuanian parliament ratified it on 19 October 1999).

As a consequence of all of these factors, EU–Russia cooperation in the JHA field has been developing very slowly and only limited progress had been achieved by the time of enlargement on 1 May 2004. The EU's response has been to focus on developing a stronger barrier against soft security threats to the European Union, rather than on addressing the problems at the source (including in Russia and the countries of the CIS). The EU has allocated some Tacis funds to help with legal reforms and initiatives, such as the training of judges, but the scale of the assistance allows for little more than small pilot projects, rather than major changes to Russian norms and procedures to address internal security problems.

In an enlarged Europe, neither the EU nor Russia can justify any longer engaging in merely limited cooperation in the area of JHA; the result of minimal cooperation will be negative for both parties. For Russia, a 'hard border' with the enlarged EU entails significant economic and political costs. For the EU, erecting hard borders with the new Eastern neighbours, including Russia, contradicts its political aim of undertaking enlargement in order to unify the European continent, as opposed to creating new divisions. As the events of 11 September 2001 demonstrated, furthermore, borders are not effective barriers against transnational security threats. They can only be effective if the developed states take the solutions directly into the regions from where the problems emanate – that is, Russia and Russia's neighbours in Central Asia or the Far East (Chinese illegal immigrants transit Russia en route to Europe). The third reason is economic. The introduction of new barriers is likely to have significant ramifications for the new EU members, disrupting trade and human contact with Russia.

In addition to the political, economic and security rationale, on a practical level, the conditions for improving EU–Russia cooperation in the JHA field started to improve before 2004. On the one hand, the EU enhanced its own integration strategy under the JHA area, including the introduction of integrated border management.[10] This generated an important impetus for strengthening EU–Russia cooperation in this area. On the other hand, Russian President Vladimir Putin has recognised the importance of soft security threats for Russia, has made efforts to reform the Russian security sector, has introduced new legislation, and has encouraged international cooperation on security matters, including trans-border threats.

Under these circumstances, the portrayal of Russia as insecure neighbour has been gradually replaced by one of partner on internal and cross-border security matters. Progress has been achieved in a number of fields. Originally, cooperation on domestic security issues had been flagged as a priority area in the PCA, which entered into force on 1 December 1997. The PCA included references to cooperation in the fight against organised crime, illegal migration, nuclear proliferation and environmental hazards.[11] All of these issues came under the rubric of 'common challenges on the European continent', which constituted one of the four principal objectives of EU policy, as outlined in the EU Common Strategy towards Russia, adopted on 4 June 1999.[12] However, the first practical agreement between the EU and Russia in the JHA sphere was the Action Plan on Combating Organised Crime, which was adopted by the EU–Russia Cooperation Council on 25 April 2000. It was followed by the first meeting between EU and Russian Ministers of Justice and Home Affairs (interior) and members of the EU Troika (the actual and the incoming presidencies of the EU and the European Commission) in Stockholm, Sweden, on 6 April 2001. The gathering resulted in a joint declaration on contact points for the exchange of information on organised crime.

EU–Russia cooperation on border security has been developing mostly on a bilateral level, including with Finland, an EU member state, or under a sub-regional framework, such as the Task Force on Organised Crime in the Baltic Sea Region, of which the EU and Russia are both members.[13] The first document adopted by the EU and Russia on border issues was the Joint Statement on Transit between the Kaliningrad Region and the Rest of the Russian Federation, which was released at the tenth EU–Russia Summit on 11 November 2002.[14] The concept of common spaces, including the common space of freedom, security and justice, was agreed upon at the eleventh EU–Russia Summit in May 2003. Finally, Russia signed an agreement to join Europol at the twelfth EU–Russia Summit in November 2003.

Cooperation on JHA issues is becoming one of the main priorities for collaboration between the EU and Russia. On the basis of decisions taken at the May 2003 summit, the EU and Russia are establishing a Permanent Partnership Council (PPC) dealing with JHA matters as well as energy, the environment and transport.[15] The PPC will involve meetings at the ministerial level, including ministers of Justice and Internal Affairs. While in the field of JHA ministerial troikas have been convened since April 2001, ministerial meetings under the new PPC will bring together the European Commission, the Presidency of the European Union, and the Russian Presidential Administration (which can coordinate all relevant Russian ministries). At the May 2004 EU–Russia summit, President Putin appointed Victor Ivanov, an influential member of the Presidential Administration, to oversee preparations for a road map for a common space on JHA. As a result, some JHA matters will come to the fore in discussions at the highest level. Furthermore, the European Commission is considering setting up a sub-committee under the PCA comprising technical experts and dedicated solely to JHA matters. Thus, the JHA might become one area where cooperation is institutionalised on every level and which utilises all of the political instruments associated with EU–Russia cooperation.

All of these agreements and proposals provide a political and legal foundation for EU–Russia cooperation on internal and cross-border security issues. However, practical cooperation continues to face difficulties. On the EU's side, one of the main constraints is limited resources; the priority is to provide assistance to the new member countries, not to Russia. In addition, the EU suffers from an information deficit on two key issues that have implications for EU member states that border Russia. First, although the EU operates a network of law-enforcement liaison officers in Russia, it still has inadequate information on organised criminal groups in the former Soviet Union that are responsible for the majority of cross-border threats, ranging from people smuggling to drug trafficking to trade in stolen vehicles. Second, it has had little success in monitoring soft security problems in Russia, ranging from environmental challenges to health risks. As for Russia, the key impediments to cooperation remain the same as they were in the 1990s, although on a smaller scale. These include incomplete reform of the security sector (particularly of law-enforcement bodies), the need to adopt additional legislation regulating soft security issues, and confusion over the division of powers between various branches of government, particularly between central and regional authorities, in relation to internal and soft security policies.

All of these difficulties will contribute directly to the extent that Russia will remain an insecure neighbour or will emerge as a security partner of the enlarged European Union. The main challenges stemming from enlargement relate to the following areas: border security and new border regimes; illegal migration; organised crime and trafficking.

New border regimes

Enlargement means that the EU is replacing its relatively secure Eastern frontiers (in the form of small CEE states), with a much less stable and less controllable zone, encompassing the WNIS and Russia. While the EU had a visa-free arrangement with many CEE countries for several years prior to enlargement, neither Russia nor any of the WNIS enjoy such a waiver. Furthermore, Russia has not completed the process of legalising its Western borders with the new EU member states. Unlike the CEE states, Russia is a vast country stretching across 12 time zones from the edge of the European Union to the Pacific Ocean and bordering such unstable regions as Central Asia and the south Caucasus. Russia has visa-free travel agreements with some of these nations. Its land border has been transformed in the post-Soviet period, but it remains the longest in the world, spanning over 61,000 kilometres. Russia borders 16 states; the new EU–Russia border incorporates five of them.

Of these five borders, only the Finnish–Russian (1,313km) and the Polish–Russian (206km) frontiers were properly demarcated and equipped prior to 1991, although the Polish border did require significant modernisation. The other countries' borders with Russia – Estonia (294km), Latvia (217km) and Lithuania (227km) – have undergone de facto delimitation and have been equipped with border-control infrastructure over the past decade. This was mostly carried out by the individual accession states, although significant EU financial assistance was allocated to border security during the accession process. On 1 May 2004, when the new members acceded to the European Union, the EU's common land border with Russia was extended to 2,257km in length. While this is not the longest EU external border with a single country, it is the longest land border with a state that is not a member of the European Economic Area (EEA) or the Schengen regime (Norway's border with Finland and Sweden measures 2,348km). The EU–Russia border is the longest of all of the EU's post-enlargement frontiers in the East.[16]

By 2002, the EU was satisfied that the three Baltic States and Poland had established border regimes that met European Union standards (see Table 4.1). By 1 July 2003 (1 October 2003 for Poland), they had introduced visa regimes that met the requirements of the Schengen *acquis*. Notwithstanding a special agreement on Kaliningrad transit, the EU made it clear that candidate states had to comply with all JHA requirements in time for accession, with no exceptions or delays. The EU introduced this stipulation despite the fact that, even after accession, the new members will retain internal border controls with their Western neighbours and will not be full members of the Schengen zone until 2006 at the earliest, when the Schengen Information System (SIS) II is due to be finalised. The tightening of the visa regime by CEE states, which had more liberal visa policies vis-à-vis Russian citizens, is expected to have a significant economic impact both on the new members and on some Russian regions, particularly those that depend on cross-border trade.

In recognition of this problem, Wider Europe[17] emphasised that both the EU and its neighbours have a common interest in ensuring that the new external border is not a barrier to trade, social and cultural interchange, or regional cooperation. Therefore, the European Commission proposed that the Council of the EU should develop a special *acquis* on local border traffic, including the introduction of a special local visa. Local border traffic is defined in the Wider Europe communication as regular crossing of the external land border of a member state by persons lawfully resident in the border region of a neighbouring third country, who are permitted to stay in the border area of that member state for a limited period.[18] According to the European Commission, efficient rules for local border traffic will help to promote the development of border regions and facilitate the crossing of the frontier by genuine border residents, while at the same time taking into account the need to prevent illegal immigration into the EU, as well as potential threats to security emanating from criminal activities.

In order to implement this arrangement, the EU has called on its member states to maintain or conclude bilaterally, if necessary, agreements with neighbouring third countries to facilitate local traffic between their border regions. Indeed, such an agreement did exist for some categories of border residents living in Russia's Pskov *oblast* and neighbouring border regions in Estonia and Latvia, whereas all other Russians had been obliged to have Estonian or Latvian visas since the early 1990s. These arrangements were annulled during the accession negotiations: one of the requirements to finalise Chapter 24 (JHA). Similar agreements for a simplified visa regime and special local border crossings exist between Finland and Russia (for residents of the Republic of Karelia). But special provisions for Lithuanian and Kaliningrad border

Table 4.1 The borders of Estonia, Latvia, Lithuania and Poland

Country	Length of border	Number of border-crossing points with Russia	Status of re-admission agreements with Russia	Date of introduction of new visa regulations for Russians	Completion date of JHA Chapter
Estonia	Latvia: 339km Russia: 294km	5	Not signed	July 2002	Chapter opened: May 2000 Status: closed December 2002 (provisionally closed in March 2002)
Latvia	Belarus: 141km Estonia: 339km Lithuania: 453km Russia: 217km	6	Not signed	1 May 2003	Chapter opened: June 2001 Status: closed December 2002 (provisionally closed in June 2002)
Lithuania	Belarus: 502km Latvia: 453km Poland: 91km Russia (Kaliningrad oblast): 227km	9	Ratified by Lithuanian parliament (19 October 1999) and Russian parliament (21 May 2003)	1 July 2003	Chapter opened: June 2001 Status: closed December 2002 (provisionally closed in June 2002)
Poland	Belarus: 407km Czech Rep.: 658km Germany: 456km Lithuania: 91km Russia (Kaliningrad oblast): 206km Slovakia: 44km Ukraine: 526km*	5	Not signed	1 October 2003	Chapter opened: May 2000 Status: closed December 2002 (provisionally closed in July 2002)#

Source: *Prozrachnye granitsy: bezopasnost I transgranichnoe sotrudnichestvo v zone novykh pogranichnykh territorii Rossii (Transparent Frontiers: Security and Transboundary Cooperation in Russia's New Borderlands)* (Moscow: 2002, Academic Educational Forum on International Relations), pp. 551–552.

* Central Intelligence Agency (CIA) World Factbook 2002, www.cia.gov/cia/publications/factbook
# http://europa.eu.int/comm/enlargement/negotiations/chapters/chap24/

residents were dropped as part of the Kaliningrad transit agreement (although one current concession is that citizens of Kaliningrad are entitled to multiple visas to enter Poland at no charge but this arrangement is likely to be annulled when Poland joins the SIS II in 2006).

The introduction of a local border-traffic facilitation visa regime is likely to have a positive impact on cross-border trade and exchanges while at the same time curbing illegal cross-border trade and smuggling. According to Russian Deputy Minister of Foreign Affairs Vladimir Chizhov, however, 'emphasis on promoting the development of border regions [as stated in Wider Europe] is likely to have a negative impact on other regions [within Russia] and thus instead of promoting stability in the entire neighbouring country it could provoke the exact opposite effect by increasing the development gap between different regions'.[19] The problem highlighted by Chizhov, though, appears much less acute, at least in the short and medium terms, than the growing economic disparity between Russia's north-west border regions and the contiguous border areas in the enlarged EU. This development gap is likely to have immediate security ramifications.

Russia's view is that, instead of introducing additional specialised local instruments into its border arrangement with Russia, the EU should develop a road map specifying the policy steps that have to be taken to establish a visa-free regime between the EU and Russia. This perspective ignores the short-term needs of those Russian border regions affected by enlargement. In fact, furthermore, it prevents progress in regard to cooperation between the EU and Russia on border and visa regimes, since many EU member states, including Finland, are reluctant to take the visa-free proposal seriously because of political and security concerns. Instead, Finland supports the idea of a local traffic visa in order to improve cross-border contacts between residents of the border regions. Estonia, Latvia and Poland now hold similar positions.

While it is anticipated that more stringent border regimes will have a negative impact on legitimate economic and human contact between Russia and the new EU members, it is not clear whether the tightening of border regimes will significantly diminish cross-border security risks, such as illegal migration and the trafficking in human beings and drugs, and criminal pursuits like trade in stolen vehicles. It is clear that, in order to address such threats, visa regimes are not enough. Other steps that need to be taken include:

- improvement in the administrative capacity, the technical base and the infrastructure of Russia, allowing the authorities to monitor, process and repatriate illegal migrants who have been smuggled from third countries via Russia into Europe;

- modernisation of border infrastructure and the strengthening of border controls on the Russian side of the frontier; and

- facilitation of an information exchange between border officials from Russia and its neighbours (as is occurring between the Finnish and Russian border services).

None of these policies can be implemented successfully until the EU and Russia reach a final agreement on the legal status of all of the new shared borders. While the three Baltic States have introduced modern border infrastructure and controls with EU financial and technical assistance,[20] the legal status of these frontiers with the exception of Lithuania has not been resolved. Russia has not signed border treaties with Estonia and Latvia, although bilateral commissions have finalised actual border delineation on maps and agreed that there are no outstanding territorial claims between the two parties. Lithuania is the only one of the three Baltic States to have a ratified border treaty with Russia.

Russia's past refusal to conclude and ratify border treaties with the three Baltic States was believed to be linked to its opposition to their membership of NATO. Russian obstinacy was seen as a tactical attempt to delay their accession to the Alliance.[21] An alternative rationale was that Russia delayed signing a border treaty with Lithuania in order to put pressure on the country in regard to Kaliningrad. Similarly, Russian procrastination with respect to Estonia and Latvia was due to concerns about the rights of Russian ethnic minorities in those two states and to its annoyance at territorial claims that they had made (which Estonia and Latvia had to drop when they became a barrier to membership of the EU and NATO).[22]

In addition to the border accord, Russia signed a re-admission agreement with Lithuania on 12 May 2003. This was part of a compromise on Kaliningrad transit that was reached at the EU–Russia Summit in November 2002. It was ratified by the Russian Duma on 11 June 2003 and the Federation Council on 25 June 2003. This agreement was the first re-admission agreement to be signed by Russia with an EU candidate or member state and it is expected to pave the way for a more comprehensive EU–Russia re-admission agreement, like the one signed by the EU and Ukraine. According to the Russian government, it is expected that Russia will spend R1.7 million ($570,000) a year on the agreement[23] and that it will admit back into Russia between several dozen and 100 people per annum.[24] The Russian Federal Migration Service, which was placed under the Ministry of Internal Affairs in 2001, has been put in charge of implementing the re-admission agreement.[25] However, lack of capacity to house illegal migrants and still too liberal laws on human trafficking are likely to complicate the fulfilment of Russia's treaty obligations.

Even if a comprehensive re-admission agreement is signed, deficiencies in the Russian security sector will hamper its effective implementation. In the absence of the security guarantees that an effective agreement should provide, the EU's main concern will remain the state of Russia's porous southern frontiers. Russia's least secure and most poorly equipped borders are those with Azerbaijan (284km), Georgia (723km) and Kazakhstan (6,846km).[26] These constitute the main gateways for illegal migration, drug trafficking, the smuggling of people and weapons, and other types of cross-border crime that have implications not only for Russia, but also increasingly for the EU.

Illegal migration

Despite European concerns following the collapse of the Soviet Union, Russian citizens have not accounted for a significant proportion of migrants who enter the EU illegally.[27] According to data contained in Wider Europe, Russians made up only 3.2% of all non-EU immigrants in EU states in 2000.[28] And only 1.5% of non-EU nationals residing in the EU in 2001 were Russian citizens.[29] The majority had a legal basis for their presence in the EU. According to the International Organisation for Migration, between 1998 and 2000, 227,901 people left Russia. The majority (59.1%) of the emigrants settled in Germany (mostly Russians and ethnic Germans who were residing in the Soviet Union and gained the right to repatriate to Germany after the end of the Cold War). Approximately 50,000 Russian specialists were reportedly working in Germany in 2001–02,[30] but these legal labour migrants do not represent a major concern for EU states and are often welcomed by countries in need of highly skilled professionals to meet labour shortages.

In addition to recorded flows, though, there are of course illegal immigrants and asylum seekers. The Russian Federal Border Guard Service revealed in June 2003 that the number of illegal migrants detained along all of Russia's state borders doubled between 1999 and 2002 – the total stood at over 63,000 by the end of 2003. But not all of these individuals were stopped along Russia's new borders with the EU. It was estimated in 2000 that, of the 1.5 to two million Russians who go to work abroad every year, only 45,800 had work permits. The EU is disconcerted by the number of these Russian illegal labour migrants, although the figure is still smaller than the potential number of legal labour migrants who are expected to move to old EU members from the new member states.

Those who seek illegal entry into Europe across Russia's borders are not necessarily Russian. Russia's geographical location makes it a transit route for illegal migrants travelling from third countries to Europe. International criminal groups exploit this fact. United Nations (UN) experts believe that Russian transnational crime nets over $1 billion per year from transporting illegal migrants to EU nations.[31]

One form of illegal labour is prostitution. It is estimated that more than 50,000 women, assumed to be from Russia, are working as prostitutes in the West. In fact they come not only from the Russian Federation, but also from the Baltic States and countries of the CIS.[32] It is hard to calculate what percentage of these women is actually Russian, but it is clear that many traffickers in women are either Russian citizens or base their operations on Russian territory. The reason is that Russia has liberal laws that do not impose a significant penalty for the trafficking in women. The EU is pressing Russia to increase the penalties. In January 2004, Putin highlighted amendments that have been made to the Russian Criminal Code, establishing liability for the trafficking in human beings and in principle making it impossible for such activity to go unpunished.[33]

The number of Russian citizens who sought asylum in European countries more than doubled between 1998 and 2000. In 1998, the figure was 6,068, in 1999 8,240, and in 2000 14,332. The preferred destinations were Belgium, Germany, the Netherlands, Poland and the UK.[34] Recent years have seen changes both in terms of numbers and, to some extent, destination, with EU accession states receiving more applications. The five countries that received the largest numbers of Russian asylum seekers in 2003 were Austria (6,700), Poland (5,600), the Czech Republic (4,900), Germany (3,400) and Slovakia (2,700); three of which acceded to the EU on 1 May 2004.[35] In 2003, according to data obtained from 36 industrialised countries by the United Nations High Commissioner for Refugees (UNHCR), 33,400 Russians sought asylum in 29 of these 36 industrialised countries, including EU member states (the majority of them Chechens). Therefore, Russia was the world's largest source of refugees seeking permanent asylum in the EU. In 2003, the number of Russian asylum seekers in the EU rose to 34%, compared to the previous year (although the increase was 73% for the whole of Europe).

Since Russia itself is a destination for illegal labour migrants, mainly from CIS countries, but also from Afghanistan and China, there is concern in Europe that some of these people intend to travel on to the EU. This fear is compounded by the prediction of further growth in the number of illegal immigrants entering Russia. According to Roger Plant of the International Labour Organisation (ILO), 'Russia… is not only a country receiving illegal immigrants, but also a source of them.' The ILO forecasts that the Russian economy will become dependent on immigrant manpower. The shadow economy and lack of legislation regulating migration are reasons for the rise in illegal immigration into Russia.[36]

The Russian Interior Ministry estimates that there are between 1.5 and five million illegal immigrants in Russia at the present time. The

Table 4.2 Migration from the Russian Federation

Countries	1995	1996	1997	1998	1999	2000	2001	2002
Departures from the Russian Federation (total)	**339,600**	**288,048**	**234,284**	**216,691**	**237,967**	**161,046**	**137,573**	**N/A**
Including to:								
CIS countries and the Baltic States:	**229,287**	**191,383**	**149,461**	**133,017**	**129,704**	**83,438**	**62,545**	**52,969**
Estonia	877	822	702	550	564	385	402	321
Lithuania	1,367	1,252	1,162	805	721	376	262	293
Other nations excluding CIS countries and the Baltic States:	**110,313**	**96,665**	**84,823**	**83,674**	**108,263**	**77,608**	**75,028**	**53,716**
Germany	79,569	64,420	52,140	49,186	52,832	45,264	N/A	42,231
Greece	1,278	1,298	955	794	868	528	N/A	190
Poland	226	196	186	274	191	99	N/A	80
Finland	603	728	755	798	1,068	1,078	N/A	1,110
Sweden	106	138	102	146	172	144	N/A	16

Sources: *The Demographic Yearbook of Russia, 2001* (Moscow: Goskomstat of the Russian Federation, 2001), p. 339; Chislennost i migratsiya naseleniya Rossiiskoi Federatsii v 2002 godu (Moscow: Goskomstat of the Russian Federation, 2003).

majority originated in CIS countries, but a significant proportion has come from China.[37] Data on the number of illegal migrants who have entered Russia from other CIS nations vary, but it is known that over 20m people from Azerbaijan, Georgia, Kazakhstan, Tajikistan and Ukraine migrated to Russia between 1997 and 2001.[38] According to some studies, the majority of these immigrants do not wish to settle in Russia for the long term and might be seeking to move to the West.[39] Yet, it might be assumed that illegal immigrants from CIS countries will not endeavour to move to the EU because in Europe they would neither have similar language skills nor organised ethnic communities to help them find illegal employment.

It is clear that illegal migration is a problem for Russia and one that the EU is right to be concerned about, since Russia is one of the routes for transporting illegal migrants to the EU. Recent data concerning old and new borders between the European Union and Russia reveal that regular attempts are made to cross the border illegally, although the number of incidents does not appear to be high. According to a report by the Finnish Frontier Guard, only 47 illegal attempts to cross the border into Finland from Russia were detected in 2000.[40] However, additional persons were apprehended on the Russian side of the frontier. The Russian Border Guards apprehended 190 people trying to cross into Finland in 2000, 90% of whom were trying to gain access to the country illegally. Major-General Alexei Stepanov, the head of the North-west Regional Administration of the Border Guards of the Russian Federation, confirmed that they were by no means all Russian. He reported that these 190 people represented 23 nationalities.[41] As for the new EU–Russia border, some sources indicate that the number of illegal migrants attempting to cross into Europe from Russia via the Baltic States has declined significantly, even in the period before the new EU members tightened their borders to meet their accession criteria. The number of illegal migrants apprehended in Lithuania declined from 1,353 in 1995 to 100 in 2000, while the number of illegal migrants detained in Estonia remained low and stable over the same period (21 in 1995 and 27 in 2000).[42] Lithuanian experts believe that, following the signing of the re-admission agreement with Russia, no more than several dozen illegal migrants will be deported to Russia annually.[43] The accuracy of their assessment will be clear only by the end of 2004 after the first batch of data is collected and analysed.

Despite these figures, there are a number of reasons why the border authorities on either side of the borders between the EU and Russia will need to continue to be alert to attempts to gain illegal entrance to the EU from Russian territory. There are several factors that are driving this phenomenon:

- Russia's open, porous borders with Central Asia. In 1997–99, Russian Border Guards apprehended 1,965 illegal migrants (of whom 1,538 were Afghans) on the Kazakh–Russian border and 2,618 on the Russian–Ukrainian border. It is assumed that those seeking entry to Ukraine were en route to the EU.[44] During the first six months of 2003, the number of illegal migrants detained on Ukraine's borders grew by 70% to 3,555, compared with the same period in 2002. Of those, 85% were detained along the Russian–Ukrainian border, and 61% of those who tried to leave Ukraine illegally were stopped on the Slovak border, which does imply that they were heading westward towards the EU.[45] In January 2004, 428 illegal migrants were apprehended by Ukrainian border guards.[46]

- The increasing sophistication of criminal networks involved in human trafficking. (In August 2003, five Russian citizens were arrested on charges of transporting illegal migrants to Spain.)[47]

- The still inadequate level of cooperation and coordination between Russian border and law-enforcement services and those of Russia's neighbours.

- The relative ease of acquiring Russian passports and even diplomatic passports. These papers may be genuine or fake. Fraudulent travel documents add to the challenge confronting the EU in terms of dealing with criminals with multiple identities. The EU's JHA Troika is demanding that passport issuance procedures be made stringent in order to prevent this.

- The absence of a re-admission agreement between the EU and Russia, as well as between Russia and other CIS nations, making it difficult to regulate illegal migration using internationally recognised legal mechanisms.

- The Russian Federal Migration Service has limited capacity to deal with illegal migration (as well as to register and monitor legal migrants). Deficiencies include: a shortage of funds for repatriating illegal migrants; a lack of facilities for processing applicants with refugee status (stipulated in the 1951 United Nations Refugee Convention); and a dearth of effective procedures for monitoring migration and travel flows. (The introduction of a migration form in 2002 for all foreign citizens entering Russia is a sign of progress, although there are many reported cases of these forms not being issued to those crossing the border between Kazakhstan and Russia.)

All of these factors represent a major cause of concern for the EU and a key obstacle to progress towards the establishment of a visa-free regime between the Russian Federation and the EU (particularly its Schengen zone). A visa-free travel initiative proposed by Putin in August 2002 has since become a primary Russian objective in relation to its relationship with the EU – this was restated as a long-term goal at the EU–Russia Summit in St Petersburg in May 2003. A similar aim was reiterated at the EU–Russia Summit in Rome, Italy, on 6 November 2003. The EU reaffirmed that it will support meetings of experts to examine conditions for visa-free travel in the long term and look at existing flexibilities within the Schengen *acquis* in order to facilitate travel in the short term.[48] The European Commission is developing a proposal to facilitate the issuance of visas to third-party (non-EU) experts, which will include Russia, to conduct this research. However, any advancement in regard to other forms of facilitated visa issuance depends on improvements in travel document security in Russia. Moreover, the EU expects Russia to introduce reciprocal measures, making it easier for EU citizens to obtain a Russian visa (for example, by reducing the bureaucracy involved in acquiring an official invitation letter from the Russian Ministry of Foreign Affairs). So far Russia has not relaxed any of its visa issuing and registration procedures. In 2004, Russia and Italy signed a bilateral agreement on simplifying visa rules for travel by their citizens but doubts remain as to how it might be implemented without a new EU–Russian agreement on visas.

As for other EU requirements in regard to upgrading Russia's border infrastructure, the former Prime Minister of the Russian Federation, Mikhail Kasyanov, stated in 2003 that it would take Russia between five and seven years to build border infrastructure that would meet European demands concerning visa-free travel from Russia.[49] With the introduction of local traffic visas by the EU, regions of Russia that border the enlarged EU will become the first areas in which simplified visa procedures will be tested. Border control structures will need to be modern and efficient to facilitate this.

Transit between Kaliningrad and the rest of Russia is exempt from Schengen restrictions; an agreement on this was reached between the EU, Lithuania and Russia at the EU–Russia Summit on 11 November 2003, which has since entered into force. However, the facilitated travel document (FTD) that Russian citizens have to obtain – in accordance with the November 2003 agreement – in order to travel across Lithuanian (EU) territory represents a kind of visa in all but name; it gives Lithuania the right to deny any Russian citizen who is under suspicion by the authorities the right of transit. In addition, Russian citizens who have been granted a Schengen visa (for example to Germany) are exempt from obtaining a transit visa for Poland.[50] It would be wise to extend similar arrangements to other new member states. Prior to the 2004 round of enlargement, the EU was not prepared to consider any other exceptions for Russian citizens, unless re-admission agreements were concluded and anti-counterfeit measures implemented for holders of Russian foreign passports. Nor was the EU prepared to produce a road map (which Russia advocates), specifying all of the EU requirements that Russia must meet in order to be considered for visa-free travel status within the Schengen zone. For now, all that the EU and Russia have agreed on is that visa-free travel is a long-term goal.

In the meantime, though, both sides have an interest in closer cooperation to combat illegal migration, as well as to aid the introduction of internationally recognised legal norms and practices to deal with illegal labour migration to Russia. This will necessitate cooperation on four levels:

1. EU assistance to improve Russia's border controls and migration policies. For example, assistance is being provided to the Russian Federal Migration Service, which is developing a single database to register all foreign citizens entering and exiting the country. It is expected to be operational by 2005.
2. Bilateral cooperation between Russia and its neighbours to track illegal migration flows. This should include regular exchanges of information (possibly via a shared database), joint training, and combined operations to apprehend those involved in trafficking.
3. Multilateral cooperation. This not only covers Russian cooperation with EU institutions working in the area of JHA, but also greater EU involvement (possibly as an observer) in multilateral mechanisms like the Council of Interior Ministers (under CIS auspices) and the 'Bishkek Group' (under the Shanghai Cooperation Organisation, comprising China, Russia and four Central Asian states).
4. Inter-agency approach. To combat human trafficking, the EU and Russia should increase the level of cooperation between their border, migration and law-enforcement services.

Security implications of the development gaps

Illegal migration is linked not only to security issues and organised crime, but also to development gaps. Illegal labour migrants will continue to enter the EU as long as the economic disparity between the EU and Russia, particularly along the new borders, remains large. In the enlarged EU, the EU borders six Russian federal entities (*oblasts* and republics): the Republic of Karelia (Finland); Murmansk *oblast* (Finland and Norway, which is in the Schengen zone); Leningrad *oblast* (Finland and Estonia); the city of St Petersburg (maritime border with Estonia and

Finland); Pskov *oblast* (Latvia and Estonia); and Kaliningrad *oblast* (Poland and Lithuania). The Kaliningrad and Pskov regions that border the territory of the new EU members have a much lower standard of living than their neighbours. A reported 30% of Kaliningrad's population is living below the subsistence level and the standard of living in Kaliningrad *oblast* is 1.4 times lower than that in the rest of Russia.[51]

The economic weakness of Russia's border regions is compounded by the fact that areas on the other side of the border – Warminsko-Mazurskie in Poland, Aluksnes, Balvu and Ludzas in Latvia and Ida-Virumaa in Estonia – are among the most economically underdeveloped and least politically integrated regions within those states. As a result, the economic wellbeing of residents in these areas is dependent on a variety of illegal pursuits, primarily smuggling. While these activities are likely to be curtailed as a result of the introduction of stricter border and visa regimes, the economic discrepancy (between neighbouring countries and between central and peripheral regions within a country) will be frozen or might even widen. Consequently, borders are likely to remain a source of instability and criminality in all its manifestations. This problem will require a more comprehensive response, such as by making it easier for skilled workers from border regions who are in demand in the EU (like doctors and nurses) to obtain temporary employment permits, while, at the same time, legalising shuttle trade, developing special economic-development and job-creation programmes that target the border regions of north-west Russia.

In addition to illegal migration, cross-border development gaps produce a number of other soft security challenges for the more wealthy neighbours, in this case the EU. Table 4.3 illustrates the differences in health and environmental indicators in Russia's border regions, which might represent a challenge for the EU and need to be addressed through special programmes under the Wider Europe concept or the common-spaces initiative.

Environmental- and health-related threats originating in Russia and in other countries of the former Soviet Union represent a major cause of concern for ordinary people and policymakers in north-east Europe. The Chernobyl accident of 1986 and revelations about poor environmental standards in East Germany, Poland and other former Eastern bloc nations have had a lasting impact on EU policy priorities in regard to the East. The poor public health situation is seen both as a risk, particularly as far as infectious diseases are concerned, and as a humanitarian worry. Even prior to enlargement, a number of Russia's European neighbours, especially the Baltic and Nordic states, became actively engaged in assistance programmes aimed at improving environmental and health indicators in Russia.

Table 4.3 Environmental and health indicators, North-west Russia, 2001

Regions	Murmansk oblast	Republic of Karelia	St Petersburg	Leningrad oblast	Pskov oblast	Kaliningrad oblast	Total/average for Russia
(R) indicates rank in Russia's 89 regions							
Environment							
Air pollution (1,000 tons)	369	139	57	182	20	43	*Total* 19.1 million tons
Production of toxic waste (1,000 tons)	469	161	1,878	3,764	30	54	*Total* 139,194 tons
Health							
Number of doctors per 10,000 people	44.3 R 37	46.9 R 28	76.2 R 2	30.9 R 77	34 R 71	35.8 R 63	*Average* 47.3
Number of hospital beds per 10,000 people	108.3 R 63	116.6 R 43	102.2 R71	99.5 R73	126.6 R 22	113.7 R 51	*Average* 115.4
Number of infectious diseases per 1,000 people	52.2	57.6	54.6	35.5	27.1	53.5	*Average* 44.2

Source: Regioni Rossii: sotsialno-ekonomicheskie pokazateli 2002 (*Russian Regions: Socio-Economic Indicators for North-west Federal District 2002*) (Moscow: Goskomstat of the Russian Federation, 2002), pp. 232–292.

Enlargement is likely to provide further impetus in this area. Wider Europe gives credit to the EU's Northern Dimension initiative to address environmental issues and seeks to apply the positive lessons from that framework to the EU's relations with its new neighbours. In future, therefore, environmental and health issues in the north-west regions of Russia are likely to be included in the Northern and Eastern Dimension programmes of the European Union.[52]

Insecurities of transition: organised crime and drug trafficking

There is no doubt that, over the past decade, Russia has become a more open society but that, equally, it has become less secure both for its citizens and for its neighbours. For Poland and the Baltic States, as for other EU members, the present insecurity is rooted in Russia's position of weakness, rather than in its position of strength. Over the past decade, Russia's difficult transition from a Soviet security system to a new arrangement that is yet to meet European standards in technical, legal and professional terms has been the source of new security challenges. Institutional weakness, corruption and inadequate funding have given rise to many problems that are having an impact beyond Russia's borders. These include criminality linked to a variety of cross-border threats, such as trafficking in drugs, weapons and human beings, as well as to the activities of Russian organised-crime networks, which are believed to be operating throughout Europe.

In the past decade, the Russian government has managed to eradicate the rigid Soviet system of law enforcement and its military and border-security structures, but it has failed to create a well functioning new arrangement. The slow pace of reform of the judiciary and law-enforcement bodies, as well as of other branches of the security sector, means that Russia's security environment has many deficiencies not only in comparison with the most developed West European states, but also with its immediate neighbours – the EU new members. Organised crime and drug trafficking are the two non-military security threats that are perceived to be having the most negative effect on relations between the EU and Russia.

More than 105,000 cases of drug trafficking and drug-related crime were registered in Russia in the first five months of 2003. According to Viktor Cherkesov, the Chairman of the Russian State Committee for Control over the Illegal Trafficking of Narcotics and Psychotropic Substances, the number of drug-related crimes registered during that period was much larger than that registered in the whole of 2002.[53] And according to the Rosbalt information agency, organised-crime groups were responsible for 10,600 of 27,600 crimes committed in 2002.[54] The Russian Interior Ministry reported that, in 2000, organised-crime groups

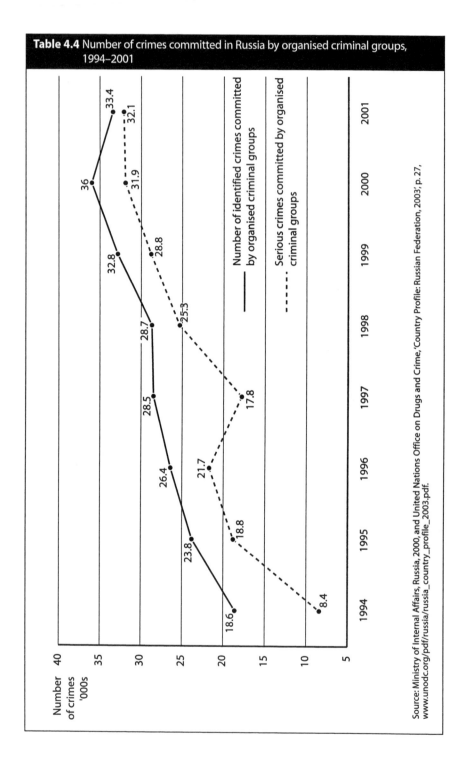

Table 4.4 Number of crimes committed in Russia by organised criminal groups, 1994–2001

Number of crimes '000s

Number of identified crimes committed by organised criminal groups

Serious crimes committed by organised criminal groups

Source: Ministry of Internal Affairs, Russia, 2000, and United Nations Office on Drugs and Crime, 'Country Profile: Russian Federation, 2003', p. 27, www.unodc.org/pdf/russia/russia_country_profile_2003.pdf.

committed 2,899 drug-related offences, an increase of 71% on the previous year (see Table 4.4).

Crime figures for Russian regions that border the EU are also on the rise. Most of these regions have recorded higher crime rates than the Russian average, although the majority remain below official levels in neighbouring European states (see Table 4.5). This statistic is likely to be misleading, though, as the methodology for calculating crime rates in the two areas differs: Russian statistics are likely to include only registered crimes, representing only a proportion of real crime. At the same time, statistics indicate that crime rates are just as high in Russian border regions as they are in the rest of Russia, and much higher, particularly in terms of serious criminal offences, than the average in the EU or in neighbouring Eastern European states.

By pointing the finger at Russia for being a source of criminality in the European Union, the EU often generates resentment on the part of the Russian government and its politicians. Russia believes that this is a speculative, overstated stereotype, which is based on prejudice. Many politicians in Russia see the European fixation with the Russian mafia as a deliberate strategy to undermine the country's international image, to separate it from Europe, and to pass on the blame for some of the failures of Europe's policies (such as controlling drug consumption or developing a better approach to asylum). Although such conspiracy theories are a clear distortion of the true state of affairs, they do reflect the fact that the two sides still have a lot of work to do to develop common strategies to address security problems. There are a number of controversial issues that complicate dialogue between the EU and Russia on crime-related matters. The main ones are set out below.

First, the European press and EU officials blame the Russian mafia for all criminal activity involving post-Soviet nationals. This is also true in regard to the trafficking in women who come from other western CIS nations, such as Moldova or Ukraine. It is correct, however, that the criminal networks that are responsible for trafficking often include Russian criminal groups.

Second, Russia sees itself as a victim of drug trafficking, not as a source of it. Most of the drugs that originate in Afghanistan are destined for consumption in Western Europe. Russia, therefore, serves as just one of many transit routes. The rise in drug production in Afghanistan following the fall of the Taliban regime in 2001 has meant that an increasing volume of narcotics is being transported through Russia; this serves to boost crime rates in Russia and to exacerbate already high levels of drug abuse there. Russians often criticise the US and West European members of the anti-terrorist coalition for failing to reduce drug production in Afghanistan. At the same time, Europe itself is increasingly

Table 4.5 Comparative regional statistics on registered crimes per 100,000 people

Regions of the Russian Federation	1990	1997	1998	1999	2001	2002
Russian Federation as a whole	**1,240**	**1,627**	**1,758**	**2,052**	**2,051**	**1,750**
Murmansk *oblast*	1,071	1,171	1,457	1,865	1,871	1,616
Republic of Karelia	1,478	2,028	2,329	2,517	2,501	1,765
St Petersburg	1,144	1,652	1,898	2,181	1,959	1,561
Leningrad *oblast*	1,624	2,121	2,228	2,728	2,662	1,899
Pskov *oblast*	1,650	2,155	2,308	2,629	2,320	1,690
Kaliningrad *oblast*	1,387	2,019	2,290	2,515	2,610	2,148
European countries						
Estonia		2,802	3,144	3,565	4,313	3,930
Latvia		1,486	1,491	2,097	2,158	1,633
Lithuania		1,995	2,056	2,029	1,629	-
Finland		7,667	7,835	8,400	14,526	-
Germany		8,030	7,868	7,682	7,736	7,893

Source:'Regions of Russia 2002' (Moscow: Goskomstat of the Russian Federation, 2002); 'The Socio-economic situation of the North-west Federal District in 2002' (Moscow: Goskomstat of the Russian Federation, 2003); and Interpol, www.interpol.int/Public/Statistics/ICS/downloadList.asp.

Table 4.6 Drug-trafficking routes through Russia

	Source	Destination
Poppy Straw	Belarus, Lithuania, Moldova, Ukraine	Estonia, Poland
Opium	Afghanistan, Azerbaijan, Kyrgyzstan, Pakistan, Tajikistan, Turkmenistan, Uzbekistan	Canada, Europe, Israel, Japan, US
Heroin	Afghanistan, Azerbaijan, Kyrgyzstan, Pakistan, Tajikistan, Turkmenistan, Uzbekistan	Australia, Canada, Europe, Israel, Japan, US
Cannabis	Afghanistan, Azerbaijan, Kazakhstan, Kyrgyzstan, Turkmenistan, Uzbekistan	Canada, China, Europe, Japan, Republic of Korea, US
Cocaine	Bolivia, Brazil, Colombia, Europe, Venezuela, US	Benin, Europe, Ghana, Guinea, Oman, South Africa, Zambia
Medical drugs	Azerbaijan, China, India, Republic of Korea, Turkey	Denmark, Finland, Latvia, Lithuania, Sweden

Source: Ministry of Internal Affairs, Russia, 2000 and United Nations Office on Drugs and Crime, 'Country Profile: Russian Federation, 2003'; p.16; www.unodc.org/pdf/russia/russia_country_profile_2003.pdf.

becoming a source of synthetic drugs, which are exported to Russia. The largest amphetamines factory ever discovered in the Nordic and Baltic countries – with a capacity to produce some 12,000 ecstasy tablets per hour – was uncovered in Estonia in 2003.[55]

Drug trafficking is, therefore, an area where Russia wants to see more genuine cooperation with, and assistance from, the EU. For its part, the Russian government has recognised that the scale of drug consumption and drug-related crime is having a very negative impact on its development. In March 2003, Putin established the Russian State Committee for Control over the Illegal Trafficking of Narcotics and Psychotropic Substances, which is charged with developing a more coordinated and aggressive policy to combat this threat. From July 2003, furthermore, a special department on drug trafficking – the Main Office for Combating Organised Crime — was established under the Interior Ministry to counter organised crime. In March 2004, Putin stated that more than 40,000 staff work in the federal service for combating drug-trafficking.

Organised-crime networks, even if they originate in Russia, often involve key actors in the European criminal world. Few purely 'Russian' organised-crime networks operate in Europe, and most of these are engaged in the trafficking of stolen vehicles. This is the most advanced area of EU–Russia cooperation, including joint police operations and regular information exchanges. Finnish and Swedish organised-crime groups are in close contact with Russian groups in relation to their drug-trafficking operations.[56] According to Mark Galeotti, 'neither in Estonia, nor in Finland has Russian organised crime colonised either the political and economic spheres or the criminal world'.[57] He adds that 'claims of the increase of Russian organised crime originating in Finland carries little evidence, instead Finnish organised criminal groups have become more activated and sought links to Russian organised crime'. At the same time, the activities of Russian organised-crime groups are more pronounced in countries that do not border Russia, but which represent lucrative markets, such as Germany and the Netherlands. Hence, as with drug trafficking, the fight against organised crime should be approached in a comprehensive way; simply tightening the border regime is unlikely to have any kind of significant effect on the actions of international organised-crime entities.

Money laundering is closely linked to the controversy surrounding the illegal export of capital from Russia, which has been detrimental to the economy since the early 1990s. However, for Europe, Russia's weak record on tackling money laundering represents a security concern. Consequently, EU states have insisted that Russia adopt tougher measures to solve the problem. Russia has been working towards bringing its anti-

Table 4.7 Drug-related crimes registered in Russia

	1995	1996	1997	1998	1999	2000	2001
Drug offences (total)	79,819	96,645	184,832	190,127	216,364	243,572	241,598
Drug trafficking	11,448	19,982	28,979	33,562	42,883	57,720	45,000
• committed by a group	5,205	6,489	7,549	6,499	10,199	12,132	13,907
• committed by an organised-crime group	-	562	1,439	913	1,763	3,092	4,234

Source: Ministry of Internal Affairs, Russia, 2000, and United Nations Office on Drugs and Crime, 'Country Profile: Russian Federation, 2003', p. 17, www.unodc.org/pdf/russia/russia_country_profile_2003.pdf.

money-laundering policies into line with international standards. On 19 June 2003, Russia was finally admitted into the Financial Action Task Force (FATF), one year after it was removed from the FATF's 'blacklist' of countries failing to fight money laundering. EU demands that the new members tighten their border and visa regimes and introduce strict measures to curb money laundering have resulted in a significant drop in Russian capital flight via Cyprus. Unlike Cyprus, the Baltic States have not registered any negative effects from this on their economies.

Regardless of their differences on assessing the extent to which Russian organised crime and other forms of crime impact on the European Union, the EU and Russia have been deepening their cooperation to combat organised crime, which is likely to be enhanced further in the post-enlargement environment. The EU and Russia have established a sub-committee on fighting organised crime within the framework of the PCA to coordinate anti-crime policies. The main mechanism for this type of cooperation is the joint EU–Russia Action Plan on Combating Organised Crime, which was adopted in April 2000. The areas that it covers range from information sharing to joint operations specifically targeting trafficking in stolen vehicles. It also established a framework for judicial cooperation on criminal matters. Since April 2000, cooperation on issues related to organised crime has been discussed at all EU–Russia summits and ministerial meetings under the JHA umbrella. Moreover, the EU Tacis programme allocated €10m in 2001 and €11.5m in 2002 to assistance programmes related to JHA issues, which, among other things, have focused on combating organised crime. An additional

€12m was earmarked in the indicative budget, adopted by the European Commission on 21 May 2003, for combating organised crime and terrorism, while €10m was allocated to migration and asylum management and €27m to border management.[58]

Is a common space possible?

In the context of an enlarged European Union, the EU faces a major challenge in terms of how to combine two strategies in relation to its policies towards Russia. On the one hand, the EU wants to reassure the citizens of the Union, as well as people residing in the new member states, that it is able to protect the integrated ('borderless') area (particularly the Schengen zone) from any security threats originating outside the EU – that is, in Russia and in the territory of the other new neighbours to the east and the south. On the other hand, the EU is politically committed to ensuring that enlargement does not result in Russia becoming (or even perceiving that it is) isolated from Europe, and that the special relationship between the two parties – in the economic, political, human and security realms – is maintained and widened. In order to reconcile these policy objectives and to address the range of security issues, from soft security matters to new global security threats, the EU should incorporate the following points into its dealings with Russia.

Concentrate on threats common to both Russia and the integrated European area instead of threats from Russia. Common threats include organised crime, illegal migration and human trafficking. To achieve this goal, greater cooperation should be promoted in the field of justice and home affairs, the legal basis for EU–Russian relations (such as border treaties and re-admission agreements) should be improved, assistance should be targeted at security-sector reform in Russia, and the economic gap should be narrowed. The short-term objective should be to achieve legislative compatibility and to strengthen Russia's administrative capacity. The medium-term aim should be to forge an integrated EU–Russia security culture, which would involve regular contact between officials and the creation of joint databases for tracking crime and migration. In the long-term, the goal should be to establish a visa-free regime and simplified border controls between the EU and Russia.

Enhancement of cooperation to counter 'human-security' threats in the fields of the environment, health and disaster relief. Cooperation should increasingly be established on a joint basis; greater Russian commitment is required, both political and financial, in regard to improving human-security practices in Russia. EU assistance should be directed at the micro-level, with priority given to the north-west regions of Russia. The Northern Dimension programme, together with sub-regional organisations in the Baltic and Nordic areas, should play a central role in this, with more active participation by the new EU members, such as the Baltic States and Poland. Finally, policies should seek to engage non-governmental organisations (NGOs), particularly from the border regions of both EU member states and Russia.

Expansion of civilian and police cooperation under the umbrella of the ESDP. Here, the focus of cooperation should shift from addressing global security challenges to tackling sources of regional instability, including unsettled conflicts and associated criminality in the WNIS and the south Caucasus. Moreover, joint peacekeeping and police operations, involving Russia and EU member states, to buttress political solutions to these crises should be founded on political agreement, should enjoy regional support, and should be operationally feasible. Cooperation between Russia and the new EU member states should be encouraged.

While the EU does not view Russia as a major security threat, it is convinced – as is clear from the Common Strategy – that the country's long-term stability and security is contingent on, first and foremost, economic and democratic reforms. The EU supports these processes and Russia's integration into a common economic space. At the same time, the EU is increasingly concerned about the slow pace of reform in the judicial, law-enforcement and border-security sectors. Improvements to Russia's migration, healthcare and environmental policies (the soft security threats) are hoped for, but so too, importantly, is an end to human-rights violations in Chechnya.

Fulfilling these hugely challenging tasks, though, is seen primarily as the responsibility of Russia, with the EU playing only a supportive role. Unlike the new EU members from Central and Eastern Europe, the EU will not provide institutional assistance (the prospect of membership) or substantial financial aid, even though this could be decisive for the reform of Russia's security sector and the transformation of its domestic security policy. EU assistance for security-sector reform in Russia, particularly of its law-enforcement apparatus, is dependent on mutual agreement on priorities and on the political will of both sides, rather than on the strict conditionality that the EU applied to CEE countries for their accession. In the short and medium terms, therefore, there is unlikely to be any major progress in relation to EU–Russia cooperation on soft security issues. Yet, enlargement is likely to be a generator of long-term cooperation rather than a hurdle.

Notes

[1] The WNIS are Belarus, Moldova and Ukraine.

[2] Communication from the European Commission to the Council of the EU and the European Parliament, *Wider Europe – Neighbourhood: A New Framework for Relations with our Eastern and Southern Neighbours*, COM (2003) 104, 11 March 2003, p. 3.

[3] Joint Statement, Eleventh EU–Russia Summit, St Petersburg, 31 May 2003; at http://europa.eu.int/comm/external_relations/russia/sum05_03/js.htm.

[4] Russian Minister of Foreign Affairs Igor Ivanov stated that there were 1,200 Russian servicemen stationed in Moldova in December 2003.

[5] See chapter by Dov Lynch in this volume, pp. 15-33.

[6] See Kujat, H., 'Enhancing interoperability', 26 February 2004, www.nato.int/docu/articles/2004/a040226a.htm.

[7] The Berlin Plus agreement comprises a series of accords between NATO and the EU, leading to the EU taking over responsibility from NATO for crisis-management operations.

[8] For more details on EU internal debates on JHA, see Townsend, A., *Guarding Europe* (London: Centre for European Reform, 2003).

[9] In 2000, the Federal Migration Service of Russia was abolished by presidential decree and migration problems came under the auspices of the newly created Ministry for the Affairs of the Federation, National and Migration Policies. On 16 October 2001, this ministry was abolished and migration was handed over to the Ministry of Internal Affairs. Regional organs of the migration service of the former Ministry of the Federation were subordinated to the Federal Migration Service of the Ministry of Internal Affairs on 21 May 2002.

[10] EU Commission communication, *Towards integrated management of the external borders of the Member States of the European Union*, COM (2002) 233, 7 May 2002. The plan for the management of the external borders of the member states of the European Union was approved by the JHA Council on 13 June 2002.

[11] At www.europa.eu.int/comm/external_relations/ceeca/pca/pca_russia.pdf.

[12] At www.europa.eu.int/comm/external_relations/ceeca/com_strat/russia_99.pdf.

[13] The members of the Task Force on Organised Crime in the Baltic Sea Region are:

Denmark, Estonia, Finland, Germany, Iceland, Latvia, Lithuania, Norway, Poland, Russia, Sweden and the European Commission Directorate-General for Justice and Home Affairs.

[14] Available online at http://europa.eu.int/comm/external_relations/russia/summit_11_02/js_kalin.htm.

[15] Communication from the European Commission to the Council of Europe and the European Parliament on relations with Russia, COM (2004) 106, 9 February 2004, p. 5. Available online at www.europa.eu.int/comm/external_relations/russia/intro/ip04_187.htm.

[16] As of May 2004, the common land border between the new member states and Ukraine will be 726 km, increasing to 1,257 km if Romania joins the Union in 2007. Poland will also have a long border with non-EU countries, totalling 1,139 km.

[17] *Wider Europe – Neighbourhood*, op. cit.

[18] Proposal for a Council Regulation on the establishment of a regime of local border traffic at the external land borders of the Member States, COM (2003) 502, 14 August 2003, p. 4.

[19] Presentation by Russian Deputy Minister of Foreign Affairs Vladimir A. Chizhov at the international conference 'Wider Europe: Strengthening Trans-border Cooperation in Central and Eastern Europe', Kiev, Ukraine, 10 November 2003; at www.mid.ru/brp_4.nsf/.

[20] Under the Phare programme, Latvia will receive €36m in 2003; in 2002, Lithuania received €43.7m and Estonia €30.4m.

[21] Golunov, S. and Vardomsky, L. (eds), *Prozrachnye Granitsy bezopasnost' i transgranichnoe sotrudnichestvo v zonakh novykh pogranichnykh territoirii Rossii* (Moscow: Academic Forum on International Relations, 2002), p. 221.

[22] See Mite, V., 'Moscow reluctant to finalise border agreements with former Soviet republics', RFE/RL report, 2 April 2003; at www.rferl.org/nca/features/2003/04/02042003152932.asp.

[23] BBC Monitoring Global Newsline Former Soviet Union Political File, 18 June 2003, citing Interfax, Moscow, 'Russian Duma ratifies readmission agreement with Lithuania'.

[24] Interview with Russian Deputy Foreign Minister Sergei Razov, first appeared in *Vremia novostei* under the title of 'V Kaliningrad po proezdnomu', 1 August 2003; also at www.ln.mid.ru/Bl.nsf/arh/C21D75B903347CC643256D7

50027A4E0?OpenDocument.
25 Daneiko, E., *Grazhdanin po 100 tysiach rublei: Rossiia podpisala pervoe soglashenie o readmissii Izvestiya*, 12 May 2003; at www.izvestia.ru/politic/article33601.
26 Golunov and Vardomsky, p. 86.
27 Pursiainen, C., 'Soft Security Problems in North West Russia', in Moroff, H. (ed.), *European Soft Security Policies: the Northern Dimension* (Helsinki and Berlin: Finnish Institute of International Affairs and Institut für Europäische Politik, 2002), p. 122; Vladimir Chizhov, 'Za Evropu bez razdelitelnykh linii', *Evropa*, 7(30), July–August 2003.
28 *Wider Europe – Neighbourhood,* op. cit., chart 8, p. 23.
29 Ibid., chart 10 pp. 24–25.
30 *Migration Trends in Eastern Europe and Central Asia 2001–2002 Review* (Geneva: International Organisation for Migration, 2003), p. 119.
31 BBC Monitoring Global Newsline Former Soviet Union Political File, 24 June 2003; citing ITAR-TASS, Moscow, 'Sharp rise in number of illegal migrants detained on Russian borders'.
32 Ganzle, S. and Kungla, T., 'Illegal Migration and Transnational Organised Crime: Factors of Instability in the Baltic States?', in Moroff, *European Soft Security Policies,* p. 65.
33 BBC Monitoring Global Newsline Former Soviet Union Political File, 27 January 2004, citing ITAR-TASS, Moscow, 'Putin sends message of support to conference on people trafficking'.
34 *Migration Trends in Eastern Europe,* op. cit., p. 119.
35 UNHCR Press Release, 'Annual Asylum Numbers Plunge in Industrialised States', 24 February 2004; at www.unhcr.org.
36 BBC Monitoring Global Newsline Former Soviet Union Political File, 5 March 2004, citing, ITAR-TASS, 'Experts predict growing influx of illegal immigrants into Russia'.
37 Ibid.
38 Statistics issued by the Russian Federation reveal that over 22m people who arrived in Russia from CIS countries between 1997 and 2001 are still residing in the country.
39 Ganzle and Kungla, 'Illegal Migration', p. 63.
40 Pursiainen, 'Soft Security Problems', p. 125.
41 See www.helsinki-hs.net/news.asp?id=200012181E1.
42 Ganzle and Kungla, 'Illegal Migration', p. 80.
43 Interview with Russian Deputy Foreign Minister Sergei Razov.

44   Kulikov, A., 'On some
problems of migration in the
Russian Federation', August
2002. Available online at
www.dpr.ru.

45   BBC Monitoring Global
Newsline Former Soviet
Union Political File, 22 July
2003, citing Interfax-Ukraine
news agency, Kiev, 'Number
of illegals detained in
Ukraine grows'.

46   Unlike Russia, Ukraine has
signed a readmission treaty
with the EU. The difficulties
that it is now facing with
housing and repatriating
illegal migrants deter Russia
from following Ukraine's
example.

47   BBC Monitoring Global
Newsline Former Soviet
Union Political File, 19
August 2003; citing Russian
Information Agency Novosti
(RIAN).

48   Joint press statement,
EU–Russia Summit, 6
November 2003; at
www.europa.eu.int/comm/e
xternal_relations/russia/sum
mit11_03/jps061103.htm.

49   BBC Monitoring Global
Newsline Former Soviet
Union Political File, 'Russia
PM sees visa-free EU travel in
5–7 years', 4 December 2003,
citing ITAR-TASS, 'Russians
will travel to Europe visa-free
in 5–7 years, says premier'.

50   For more information, see
Cichocki, B., 'Poland's

Accession to the EU and Its
Impact on the Movement of
People and Goods over the
Kaliningrad–Poland Border',
in this volume, pp. 197-210.

51   Pirogov, V; 'V Kaliningrade
aproburuetsia budushchee
vcei Rossii', 11 October 2001;
at www.2001.novayagazeta.
ru/nomer/2001/74n/n74n-
s05.shtml.

52   See Hiski Haukkala in this
volume, pp. 35-50.

53   'Over 105,000 drug-related
crimes registered in Russia
over five months', 26 June
2003; at
www.english.pravda.ru/acci
dents/2003/06/26/48708.ht
ml.

54   See www.rosbalt.ru/2003/
04/15/94020.html.

55   BBC Monitoring Global
Newsline Former Soviet
Union Political File, 26
August 2003. See 'Estonian
police find largest ever
Ecstasy factory in Nordic,
Baltic Countries', Postimees,
21 August 2003.

56   Galeotti, M., 'Organised
Crime in Russia: The
Emergence of Russian
Organised Crime'; at
www.ex.ac.uk/politics/pol_d
ata/ undergrad/jaakko/
caserussia.htm.

57   Ibid.

58   See
http://europa.eu.int/comm/
external_relations/ceeca/rsp
/ 04_06_en.pdf.

5. Russia–EU Relations and the Common European Economic Space

Vladimir Mau and Vadim Novikov

The foreign dimension is becoming increasingly important to Russia's economic policy. At the European Union (EU)–Russia summit in May 2001, the two sides declared their intention to move towards a Common European Economic Space (CEES). This put an end (on paper at least) to debates in Russia about the key directions of the country's foreign policy. Europe had clearly been designated a priority.

However, Russia's identification with Europe is by no means final; rather, it is a starting-point for future development. Even today, and following the EU–Russia summit of 6 November 2003 in Rome, many serious problems are yet to be resolved. First, the idea of a CEES has so far been formulated only in the most general terms, and a significant amount of intellectual and political work remains to be done in order to give it real content. At the November 2003 EU–Russia summit the concept of a common European economic space did not receive firm and unequivocal support; the leaders of the EU and Russia only went as far as to 'welcome' the concept.[1] Second, Europe's attitude to Russia is far from unambiguous. Influential groups, both in Europe's business community and among politicians in Brussels, are extremely sceptical about the prospects for economic convergence (*sblizheniye* in Russian).[2] Third, unlike the countries of Central and Eastern Europe, which are moving towards full integration with the EU, Russia must develop a European policy that allows it to take advantage of the benefits of integration without undermining its ability to develop close relations with other parts of the world, especially North America and the Asia–Pacific region.

This chapter assesses the key problems in the way of progress towards a common economic space and the eventual creation of a Europe 'from the Atlantic to the Urals' (or, to be more precise, from the Atlantic to the Pacific).[3]

The framework for EU–Russia relations

The idea of a free-trade zone between the EU and Russia was first mentioned in the Partnership and Cooperation Agreement (PCA). The PCA was signed in Greece on 24 June 1994, and entered into force on 1 December 1997. One of its objectives is 'to create the necessary conditions for the future establishment of a free trade area between the Community and Russia covering substantially all trade in goods between them, as well as conditions for bringing about freedom of establishment of companies, of cross-border trade in services and of capital movements'.[4] Two years later, in 1999, the EU Common Strategy Towards Russia set as a goal the 'integration of Russia into a common European economic and social space',[5] and spoke of 'the establishment of a *free trade area*' between the EU and Russia, and then of a *single economic space* (authors' italics) resulting from the gradual adoption of compatible laws and standards.

From the very beginning, these proposals included ambiguities and had deliberate omissions. For example, Europe already has a European Economic Area (EEA), which comprises the EU member states, Iceland, Liechtenstein and Norway. However, in the English-language version of the joint declaration from the May 2001 summit, a far less definite term was used: 'the European economic *space*'. This term is open to interpretation, and there are disagreements over its definition.

The main question is whether the CEES represents a process, or an objective. If it is an objective, then it implies some form of integration, such as a free-trade zone or customs union. Negotiations on the CEES could be structured around the Four Freedoms (of movement of labour, capital, goods and services), or in terms of developing conditions for convergence between the EU and Russia in different sectors of the economy. If it is not an objective then it is a process, in which the two sides take steps to improve the conditions for economic convergence. If the CEES is a process, it could be 'closed' (that is, limited to creating better conditions for Russia's relations with the EU); or 'open' (developing measures for improving conditions for Russia's economic convergence with all international markets). Some Russian experts believe that a CEES, as a process, should involve concessions and actions by both parties, rather than unilateral steps by Russia to further liberalise its economy.

Regardless of these ambiguities, the decision to move towards a common economic space is important given the EU's internal processes and the development of Russia's economic policy.

1. The CEES concept is linked with the issue of Russian membership of the World Trade Organisation (WTO). As was reiterated at the 6 November 2003 summit, 'the CEES will be based on existing and future commitments of the Parties in the PCA and WTO. Its scope shall

be broader and deeper in comparison to the WTO and PCA provisions. Both Parties shall ensure that the CEES is compatible with existing or future commitments undertaken by the Parties in the context of WTO.'[6] Progress towards a CEES affects Russia's domestic policies since it implies liberalisation of the Russian economy on the basis of the government's strategies from 1992 onwards.

2. The CEES concept is grounded in the PCA and the Common Strategy, the main documents of Russian–European cooperation. It offers a comprehensive application of PCA principles to economic relations between Russia and the EU.

3. The CEES presupposes deeper economic integration between Russia and the EU, without contemplating Russia becoming a member of the European Union.

4. The EU–Russia summit of November 2003 concluded that the creation of a CEES should be viewed as part of a wider context: the idea of creating four common spaces (an economic space, a space of freedom, security and justice, a common space of cooperation in the field of external security, and a common space of research, education and culture) which should be set up in the long term.

Russia's economic challenges and its relations with the EU

An important feature of Russia's integration into the world economy relates to the problem of accelerating economic development and structural reform.[7] Economic development in Russia should not be defined merely according to per capita gross domestic product (GDP), because the rapid changes taking place in the economy mean that macroeconomic indicators do not reveal the full picture.[8] The flexibility and adaptability of the economic system are the main indicators of economic development, along with the capacity of economic actors to react to challenges. This adaptability ought to be the key determinant of the Russian government's economic policy.

As far as industrial policy (or structural policy) is concerned, this ought not to be oriented towards protecting markets or companies. This would only add to the current distortions in the economy. If instead there were a strategy which could be constantly adjusted, the government would support by political means (foreign policy included) Russian companies which already compete successfully on international markets.

For Russia to achieve an economic breakthrough there will need to be changes in its foreign economic relations. The negotiations on Russia joining the WTO and on achieving a CEES should aim to promote post-industrial transformation, rather than protectionist policies for Russian producers. Policy ought not to protect inefficient industries, but rather help Russia's competitive products such as high-technology services to gain better access to international markets. Russia's cooperation with the WTO would subsequently require a radical re-thinking of rationale: Russia should not only focus on removing the antidumping barriers for her primary products but should not lose sight of the opportunity WTO provides for access to global markets.

One of the priorities for economic convergence between the EU and Russia should be Russia's access to modern technology through foreign direct investment (FDI), and better access to European markets for Russian firms. The experience of the Central and East European countries shows convincingly the exceptional importance for sustainable economic growth of access to the markets of the most developed nations.[9] Giving financial assistance to post-communist countries in transition ('cheap money', as it is known) is ineffective; what is needed is better access to foreign markets. The former East Germany obtained virtually unlimited finance from one of the most advanced countries in Europe, but its negative experience proves the point.[10]

Areas for EU–Russia cooperation

Convergence means that both the EU and Russia reduce and ultimately remove barriers to the free movement of goods, services, labour and capital. In Russia, pursuing economic convergence would require:

- the consistent unilateral liberalisation of the economy, including foreign economic relations;
- launching negotiations with the EU on changes to its regime regulating economic convergence with Russia; and
- an assessment of the impact of these changes on Russians themselves, in order to promote broader political support for reforms and liberalisation.

If this is how convergence is defined, then a CEES would have the following characteristics:

First, a CEES, as a final objective, should mean that political barriers separating businesses and private individuals in Russia and the EU no longer exceed those that exist for the citizens in their home state. But it does not mean that Russia becomes a member of the EU. Second, in negotiations on a CEES, Russians are more interested in determining the parameters for integration into Europe than in negotiating a legal definition of CEES. Third, a CEES should be developed on the basis of the 'open' scenario described above, because for Russia it is important to remove barriers not only with the EU, but also with other economic partners including the Commonwealth of Independent States (CIS), the US and the Asia-Pacific Economic Cooperation (APEC) states. This would mean that Russia and the EU should not seek to find trade liberalisation arrangements which could benefit them against third countries, but should make arrangements which could then be applied to Russia's relations with other trade partners.

The process of economic convergence between Russia and the EU can be viewed not as a bilateral process, but more as the sum of two unilateral ones. On the one hand, it is a domestic process for Russia, and it includes implementing and developing a government reform programme aimed at improving the conditions for private business (not just European) and the development of foreign economic relations (not just with the EU). On the other hand, Russia would like the EU to lift its trade barriers. Thus, in making a final decision on any issues of EU–Russia economic convergence, two factors should be considered: whether this convergence corresponds with the aims and strategies of the reform programme within Russia; and how it could influence the liberalisation of EU trading practices. Progress in either of these two areas could significantly increase the prosperity of the Russian people. Finally, the fact that CEES negotiations between the EU and Russia are structured according to sectoral groupings, rather than thematic ones (like the Four Freedoms of movement), increases the influence of industry lobbyists and underlines the political, rather than economic, rationale behind negotiations.

Should Russia adopt the *acquis communautaire*?

In order to develop a set of measures for Russia's convergence with the EU's standards and laws, it is important to compare the current state of the country's economic and political development with the so-called Copenhagen criteria for EU membership that were applied to EU candidate countries. These criteria are:

1. Democracy, observance of human rights and the protection of national minorities.
2. A market-based economy.
3. The ability to function under conditions of competition.
4. The possibility of fulfilling the obligations of membership (that is, applying *acquis communautaire*, the official compilation of EU and European Communities law).

Financial standards were set by the Maastricht Agreement of 1992, and the following criteria specified:

1. Price stability: the level of inflation cannot exceed by more than 1.5% the average level of inflation of the three countries with the lowest levels of inflation.

2. Deficit: national budget deficits should be lower than 3%.
3. Indebtedness: government debt cannot be higher than 60% of GDP.
4. Exchange-rate stability: the national currency ought not to have been devalued in the last two years, and should remain within the 2.5% limit of exchange-rate fluctuation provided for by the European currency system.
5. Long-term interest rates should not be more than two percentage points over the average level for this indicator in the three EU countries with the most stable prices.

In political terms, Russia meets the membership criteria to some extent. Additional proof of this is Russia's membership of the Council of Europe. The EU usually follows the Council in assessing observance of human rights and the protection of national minorities. Significant progress is also being made in creating a market-based economy. However, it is still too early to consider the majority of Russian firms as competitive on the global market. It is also obvious that Russia only partially meets the Maastricht criteria. Despite the fact that Russia has made great progress concerning state debt and the budget deficit, inflation is still a major problem.

The greatest obstacles to compatibility between the EU and Russia lie in Russian law, which does not correspond to European legal standards, and still constitutes a serious hindrance to the development of business. In practical terms, the criteria described above for EU accession may be interesting not only in the context of Russia possibly joining the EU, but rather as criteria the Russian government might adopt for conducting a rational policy. This demands some clarification. First, using these parameters as basic guidelines ought not to be equated with the issue of joining the EU. Russia might adopt some of them unilaterally if doing so would help with economic liberalisation and the development of economic cooperation with the EU. Second, these parameters remain vague. Russia should refine the Maastricht and Copenhagen criteria and examine the European Commission's evaluations of countries' readiness to accede. Then Russia could work out more concrete proposals for its own economic policy, with the proviso that not all the criteria will be relevant in the short or medium term. Third, these policies should be developed in Russia, for Russia. But this does not preclude discussion with EU and new EU member states on their experiences of adopting the *acquis*.

The following factors will be crucial for Russia's decision to adopt (unilaterally) any of the EU policies in the *acquis*:

1. The existence of an effectively operating market-based economy.
2. The ability to guarantee the effective functioning of a competitive mechanism and of market forces (deregulation of the economy,

favourable conditions for competition, a reliable and strong legal framework and transparent budgetary policies).

3. The implementation of structural reform, with special emphasis on the protection of property, effective bankruptcy legislation, an efficient tax system, a stable banking system and stable financial markets.
4. Monetary and budgetary policies that can secure sustainable economic growth.
5. The establishment of administrative and governmental institutions that meet European standards.

It is clear that, in a range of areas, Russia has either already met the criteria for EU membership (in the parameters of budgetary policy, for example), or has regulations that are significantly more favourable to economic growth than the EU's rules (on budgetary matters, taxation and social legislation, for example). Russian law might even appear attractive to some European countries, though while the economic and social situation in Europe remains stable, one can hardly expect the EU to refer to Russian experience.

Russia must define the role of European legislation in furthering its own institutional reform. Often, European law appears too socialist (or socially oriented), placing too great a burden on the state, and is therefore not conducive to speeding up economic growth within Russia. Russians currently prefer to spend money not on private healthcare or education but on other factors (material goods) which improve their standard of living. Expenditure on social security by the government could impede economic growth.[11] However, Russia's status as a partner of the EU, rather than as a candidate for membership, means that it can adopt those European standards which will facilitate economic growth, while rejecting standards and procedures which do not. By avoiding unhelpful elements of European regulation, Russia will have a lower tax burden than EU countries, and a more favourable investment climate.

Which sections of European law should Russia adopt in order to create a CEES, and which are undesirable or irrelevant? Table 5.1 divides the policies into four groups: irrelevant, inadvisable, unimportant and essential. The irrelevant group includes such things as the Economic and Currency Union (ECU). Although ECU standards are entirely economic in nature, they are not related to the concept of a common economic space. The second group includes legislation on economic policy which, if implemented by Russia, might weaken its competitiveness and so should be excluded. Examples are agrarian, social and environmental policies, plus legislation on the protection of consumers' rights. The third group comprises *acquis* chapters whose adoption would, on the whole, be useful, but which would not have a substantial influence on the economy. The

Table 5.1 Potential Russian conformity with the *acquis* in a CEES

Group 1 Policies irrelevant to Russia–EU integration	Group 2 Policy changes inadvisable for Russia	Group 3 Policy areas with little influence on CEES	Group 4 Policy areas essential for establishing a CEES
Economic and currency union	Competition policy and government assistance (competition policy only)	Transportation policy	The free movement of goods
Industrial policy	Agriculture	Statistics	The free movement of people
Small- and medium-sized businesses	Fishing	Energy	The free movement of services
Science and research	Taxation	Telecommunications and information technologies	The free movement of capital
Education and training	Social policy and employment	Culture and audio-visual policy	Company law
Regional policy and the government of structural measures	The environment	Foreign relations	Competition policy coordination and assistance (government assistance)
Cooperation in justice and home affairs	Protection of consumers and their health		Customs union
Common foreign and security policy			
Financial controls			
Financial and budgetary issues			
Institutions			

fourth group contains those chapters whose adoption is most closely connected with the concept of a common European economic space, and which therefore would need to be adopted.

Steps towards integration

Norway's relations with the EU could provide a model for developing a common economic space between the EU and Russia. While not a member of the EU, Norway is part of the EEA, and so is an integral part of the European common market.[12] True, Norway has set out to fully adopt the *acquis communautaire*, which would be inadvisable for Russia. However, Russia's membership of the WTO and the Organisation for Economic Cooperation and Development (OECD) would be natural stages on the road to joining European institutions (Russia formally applied for OECD membership in 1996). However, unfortunately, entry into the WTO is not entirely synonymous with the opening of markets to Russian goods. The WTO in many ways is a 'club' for discussing the trade regime and not for unifying countries who follow a free trade policy.[13]

It is difficult to say when the formation of a single European market between the EU and Russia will become possible. The main obstacle here is not fear within the Russian business community about competition from European manufacturers; indeed, past experience suggests that Russia's Western partners are much more afraid of Russian goods appearing in their markets. The EU's fear of competition with Russia was seen particularly clearly in the way that the EU prolonged its decision on giving Russia Market-Economy Status (MES). The EU finally pledged to do so on 30 May 2002, and MES was granted at the November 2002 EU–Russia summit. However, the way in which the decision was taken is evidence of the gloomy prospects for liberalising trade and economic relations between the EU and Russia. When the European Commission lifted its categorisation of Russia as a non-market economy, it made a number of complaints ostensibly about market conditions. In fact, these concerns were closely linked to the terms of Russian exports to European markets (gas exports, for example). On granting MES, the EU stated that it would make dumping calculations based on Russian companies' costs and prices, rather than on prices in a proxy or third country with a market economy, but would use information from other markets if it decided that a company did not 'reasonably' reflect its production and sales costs in its accounts.[14] This means that Russian companies – even the country as a whole – could still face anti-dumping sanctions even though Russia is officially recognised as a market economy. These amendments to the EU's anti-dumping legislation were done for effect, and were connected with the EU's political decision to give Russia market-economy status. The trade advantages Russia is expected to receive as a newly designated market economy could be negated as a result of these changes.

A radical breakthrough in relations between Russia and the EU and a step towards a single economic space could be forthcoming if, instead of discussing the status of different sectors of the economy, the two sides might agree on a mutual opening up of the goods and services markets, including financial and insurance services (which were always contentious issues in Russia's domestic politics). At the May 2004 EU–Russia summit, Russia promised to open up the financial services sector to foreign competition. This will make possible an increase in the overall level of competition in the two markets, and facilitate economic growth, including a sharp rise in the quality of financial services in the Russian market. The date on which markets would open up to one another might become the subject of negotiations, rather than a scrupulous comparison of individual sectors of the economy. Businesses would then have to focus their efforts on working out the problems of improving their competitiveness themselves. Many people might think this impossible at the moment, but not so long ago the idea of a common economic space was also considered impossible.

Conclusion

In developing a policy for economic convergence with the EU, Russia should seek to solve two sets of problems: removing obstacles to the free movement of goods, services, labour and capital by both Russia and the EU; and improving the conditions for stable economic growth. Strategically, finding answers to these problems will make it possible to solve the fundamental problem of how to enable Russia to draw closer to the more advanced countries of the West. Russia should take advantage of the EU's institutional experience, including elements of EU legislation. It should be re-emphasised that the full-scale adoption of European law is not a prerequisite for the integration of Russia's economy into Europe. European economic policy is important for Russia primarily because the EU is Russia's nearest competitor, and because Russia hopes to attract foreign capital as well as to expand trade. A single economic space comprising both Russia and the EU does not mean a 'choice of area' (defining which areas will be homogeneous), but rather an 'area of choice' offering opportunities for economic activity by Russian and European citizens. The liberalisation of the Russian economy, based on making the four freedoms a reality, alongside negotiating with the EU on liberalising its foreign economic policy, will be the base upon which these new opportunities will emerge.

Notes

1 The Joint Statement says, 'We endorsed the work of the CEES High Level Group and welcomed the annexed concept of the common European economic space.'; at www.eur.ru/en/p_400.htm.

2 There is concern that harmonising regulatory standards in the CEES might lead to protectionism. Margaret Thatcher argued that protectionism will increase in Europe if there is a combination of strictly regulated high taxes and high costs on the one hand and an absence of flexibility conditional on a single currency and interest rate on the other. Thatcher, M. *Statecraft* (London: HarperCollins, 2003).

3 The question of the economic and political advisability of the EU and Russia drawing closer together cannot be dealt with in an article of this scope. A huge discussion on this theme is under way in the political and academic community. The main issues under discussion are: historical and cultural values and their influence on the possibilities for integration; volumes of two-way trade; and the influence of European institutions on Russia's economic growth.

4 At www.europa.eu.int/comm/external_relations/russia/pca_legal.

5 At www.europa.eu.int/comm/external_relations/russia/csp/0 2-06_en.pdf.

6 Point 14, Annex 1, to the Joint Statement from the EU and Russia at their 6 November 2003 summit, The common European space concept paper; at www.eur.ru/en/p_402.htm.

7 Vladimir Mau, 'Postcommunisticheskaia Rossiya v postindustrialnom mire', *Voprosy Ekonomiki*, No. 7, 2002.

8 David Simpson, *The End of Macroeconomics?* (London: Institute of Economic Affairs, 1994).

9 Economist Peter Bauer rightly pointed to this indicator in the early 1990s in his theoretical (one might say speculative) analysis of problems in the development of post-communist countries. Opening up access to the market is, in Bauer's opinion, more important for these countries than financial assistance: 'There are several things the West can do to promote economic advance in Eastern Europe. First and foremost, Western countries should reduce their trade barriers. Eastern Europe would benefit because international trade acquaints people with the market system, helps to allay suspicions about its operation, and promotes market-oriented attitudes, habits, and conduct, which would emerge only from direct experience', Peter Bauer, 'Western Subsidies and Eastern Reform', in Dorn, J. A., Hanke, S. H. and Walters, A. A.

(eds), *The Revolution in Development Economics* (Washington, DC: Cato Institute, 1998), p. 246.

[10] See Anders Aslund and Andrew Warner, 'EU Enlargement: Consequences for the CIS Countries', paper presented at the conference 'Beyond Transition: Development Perspectives and Dilemmas' (Warsaw: CASE, 2002).

[11] Anders Aslund and Andrew Warner in particular point out the debatable effects of the Central and East European states joining the EU, from the point of view of the *acquis communautaire*'s influence on economic growth in the new EU members. Anders and Warner, 'EU Enlargement', op. cit.

[12] On Norway's relationship with the EU, see Emerson, M., Vahl, M. and Woolcock, S., *Navigating by the Stars: Norway, the European Economic Space, and the European Union* (Brussels: CEPS, 2002).

[13] See, for example, Andrew K. Rose, 'Do We Really Know That the WTO Increases Trade?', *American Economic Review*, March 2004, Vol. 94, No. 1; Andrew K. Rose, *Do WTO Members have a More Liberal Trade Policy?* (National Bureau of Economic Research (NBER) Working Paper No. w9347, Nov. 2002).

[14] The EU argument is that the Russian government regulates and artificially lowers prices, in effect giving indirect subsidies to industry, thus affording Russian companies an unfair advantage over their European competitors. Products affected include steel, fertilisers and aluminium, as well as oil, gas and electricity on the domestic market. Russia sells energy to domestic consumers at a tariff lower than the world market price, but the EU has been pressing Russia to eliminate this disparity by increasing the domestic price. Russia has insisted that strategic users will be exempt from higher gas tariffs for some time.

6. EU–Russia Economic Relations[1]

Katinka Barysch

The European Union (EU) and Russia describe their bilateral relationship as a 'strategic partnership'. Yet, in their day-to-day dealings, Brussels and Moscow rarely behave like partners. Nor do their constant squabbles and gripes support the assertion that they have joint strategic objectives. Bilateral dealings are often characterised by mistrust and frustration. Disagreements over individual issues, be they in regard to transit rights for Kaliningrad or steel export quotas, are regularly allowed to hijack the entire relationship. There is a widening gap between acrimonious negotiations on the technical details of the relationship and the heady rhetoric of the biannual EU–Russia summits.

In early 2004, EU–Russia relations took another turn for the worse. The EU is worried about authoritarian tendencies in President Vladimir Putin's Russia and setbacks to economic reforms there. It wants Russia to do more to open up its economy and to cooperate in key areas, such as environmental protection and the fight to curb cross-border crime. Russia, meanwhile, insists that the demands of the EU are unreasonable. It blames the EU for lack of progress in its accession talks with the World Trade Organisation (WTO). It worries about the implications of the eastward enlargement of the Union, which has placed a larger and more powerful EU right on the doorstep of Russia. It wants the EU to commit to visa-free travel and to allow Russians a say in its emerging security and defence policy.

In early 2004, the EU and Russia aired their frustrations during a lengthy and unsavoury battle over the Partnership and Cooperation Agreement (PCA), which has formed the legal basis for their relationship since 1997. Russia presented the EU with a list of 14 demands – most of which are related to trade and economic ties – and threatened to block the extension of the PCA unless the EU met them. The EU insisted that Russia had no right to do so, issuing thinly veiled threats of trade sanctions. The PCA spat will soon die down, but it will have caused a further deterioration in an already tense relationship.

Table 6.1 Russia and the EU: basic figures

	EU-15	Russia
Population (million)	378	144
Area (1,000 square kilometres)	3,191	17,075
Gross domestic product (GDP) (€billion)	8,814	347
GDP per capita (€)	23,170	2,398
Exports as a percentage of total world exports	17.5	1.7
Imports as a percentage of total world imports	18	0.7

Note: figures are from 2001, with the exception of trade shares, which are from 2000.

Source: Eurostat (Statistical Office of the European Communities).

The poor state of relations between the EU and Russia is surprising. A cursory glance reveals a multitude of common interests and objectives. The EU is Russia's most important business partner, accounting for more than one-third of the country's external trade, a proportion that will rise to over 50% after enlargement. EU companies are now the biggest foreign investors in Russia. Two-thirds of Russia's oil and gas exports – its main source of foreign currency – go to the EU. The Union relies on Russian oil and gas to satisfy 15–20% of its total energy needs (again, this will rise after enlargement). Both sides have a strong interest in the stability of their common neighbours, such as Belarus and Ukraine, as well as in the peaceful development of the wider European neighbourhood, including explosive regions like the Balkans and the Caucasus. Both the EU and Russia have made the fight against international terrorism a priority. They see themselves as partners of the US but are worried about its global hegemonic status. Both would like to protect the role of international organisations like the United Nations (UN) and uphold the rule of international law.

Yet most Russians are dismissive of the EU and prefer the US as an international partner. They see the US as a country with which they can do business. By contrast, Europeans are viewed as weak and divided and are believed not to understand the needs of Russians. Such conclusions are short-sighted and unfair. EU–Russia relations are difficult precisely because they are multifaceted and complex. Since there is so much at stake, there is much scope for disagreement. Relations with the US, however, centre on a few strategic and military issues, for example, non-proliferation and the role of 'rogue' states, such as Iran and North Korea. The US is much less important as a trading partner (purchasing only 7%

of Russian exports). And, despite recent talk in the US about Russia becoming an alternative oil supplier to the unstable Middle East, it is by no means clear that such shipments would be commercially viable. The narrow scope of the Russia–US relationship ensures that it is relatively straightforward. It also allows for more leadership-driven policymaking. Alongside the focus on geo-strategic questions, this fits well with Russia's rather old-fashioned foreign-policy ideas.

Putin is well aware of the fact that Russia cannot choose between the EU and the US. It needs good relations with both. But while Russia's relations with the US evolve in a global political context, its dealings with the EU have assumed a more regional focus. Good relations with the US are key to strengthening Russia's shaky self-confidence. Those with the EU are crucial for the country's internal development, which will be increasingly shaped by trade and technical cooperation. The intrusive nature of EU policies is the biggest obstacle confronting the EU–Russia relationship – and perhaps its greatest opportunity, too.

Trade and the WTO: an unbalanced relationship
The value of trade between the EU and Russia has more than doubled since 1995, rising to €85 billion in 2003. However, headline figures reveal little about the true content of the EU–Russia trade relationship. As one observer has noted: 'The two key words characterising Russia's trade with Western Europe are energy and asymmetry'.[2]

The asymmetry is twofold. While the EU is clearly Russia's single most important trading partner, the same does not hold true for Russia. In 2003, Russia accounted for only around 3% of the Union's imports and 5% of its exports. The resulting trade surplus is Russia's biggest source of foreign exchange. The composition of trade flows is similarly imbalanced. Most Russian exports to the EU comprise oil, gas and other raw materials; manufactured goods make up a very small proportion. Conversely, the EU mostly ships machinery to Russia, as well as automobiles, consumer goods and food products.

For Russia, better access to the large (and enlarged) EU market, especially for non-energy goods, is the primary objective. The Russian authorities are worried about the economy's growing dependence on energy exports. Oil and gas now account for more than 60% of export earnings, some 30% of federal budget revenue and the bulk of investment spending. International commodities markets tend to be volatile; a slump in oil prices could quickly send the Russian economy back into recession and generate instability.

Russia claims that the 'protectionist' trade policies of the West make it unnecessarily difficult to diversify its economy away from oil and gas. The only areas where Russia's outdated industrial sector can compete

Table 6.2 EU–Russian trade (€bn)

	1996	1997	1998	1999	2000	2001	2002	2003
EU exports to Russia	19.1	15.5	21.1	14.8	19.8	27.8	30.3	33.0
EU imports from Russia	23.4	27.0	23.2	26.0	45.3	47.4	47.5	51.6
Trade balance	-4.3	-11.5	-2.1	-11.2	-25.5	-19.6	-17.2	-18.6

Source: European Commission

internationally are metals, basic chemicals and some labour-intensive products like shoes or clothing. These, however, are exactly the areas that developed market economies, not only the EU, but also the US, consider 'sensitive'. In 2002, 20 anti-dumping measures were imposed on Russian exports of steel and chemicals. In addition, steel exports are subject to strict numerical quotas. The EU has also introduced special restrictions on food sales from Russia and retains the right to limit textile imports (although it has not done so recently).

The EU rejects all allegations of protectionism. It points out that Russia itself has erected high barriers to some EU products, including automobiles, alcohol and meat. The EU insists that its overall trade policy is seeking to maintain economic integration with Russia. Although Russia is not a member of the WTO, the EU has granted it most-favoured nation (MFN) status through the PCA (which means that the lowest available EU tariff is extended to Russian goods). The PCA also provides for a free-trade agreement between Russia and the EU – although little progress has been made in this direction. Both sides agree that Russia should become a member of the WTO before they talk further about liberalisation.

The impact of enlargement

Most of the points on Russia's 14-point list of enlargement worries relate to trade. Maxim Medvedkov, Russia's chief negotiator in the WTO talks, has warned that extension of the EU common tariff to the ten new member states will result in Russia losing €200 million a year. However, Russian officials struggle to provide concrete examples of how enlargement will damage national exports. They cite higher tariffs on Russian aluminium exports to the East European members and on barley exports to Cyprus, as well as EU quotas on Russian steel exports. Then they grudgingly admit that enlargement is unlikely to have a big impact on Russian trade.

Most Russian exports to the accession states consist of oil and gas (up to 90% in the case of some countries), and these will continue to enter the EU market tariff-free. For industrial goods, EU tariffs tend to be lower than those that the new member states applied before. In line with the PCA, the new members will also grant Russia MFN status (only Hungary did so prior to 1 May 2004). Russia is right, however, to fear the extension of the EU's protectionist farm policies (the Common Agricultural Policy), especially since Russia is once again becoming a major exporter of grain.

Russia also worries about EU anti-dumping action. The extension of existing anti-dumping action to the new members is unlikely to do much damage. But the new members will themselves be able to apply EU anti-dumping measures if their steel and chemical companies fear 'unfair' competition from Russia. These fears should not be overstated, though. The new EU members are rapidly upgrading from heavy industry to exports of high value-added manufacturing products, for which Russia will be a lucrative market. They will, therefore, want to maintain good and open trade relations with Russia.

Ways out of the WTO deadlock
Russia first applied to join the WTO in 1993. But it was only when Putin took over the presidency in 2000 that accession became a priority. In 2001 and 2002, Russia made good progress in the talks. It reached agreement on tariffs and market access conditions for most products and rewrote dozens of laws in line with WTO requirements. One major obstacle to WTO membership was removed in May 2002, when the EU decided to reclassify Russia as a market economy for trade-policy purposes. The upgrade will allow Russia to join the WTO on the same terms as other developed economies. It also shifts the burden of proof in anti-dumping cases from Russian companies to the EU. Nevertheless, many Russians are sceptical about the upgrade, partly because they regard it as a politically motivated U-turn and partly because subsequent amendments to EU trade rules watered down the benefits that Russia was hoping for.[2]

Since late 2002, the negotiations on Russia's entry to the WTO have stalled. The Russian authorities have put the blame squarely on the shoulders of the EU. At a meeting of EU and Russian business executives in December 2003, Putin stated that 'We permanently hear assurances and EU statements in support of this process, but unfortunately in practice time and again we are facing what we consider excessively strict requirements that actually block Russia's accession to the WTO.'[3]

The Union has frequently reconfirmed its commitment to Russia joining the WTO as quickly as possible. But it insists that the speed of accession depends mainly on Russia itself. In 2002, EU Trade Commissioner Pascal Lamy wrote that 'Any new WTO member enjoys the legal rights and has to take on the obligations that have previously been negotiated by the existing members. This usually requires the

Katinka Barysch

Table 6.3 Composition of EU–Russian trade (€bn), 2003

	EU exports to Russia	EU imports from Russia
Machinery	11.5	0.4
Transport equipment	3.9	0.2
Chemicals	4.4	2.1
Farm products	3.4	1.9
Energy	29.3	0.2
Textiles and clothing	1.7	0.2

Source: European Commission

acceding country to carry out extensive legal and structural reforms, which turns WTO accession into a difficult and sometimes politically-charged process.' Russia must not forget, he added, that WTO membership is primarily in its own self-interest. Russia would gain better access to EU markets. It would consolidate economic reforms, improve transparency and create greater legal certainty – all of which would make Russia a more comfortable place for investors. Russia would acquire access to the WTO's dispute-settlement system, which would leave it better placed to challenge anti-dumping measures and other action taken against its exports. Last, but not least, Russia would get a seat at the table where global trade policy is made.

To reap these benefits, Russia will have to accept certain obligations. It is not only the EU that is making demands of Russia in the WTO talks, individual states are too. But as Russia's largest trading partner, the EU has most at stake and thus its list of concerns is long. According to the EU, Russia must improve access to its markets for certain goods and services, including banking, insurance and telecommunications. Furthermore, it must phase out discriminatory fees that EU airlines have to pay to fly over Siberia, and it must improve enforcement of trade-related legal rules.

The most intractable dispute, however, concerns energy prices. The EU claims that Russia's very low domestic energy prices (gas prices are one-fifth of those on the world market) give an 'unfair' advantage to Russian producers, particularly those in energy-intensive sectors like fertilisers and metals. Russia has protested that local energy costs are not part of the remit of the WTO. But the EU has insisted that there are no 'standard terms' for WTO accession and that latecomers have to accept the demands of those that are already members of the club.

Initially, the EU asked Russia to raise gas prices to EU levels. Russia replied that high European prices were the result of inefficient,

120

fragmented markets, high transport costs and the strong euro. Low Russian prices, however, were due to the country's 'national advantage' of sitting on one-third of the world's gas reserves. Fine, said the EU. But the claim that prices were 'naturally' lower could only be tested if Russia liberalised the energy sector and let market forces, rather than state regulators, set prices. At first, Putin talked about shaking up Gazprom, the giant gas monopoly, but then changed his mind. In 2003 and 2004, he stated repeatedly that 'Gazprom will not be broken up'.

Meanwhile, Russian industrialists lobbied hard against rapid WTO accession, claiming that the opening up of trade would bankrupt Russian companies and farmers. Russia missed its 2003 target date for accession with equanimity. Eventually, the EU reformulated its request once more. Russia should at least raise gas prices to a level that covers production and investment costs. It should also abolish gas export tariffs and end Gazprom's monopoly over gas exports and transit pipelines. The Russians remain intransigent. 'The Europeans have entered a dark room without doors and windows and are now looking for an emergency exit', quipped Medvedkov in early 2004.

Nevertheless, the prospects for Russian accession to the WTO are improving. The Putin administration knows that it needs to continue to raise gas prices anyway, to give Gazprom cash for investment and to force energy-guzzling factories to restructure. Although Gazprom's opaque structure makes it impossible to discern production costs, economists assume that they are not vastly above current price levels.[4] In early 2004, the two sides were working feverishly towards reaching a deal before the EU–Russia Summit in May. Even though this deadline was missed, Russia knows that the current members of the European Commission, including Lamy, will step down in October. WTO talks will be on hold while the ten new members of the European Commission find their feet, and they may well get even more complicated once the new members have added their demands to the EU's list.

Towards a Common European Economic Space?

Despite slow progress in the WTO talks, the EU wants to reassure Russia that it remains committed to economic cooperation and integration beyond WTO accession. Consequently, it has kept alive the project to build a Common European Economic Space (CEES) between the EU and Russia. The term first appeared in the EU's Common Strategy of 1999. The basic idea is to give Russia improved access to the EU single market, provided that Russia brings its standards and regulations into line with the *acquis communautaire* (the EU's accumulated rulebook).

In 2001, the two sides set up a high-level group to lead the process and a team of economists set to work to thrash out the details.[5] However, when

Table 6.4 Potential impact of enlargement on Russian exporters

Positive	Negative
1. Russian businesses can sell to a deeply integrated market of almost half a billion consumers	1. Trade in farm products will fall under strict CAP rules
2. Average manufacturing tariffs in the new member states will fall	2. Exports to the new member states will have to comply with tough EU product standards
3. The new members will grant Russia MFN status and remove all quantitative restrictions on Russian imports	3. The new members may lobby for EU anti-dumping action against Russian steel and chemical companies
4. Customs and transit procedures will be unified and simplified	4. Competition in the enlarged EU market will grow stronger
5. Enlargement may boost European growth and create new business opportunities for third-country exporters	5. Tougher visa requirements for business people travelling to the new member states

the high-level group reported to the EU–Russia Summit in Rome, Italy, in November 2003, it still did not have a workable road map for economic integration. It listed some guiding principles, but stated that it was still too early to set concrete targets.

Both sides agree that a WTO deal is the essential initial step for the CEES. First, many of the preparations that Russia has made in regard to membership of the WTO, such as upgrading customs and offering better protection for investments and intellectual property, are also required to secure deeper integration with the EU. Second, Russia simply does not have enough skilled trade specialists to negotiate a WTO deal and the CEES at the same time. And third, since the CEES would be a regional trade agreement, it may conflict with the WTO's non-discrimination clauses, potentially making Russia liable for paying compensation to third countries.

Nevertheless, the EU hopes to get Russia interested in legal approximation over and above WTO rules in the interim. This looks somewhat unlikely. Many economists, both from the EU and Russia, are sceptical about the whole idea of the CEES. They say that the gap between the EU's well-developed and densely regulated market and Russia's shaky, oil-dependent transition economy is so wide as to make the CEES meaningless as a framework for concrete policy measures. Some economists doubt that the CEES would reap substantial economic benefits for Russia.[6] Others think that only a small part of the *acquis* – notably the free movement of goods, services, capital and people – would be good for

Russia's development. Other EU rules, environmental and social standards, for example, could harm Russia's growth prospects. Most of the *acquis* would be either irrelevant or have little impact.[7]

The European Commission has reassured Russia that it would not have to take on the whole *acquis*. But the EU newcomers from Central and Eastern Europe beg to differ. They fear that Russia will 'cherry pick' those parts of the *acquis* that it likes and reject those that are difficult, restrictive or expensive. Such a selective approach, they fear, could give Russia an unfair advantage. The new member states also know from first-hand experience how difficult it is to adopt, implement and enforce a large number of EU rules in a short space of time. Many fear that Russia's inefficient and notoriously corrupt bureaucracy would not be up to the job. The European Commission would be in a weak position to supervise actual implementation of the *acquis*, as it did in the accession countries. If the EU did not have faith in Russian food inspectors, for instance, this could undermine trust – a vital characteristic of the EU single market.

Some observers also find the CEES concept problematic from a political standpoint. The CEES would require Russia to play according to rules, the development of which it cannot influence. The basic idea is similar to that underlying the European Economic Area (EEA).[8] The EEA gives non-EU members, such as Iceland and Norway, full access to the EU single market. In return, these countries implement the *acquis* in all relevant areas. Although the EU consults EEA countries in regard to the law-making process, it does not give them a say when it decides on new regulations. This asymmetry has led many former EEA members to apply for EU membership, including Austria, Finland and Sweden. Iceland and Norway have their own problems with the EEA model.

Given that Russians are more sensitive about sovereignty than Norwegians, for example, anything resembling the EEA model would be very difficult to accept. What is more, current plans for the CEES would not even afford Russia the consultative role that the EEA nations enjoy.[9] Russia has already made it clear that it dislikes the idea of having to adapt to EU rules unilaterally. Instead, Russians demand a more 'balanced' approach to legal approximation. 'Convergence cannot be a one-sided process', says Elena Danilova, who is in charge of the CEES project in Russia's Ministry of Economics. But the EU remains adamant that non-members cannot be part of EU internal decision-making. And it finds any suggestion that EU rules should move closer to Russian standards abhorrent.

Badly drafted and contradictory laws continue to place a huge burden on businesses in Russia. An EU-style competition and anti-subsidy policy could help to arrest the ever growing concentration of economic assets in a few hands. But Russia does not, at present, see the CEES as an opportunity. On the contrary, many officials suspect that the EU is using the CEES concept to make unrealistic demands of Russia – or else to shut Russian goods out of the internal market.

In September 2003, Russia agreed with Belarus, Kazakhstan and Ukraine to create a 'Single Economic Space', a plan that looks conspicuously like the CEES. The EU now worries that, if both plans proceed in parallel, it might end up sharing a single market with some unreformed and badly managed former Soviet economies. Such concerns are likely to be misplaced. Over the past decade, Russia has signed half a dozen agreements on free trade and regional economic integration with members of the Commonwealth of Independent States (CIS) – without any tangible results. Russia's launch of the Single Economic Space demonstrates its acute lack of enthusiasm for aligning its economy more with that of the EU.

The EU–Russia energy dialogue

Since plans for a CEES have yielded few results, some EU officials have suggested looking elsewhere for a general framework for EU–Russia relations. EU External Relations Commissioner Chris Patten and Pascal Lamy have suggested using the EU–Russia energy dialogue as 'a blueprint for wider relations'.[10] In the energy field, more than in almost any other area, the EU and Russia have very clear mutual interests. The EU-15 is the final destination for more than half of Russia's oil and gas exports. This means that the EU relies on Russia for about 20% of its gas and 17% of its oil. These shares will rise after enlargement, since some of the new members rely almost entirely on Russia to satisfy their energy needs. Further in the future, the EU expects its own energy resources to diminish, while consumption will shift increasingly from oil and coal to natural gas. Both trends will heighten the EU's reliance on Russian supplies.

In acknowledgement of the importance of this mutual dependency, the two sides launched a bilateral 'energy dialogue' in 2000, aiming 'to raise all issues of common interest relating to the [energy] sector, including the introduction of cooperation on energy saving, rationalisation of production and transportation infrastructures, European investment possibilities, and relations between producer and consumer countries'.[11] The dialogue involves regular meetings of experts, as well as high-level political discussions during biannual EU–Russia summits.

However, progress since 2000 has been mixed. There have been some notable successes, including the establishment of a technology centre in Moscow in November 2002, plans for an EU-funded investment guarantee scheme, and the start of several pilot projects to achieve energy savings. Yet on many of the more important issues – pipelines, gas supply contracts, electricity-sector restructuring, and nuclear-fuel supplies – the EU and Russia continue to disagree.

As explained above, the EU wants Russia to reform its energy market as a precondition for accession to the WTO. But the EU also fears an increasing mismatch between its own efforts to liberalise its energy markets and the supply of Russian gas through a monopolist, namely Gazprom. EU countries have committed themselves to liberalising fully their energy markets for industrial users by 2004 and for households by 2007. Russia, though, supplies its EU customers under long-term contracts, some of which contain so-called territorial restriction clauses: even if one EU state receives more gas than it needs, it is not allowed to sell it on to its neighbours. The clauses are in breach of EU single-market rules. They allow Gazprom to sell gas to different EU countries at different prices, and they prevent the EU from developing a functioning EU-wide gas market. While Gazprom has agreed to remove the territorial restriction clause governing its business with Italy, there has been no such move in relation to Austria and Germany.

Problems also plague the EU–Russia dialogue on electricity. Russia is increasingly keen on linking its own electricity grid to that of the enlarged European Union. This would enable Unified Energy Systems (UES), the electricity monopoly, not only to sell surplus electricity to EU consumers, but also to make up for temporary shortages in its own market by importing power from the EU. The latter says that, in order to sell to the European market, Russia must apply EU-level standards of competition, nuclear safety and environmental protection – which of course it does not – and that it must get rid of the 'unfair' subsidy that UES receives in the form of cheap gas from Gazprom. For now, the two sides have asked an expert panel to ascertain to what extent EU and Russian rules and policies diverge in these areas.

The dialogue on oil is less politically charged, partly because Russia has already privatised and liberalised its oil industry. Here, the dialogue focuses mainly on how to attract EU investors to the Russian oil sector. The EU has long pushed Russia to establish a workable framework for production sharing agreements (PSAs), which are commonly used in emerging market economies to make fast the legal and tax environment for large-scale investments in natural resources. The Russian government has been dragging its feet, however, and in 2003 cancelled all ongoing negotiations on PSAs and made it more difficult to conclude new ones. The government claims that British Petroleum (BP)'s decision in 2003 to commit more than $6bn to its Russian ventures is proof that PSAs are not needed. But apart from BP's investment and a couple of giant offshore operations financed mainly by Royal Dutch/Shell and ExxonMobil, there has been remarkably little foreign investment in the Russian energy sector.[12] The absence of a functioning PSA framework is only one reason for the dearth of foreign involvement; among the others are uncertain property rights and widespread public hostility to Russia selling its riches to foreigners.

Another obstacle to private investment, not only in oil, but also in the gas sector, is the state's firm grip on pipelines. The capacity of Transneft, the state-owned oil-pipeline monopolist, has failed to meet rapidly rising oil output. Russia's oil majors are complaining that lack of pipeline capacity is impeding their plans for expansion and investment. Several Russian oil companies are also sitting on considerable gas reserves. Few exploit them commercially, though, since Gazprom does not allow them access to lucrative export markets via its pipelines and domestic prices are too low. Finally, Russia refuses to grant other gas producers in the Caspian region access to its pipelines. Nor does it want privately run transit pipelines on its territory.

From the EU's perspective, the lack of investment and openness in the Russian energy sector is worrisome. The EU predicts that, by 2020, it will be buying an additional 300bn cubic metres of Russian gas per year to meet growing domestic demand. But Russia's own energy strategy foresees additional sales to the enlarged EU of only 30bn cubic metres a year by 2020, while increasing amounts of gas would go to the fast-growing Chinese market and to the US.[13] The EU, therefore, has a large stake in the development of the Russian energy market. The two sides have identified a number of projects of 'common interest', such as the development of the Shtokman gas field and a new gas pipeline under the Baltic Sea. But they have made little progress in getting EU companies to invest while the Russian state retains a firm hold on the sector.

While talks on the opening up of markets and pipelines have made little headway, other issues have moved to the top of the bilateral energy agenda, namely the 1997 Kyoto Protocol to the 1992 United Nations Framework Convention on Climate Change and quotas for imports of nuclear fuel. The EU is the main supporter of the Kyoto Protocol and has started to implement its provisions, although the treaty has not yet entered into force. With the US refusing to ratify it, Russia is the only country that could ensure its entry into force.[14] In economic terms, Russia may well gain from Kyoto, since it could sell off unused pollution rights (although some experts think that the benefits would be small unless the US joins the new market for emissions rights). The Russian administration appears split on the matter of ratification. But so is the EU. Many EU officials think that Russia's continued refusal to ratify the protocol is a thinly veiled attempt to obtain concessions in other areas, particularly in relation to the WTO talks. They want the EU to create a similar 'linkage' to WTO talks to put pressure on the Russian government. But other EU representatives, especially Energy and Transport Commissioner Loyola de Palacio, have taken a more lenient stance.

The EU has managed to dispel Russian worries that it will seek to reduce its reliance on Russian gas after enlargement. Yet Russia is still concerned about its lucrative contracts for selling and storing nuclear materials. Almost all of Eastern Europe's nuclear power stations are of Soviet build and run on Russian nuclear fuels. As a result, Russia has a near monopoly in regard to supplying the accession states with enriched uranium. This could clash with an EU rule (decided on in 1994) that says that Russia's stake in the EU's uranium market should not be greater than 20%. In November 2003, the EU member states finally gave the European Commission a mandate to negotiate with Russia on the issue.

There are several possible reasons why progress under the energy dialogue has been slow. First, the dialogue has become intertwined with other EU–Russia negotiations, in particular, the WTO accession talks and Russia's refusal to ratify the Kyoto Protocol and the multilateral Energy Charter. Second, the EU–Russia energy dialogue involves a host of participants that do not always see eye-to-eye. The Russian government and the EU may agree on the importance of bilateral cooperation, but the key players in the field are private or state-controlled companies that often have their own agendas. Third, the energy dialogue is not only, or even primarily, about country-to-country sales of oil and gas. It stretches deep into the realm of national economic policies, especially energy-market liberalisation.

Conclusion

As this chapter shows, the EU and Russia have plenty of common interests, particularly in the sphere of economics. However, there are also some fundamental differences in terms of outlook, approach and objectives, which make it very hard for the two sides to reap the full benefits of their bilateral relations.

The EU's main goal is to nudge Russia along the path of economic reform and democratisation. This is not altruism: the EU fears that trouble within Russia could quickly turn into a security threat for the whole continent, not only because the 'wrong' people may take over in the Kremlin but also because a poor, chaotic Russia could be a major source of organised crime, terrorism, weapons smuggling, illegal migration and environmental hazards. To achieve this goal, the EU has resorted to its tried and tested method of integration and association. It offers a closer relationship but attaches significant conditionality. In the case of the Central and Eastern European candidate countries, this methodology has resulted in one of the most successful instances of 'regime change' ever.

States like Hungary, Latvia and Poland have gone from post-communist upheaval to being orderly EU members (as of 1 May 2004) within a decade and a half.

Russia's case is different for several reasons.

The overriding wish to join the EU as quickly as possible served as a powerful 'anchor' for reforms in the East European accession countries. The EU has not offered Russia membership, nor is Russia interested in it. Russia very much sees itself as an independent player, a regional great power with global aspirations.

The EU has at times underestimated the enormity of the task at hand. Russia's post-communist reform process has been characterised by half-hearted measures and policy reversals. Unlike the populations of the Central and East European nations, Russians have never experienced a sustained period of democracy and market economics. The country's huge oil and gas sales have helped economic recovery but they have also fostered cronyism and corruption. Russia itself is unsure of where it is going and how fast.

The two sides have vastly different approaches to the rule of law. The EU is the epitome of a rules-based community. Its single market, competition policy and fiscal restrictions, to name but a few, cannot function without assiduous adherence and strict enforcement. Russia is still a long way from the 'dictatorship of the law' that Putin promised in 2000. Recent improvements notwithstanding, Russia's confusing and contradictory laws remain a breeding ground for corruption. Overworked and often corrupt judges cannot be relied upon to protect rights and to enforce obligations. The arrest in late 2003 of several high-profile business executives, including Mikhail Khodorkovsky, shows that, in Russia, the law of power is still stronger than the power of law.

Most Russians believe that their country is somehow unique. They argue that Russia needs to do things the Russian way, not the European or the Western way. True or false, such perceptions serve as a powerful impediment to Russia accepting EU conditionality. In addition, a resurgence of nationalism, particularly among younger Russians, leaves the country ever more sensitive about outside interference.

Large parts of the Russian policy establishment remain wedded to old-fashioned concepts, such as spheres of influence, zero-sum games and strict reciprocity. Most EU bureaucrats, however, believe in 'post-modern' ideas like mutual interest, shared sovereignty and win-win solutions.

Putin and his government will continue to resist any overt form of external influence over domestic developments. What the president wants from the EU is not policy advice, or even financial assistance. Rather, he sees relations with the EU as a way of strengthening the domestic economy through trade and, to a lesser extent, investment.

A stronger and more stable economy is the precondition for restoring Russia's former great-power status in the world. In short, Putin does not seek good relations with the West for their own sake. He sees the West, particularly the EU, as a 'modernisation resource'.[15]

This rather instrumental approach to EU–Russia relations implies clear limits to the compromises that Putin is prepared to make. Internal objectives will take priority over external ones. Another limiting factor is the continued ranking of political goals – meaning geo-strategic or military objectives – over economic ones. Putin, more than any other Russian leader before him, recognises the importance of economic relations in foreign policy.[16] But he is also fully aware that his country resembles an economic dwarf compared with the EU (Russia's entire gross domestic product (GDP) is roughly equal to that of the Netherlands). Putin will therefore resist making economics the basis of mutual relations, and continue to look for a 'political deal' even in more technical areas such as trade.

The EU's approach is the exact opposite. It is a powerful economic actor on the world stage, but a political dwarf due to its internal divisions and lack of military cooperation. The EU is developing a Common Foreign and Security Policy (CFSP) and it has recently made some headway in regard to defence cooperation. But its relations with third countries are still heavily influenced by those areas where the Union has competences, such as trade, competition, transport and energy.

This mismatch will continue to hold back EU–Russia relations. But the focus on economics also implies opportunities. Ten years after the EU and Russia signed the PCA it is becoming clear that they do not share a strategic vision. In fact, the EU does not have a clear strategy towards Russia, and nor does Russia know exactly what it wants from the EU. But cooperation in well-defined areas has the potential to link the EU and Russia through solidarités de faits – the term used by Jean Monnet, the EU's founding father, to describe how countries can develop trust and a habit of cooperation over time.

Notes

1 This chapter is an abridged and amended version of Barysch, K., *The EU and Russia: Strategic Partners or Squabbling Neighbours* (London: CER, 2004).

2 Hamilton, C.B., 'Russia's European economic integration: escapism and realities', Centre for European Reform (CEPR) discussion paper no. 3840 (London: CEPR, March 2003).

3 Kaveshnikov, N., 'Three stories about strategic partnership between Russia and the European Union'. Paper presented at 'Russia and the European Union in a Wider Europe: New Openings and Old Barriers', international academic conference, St Petersburg, 20–21 September 2002; at www.edc.spb.ru/conf2002/home.htmle.

4 Quoted by Prime-Tass and at www.wto.ru.

5 For a comprehensive overview of EU and Russian arguments, see Lamy, P., Medvedkov, M., Cottrell, R. et al., *Russia and the WTO* (London: Centre for European Reform, 2002).

6 The Office of the United States Trade Representative puts cost-recovery levels at $35–40 per 1,000 cubic metres, compared with Russian gas prices of $21–$24 per trillion cubic metres (tcm) and world market prices of $100–120/tcm. Report on World Trade Barriers (Washington, DC: Office of the United States Trade Representative, 2004).

7 Russian European Centre for Economic Policy, *Common Economic Space: Prospects for Russia–EU Relations* (Moscow: Tacis, 2002).

8 Sutela, P., *Russia and Europe: Some Economic Aspects* (Moscow: Carnegie Moscow Center, 2003), pp. 169–173.

9 Mau, V. and Novikov, V., 'Otnosheniya Rossii i ES: Prostranstvo Vybora ili Vybor Prostranstva?', *Voprosy Ekonomiki*, No. 6, 2002, and also see Mau, V. and Novikov, V. 'Russia–EU Relations and the Common European Economic Space' in this volume pp. 103–114.

10 Gould, T., 'The European Economic Area as a Model for the Wider Europe', Background paper for the European Free Trade Association (EFTA) Ministerial Meeting, 27 June 2003.

11 Vahl, M., 'Whither the CEES? Political and institutional aspects of closer integration between the EU and Russia', in de Wilde, T. and Spetschinsky, L. (eds), *La politique étrangère de la Russie et ses implications pour l'Europe* (Brussels: PIE-Peter Lang, 2004). Patten, C. and Lamy, P., 'Economic space and beyond: EU enlargement will help build closer economic ties between Russia and the rest of Europe', *Financial Times*, 5 December 2001.

12 Communiqué of the EU–Russia Summit, Paris, France, October 2000; at www.europa.eu.int/

Katinka Barysch

130

comm/external_relations/russia/summit_30_10_00/statement_en.htm.

[13] According to Russia's own energy strategy, the oil sector will require $12 billion of investment each year until 2020 in order to renew the capital stock and to sustain economic growth. Similar sums are needed for gas and electricity.

[14] Götz, R., 'Russlands Energiestrategie und die Energieversorgung Europas', SWP-Studie 2004/S (Berlin: SWP, 2004).

[15] The Kyoto Protocol would enter into force if a majority of the producers of greenhouse gases – accounting for 55% of worldwide carbon emissions in 1990 – ratified it. Trenin, D., 'Russia and the West: what you see is what you get', *The World Today* (London: Royal Institute of International Affairs, April 2004), p.13.

[16] Lo, B., *Vladimir Putin and the Evolution of Russian Foreign Policy*, Chatham House Papers (Oxford: Blackwell Publishing, 2003).

PART TWO

7. The Implications of Centre–Region Politics for Russia's North-west Border Regions

Nikolai Petrov[1]

The role of the regions in Russian foreign policy has grown enormously in comparison with the Soviet era, when all foreign-policy activity was tightly controlled and extremely centralised. At that time, there was little activity to speak of except for the twinning of cities and regions and certain forms of cross-border cooperation. Nowadays, it is not only federal ministries and offices that are engaged in international activity, but also regional governments and numerous companies, national and regional. After the collapse of the Soviet Union, the number of border regions increased dramatically, practically doubling.[2] Today, almost half of the country's regions are border regions.

Although the regions have become considerably more involved in foreign policy in recent years, the federal reforms of 2000–03 have led to a noticeable decline in the role of regional heads on the federal stage in general, and as relatively independent players in foreign policy in particular. As regards the latter, the regions are at once objects and subjects of foreign policy. It is also important to note the current plurality (the variability and complexity) of foreign policy: in Soviet times, a common policy was implemented from a single centre, while today there is scope for pluralism within the framework of the different state departments, business structures and even the regions themselves. Since, time and again, the overall policy direction is the result of a combination of many individual vectors emanating from different directions, it is extremely dynamic and varies in both time and space. The regions have a special part to play in this variation and this chapter analyses it by looking primarily at the example of the North-west regions of Russia that border the European Union (EU). This chapter not only examines how the regions affect foreign policy, but it also considers how foreign policy affects life in the regions.

Articulation of foreign-policy issues in the political life of the regions
As far as the political life of the regions is concerned, neither the governors, nor the general public, are particularly interested in foreign-policy issues, except in a few special cases when foreign policy impacts directly on domestic policy. Below are some examples:

- When regional heads see themselves as federal politicians and aspire to hold greater status. This applies primarily to Moscow Mayor Yury Luzhkov, particularly in relation to his playing of the anti-Lithuanian and Sevastopol cards in 1996–99. To some extent it is also true of the former Governor of Primorsk *krai*, Yevgeny Nazdratenko, in regard to his confrontation with the Russian Ministry of Foreign Affairs (MFA) over the Russian–Chinese border.
- When regional heads promote themselves and their regions in the international arena in order to attract foreign investment and to boost the regional economy. The most obvious examples of this are the 'showcases of reform'. That is, Nizhny Novgorod *oblast* under Governor Boris Nemtsov (1991–97), Novgorod *oblast* under Mikhail Prusak, and Samara *oblast*, which achieved supremacy over its rivals under 'Social Democrat' Konstantin Titov.[3]
- When a region's active presence in the international arena plays a significant and symbolic part in the realisation of 'state' ambitions[4] and in the exploitation of the ethnic factor in the case of Russia's national republics. The most striking case in point is Tatarstan, with, for example, its 16 official missions and trade representations outside the Russian Federation and its World Tatar Congresses. This also applies to the active exploitation of the German ethnic factor in its real, virtual and even phantom forms in the cases of Altai *krai* and the *oblasts* of Kaliningrad, Saratov, Sverdlovsk and Tomsk, among others.
- When foreign-policy issues directly affecting a region's economy and thus its citizens become more acute. Examples include the Far Eastern regions and the difficulties that they have experienced in relation to Chinese migration and shuttle trade, Kalmykiya and Buryatiya Republics in connection with the visit of the Dalai Lama, Dagestan and the divided Lezgin national group following changes to the Russian–Azerbaijan border regime, and North Ossetia and its problems associated with South Ossetian refugees and the border with Georgia.

- When migration creates a special class of problems that often make foreign policy an important factor in domestic political life. Here it is worth mentioning Krasnodar *krai* and Stavropol *krai* which are home to a large number of migrants from the Caucasus and also other Russian regions which have witnessed various forms of ethno phobia – notably Kaliningrad *oblast* and the belt of regions on the border with China, particularly Amur *oblast* and Khabarovsk *krai* and Primorsk *krai*.
- When ethno-territorial disputes exist and various groups in neighbouring states harbour claims to a region's territory. Above all, this concerns Kaliningrad *oblast* in connection with East Prussia and 'Lithuania Minor', and the Kuril Islands (northern territories claimed by Japan in Sakhalin *oblast*). However, it also applies to the Russian–Latvian and Russian–Estonian borders in Pskov *oblast* and the areas of Finnish Karelia that became parts of the Republic of Karelia and Leningrad *oblast* as a result of the 1939–40 Soviet–Finnish War.
- And when a region's economy is geared towards the development of cross-border cooperation. This is typical of a large band of regions on the Russian–Ukrainian, Russian–Kazakhstan and Russian–Chinese borders.

Trends in foreign policy and the regions
The relationship between foreign policy and the domestic life of the regions is a very dynamic one. The time factor plays a key part here, making any conclusions and generalisations relative and inevitably time-bound.

In just over ten years of rapid political development, the Russian regions have passed through several stages as foreign-policy players. At least three major stages can be identified in regard to both the nature of the regions' international relations and the way in which these have been regulated by law.[5]

- 1991–94 Transition stage, characterised by the absence of an institutional and legislative base and by individualism and chaos in the regions' pursuit of international relations.
- 1995–98 Initial stage of the institutionalisation and legislative development of international relations at the time of a weak centre and increasingly strong regions.
- 1998–present Growing centralised control and regulation of international activity pursued by the regions and standardisation of the conditions for such activity.

During the first stage (1991–94), the regions acted in the spirit of a revolutionary era. At the time, the centre was very weak and beset by contradictions. The regions themselves established the legal basis for the development of international relations in the absence of the exercise of real control by Moscow. Lack of political stability in the country at a time of deep economic crisis, insufficient professionalism and experience in the implementation of international activity both in the centre and in the provinces, and inconsistencies in the interpretation of national and regional interests, gave rise to a wide range of often contradictory foreign-policy aims, forms, methods and results.

The second stage (1995–98) saw a certain increase in political stability and with it the consolidation of the élites both in the centre and in the provinces. The MFA began to assume responsibility for coordinating the foreign policy and foreign economic activity of the regions. In order to do this, a special department was even set up, which at one time was led by Valentina Matvienko, who went on to become one of the president's deputies and then the presidential representative for the North-west Federal District.[6] The MFA's work gradually came to include the development of a legislative base comprising federal laws and bilateral agreements on the demarcation of jurisdiction and powers.[7] Despite a certain lack of clarity in this respect, the regions played an active part in international relations. Tatarstan alone entered into over 50 agreements on commercial, economic, scientific, technical and cultural cooperation with numerous foreign partners, including members of the EU – France, Germany and the Netherlands – and the federal state of Lower Saxony and the autonomous region of Madrid. With Moscow's consent, Tatarstan also signed the first direct agreement with a foreign state, Turkey, in 1995. Records show that, by the second half of the 1990s, the regions had entered into over 3,000 different international agreements, the majority of which were drawn up with the help of the MFA.[8] It was during this particular stage that the regions entered the foreign loans market and, for instance, began to dispose of Eurobonds. The volume of foreign loans held by the regions was estimated in the late 1990s by experts at over $17 billion.[9]

The third stage began with the 1998 financial default, when many regional governments suddenly found themselves all but bankrupt. This phase is characterised by significant clarity of vision and organisation, pragmatism in the pursuit of foreign relations, standardisation of the rules of the game, and greater monitoring of their implementation. Orenburg *oblast*, whose experience of cross-border cooperation was the subject of an international conference held in 1998 by the local government, the MFA and the Council of Europe, provides an excellent example of the peculiarities of the foreign-policy activity of a region during the different stages. Whereas the programme of official visits by representatives of the *oblast* read like a colourful and exotic travel itinerary in 1992–94, including Austria, Bulgaria, Czech Republic, Germany, Hungary, Indonesia, Singapore, Slovakia, Switzerland, Turkey and Vietnam, the situation was completely different in 1998 with visits being made to Belarus, Kazakhstan and Uzbekistan, all of which were major commercial partners.

The federal reforms of Russian President Vladimir Putin, which began in May 2000, gave strong added impetus to the centralisation of the decision-making process and enhanced the monitoring of its outcomes. At this stage, in particular, the bilateral agreements that many of the regions had entered into with the centre during the era of Russian President Boris Yeltsin were rescinded.[10] Whereas international relations had previously been an important part of the work performed by inter-regional organisations in regard to economic cooperation, with the creation of the federal districts, this task passed largely into the hands of the presidential representatives after 2000. It is the president's plenipotentiaries who are now responsible for foreign investment and, accordingly, for promoting their districts in key international capitals. The problem is that the military generals and KGB veterans appointed to the posts of presidential plenipotentiaries in the federal districts have staffed their administrations with their own kind. Their offices are lacking in competent specialists in the fields of economics and international relations and the presidential representatives themselves generally limit their international activities to arranging regular exhibitions in major international cities, such as Berlin, Brussels, London and Paris, only occasionally hosting foreign delegations and even more rarely making overseas visits, which are often merely for the purpose of familiarisation. Although the North-west Federal District has a Supervisory Council for Cross-Border Policy, its function is geared more towards maintaining security than promoting cooperation.

The personalities of the presidential representatives themselves have significant influence on the kind of activities that their offices pursue. The North-west has been unlucky from the standpoint of international relations. From 2000 to 2003, the president's chosen representative was ex-KGB general Viktor Cherkesov, who regarded international contacts from a very specific professional perspective. Between March and September 2003, Valentina Matvienko held the post. Even though she was previously responsible within the MFA for international relations with respect to the regions, she spent half of her term as presidential representative overseeing preparations for the St Petersburg tercentenary celebrations and the other half campaigning for the position of governor of the city. Consequently, she was left with no time for international relations no matter how close within her professional reach they may have seemed.

Foreign-policy resources and the regional infrastructure

The Russian regions have a number of important foreign-policy resources,[11] which as yet remain under-exploited. Some examples are outlined below:

- Their geopolitical, geographical and strategic locations (the last two having transport and military implications respectively), which are particularly significant in the cases of Kaliningrad *oblast* and the Far Eastern regions.
- Their considerable natural, human, scientific, technical and industrial potential.
- Historic ties and ethnic and cultural links between the border regions and their foreign neighbours. This is particularly true of Kaliningrad *oblast* (with Lithuania and Poland), the Republic of Karelia (with Finland), and the regions of southern Russia and southern Siberia (with Ukraine and Kazakhstan).[12]
- Numerous industrial ties from the Soviet era between neighbouring regions of the former Soviet republics and with members of the socialist bloc.
- The participation of many of the regions in international and regional organisations, and
- direct bilateral and multilateral cooperation with regions of neighbouring states.

The problems that the Russian regions have in common with their foreign neighbours (particularly concerning the environment, transport and cross-border issues) can only be solved through joint efforts. The very existence of common borders gives rise to a whole range of problems that require the assistance of Russia's immediate neighbours often with the involvement of border regions from other parts of the country, too. The Russian Ministry of Foreign Affairs now has representative offices in more than 30 regions of the federation including in the majority of the North-western regions: St Petersburg, Karelia and Komi republics, Murmansk, Arkhangelsk and Pskov *oblasts*. There are a lot of foreign consulates and other representative offices in these regions as well. They include:

- St Petersburg – office of the MFA[13] and missions representing 44 foreign states;
- Murmansk *oblast* – office of the MFA, Consulate Generals of Norway and Sweden, a branch of the Consulate of Finland and a branch of the embassy of the Republic of Belarus;
- Pskov *oblast* – office of the MFA, Consulate of the Republic of Latvia, and a chancellery of the Consulate General of the Republic of Estonia in St Petersburg;

- Kaliningrad *oblast* – Consulate Generals of Latvia, Lithuania, Poland and Sweden with a German Consulate set to open soon; and
- Republic of Karelia – an EU Tacis technical office and a branch of the Consulate of Finland.

Regional involvement in shaping and implementing foreign policy

In 1994, the Advisory Council of the Subjects of the Russian Federation on International and Foreign Economic Relations was set up within the MFA to provide guidance to the subjects of the Russian Federation with respect to international and foreign economic relations. Among other things, its responsibilities include giving expert legal assessments of the international agreements that the regions have entered into. The regions' representatives have their say at the highly influential Foreign Affairs Committee (FAC), which is one of the committees of the old 'gubernatorial' Federation Council (as it was from 1996 to 2002 when it comprised 89 governors and 89 regional speakers). A characteristic of the old FAC was the strong representation of the North-west: it was not only chaired by the Governor of Novgorod, Mikhail Prusak, but also included three more governors from the North-west: Vladimir Butov (Governor of Nenets autonomous district); Leonid Gorbenko (Kaliningrad *oblast*); and Anatoly Yefremov (Arkhangelsk *oblast*).[14] As of 2002, the new Federation Council no longer includes the governors and speakers, but instead is presided over by their representatives. The Foreign Affairs Committee on the other hand does still bear many similarities to the old FAC[15] but the North-west regions and the border regions as a whole are noticeably less represented. The key exception is that Mikhail Margelov, who represents the executive authorities of Pskov *oblast*, now chairs the committee. The only other parliamentarian from the regions of the North-west is a representative of Vologda *oblast*.

On 21 January 2003, at a meeting of the State Council to discuss matters concerning Russian international activity, Putin proposed establishing a Council of Heads of the Regions under the MFA, although, as of May 2004, it is still not operational. He also suggested that the regions play a greater role in Russia's cooperation with neighbouring states and that the rotation of diplomatic officials should draw upon cadres trained in the regions.

In some cases, the regions succeed in either modifying resolutions already adopted by the centre, as in the case, for example, of Kaliningrad *oblast* at the beginning of 2003 when the new Customs Code was introduced, or even shooting them down entirely, as with the prohibition of right-hand drive vehicles in 2000, which provoked a united wave of protest by all of the Far Eastern regions of the country, where there are large numbers of second-hand Japanese cars.

The regions as foreign-policy subjects

In accordance with Article 71 of the Constitution of the Russian Federation, foreign policy falls within the exclusive jurisdiction of the Russian Federation, while Article 72 places the coordination of international and foreign economic contacts under joint control. This provision of Article 72 is elaborated on and governed by a whole series of federal laws.[16] Furthermore, a large number of regions have adopted and observe their own laws regulating international activity within the scope of their own powers.[17]

Regional and national interests do not necessarily coincide. The most obvious examples of serious conflicts of interest include: the support shown by the delegations of Bashkiria, Chuvashia, Dagestan, Khakasia, Tatarstan, Tuva and Yakutia (contrary to Russia's official position) for a communiqué delivered at a meeting of Turkic states and communities in Istanbul in 1997 demanding recognition of the Turkish Republic of Northern Cyprus; the MFA's refusal to extend an invitation to the Dalai Lama to visit Russia, despite persistent requests from the heads of Buryatia and Kalmykia, for fear that such a move might aggravate Russian–Chinese relations; and recognition by Kabardino-Balkaria of the self-proclaimed Republic of Abkhazia (in Georgia), once again contrary to the line of the Kremlin.

At a State Council meeting in January 2003, no less than two regional heads from the North-west – Sergei Katanandov, the President of the Republic of Karelia, and Yury Yevdokimov, the Governor of Murmansk – addressed the issue of the role of the regions in implementing Russia's foreign policy and stimulating cross-border cooperation. Katanandov said:

> The government of the Republic of Karelia regards cross-border cooperation not as an end in itself, but as an important instrument in solving the region's social and economic problems. The key objectives of cross-border cooperation are to close the gap in the standard of living on either side of the border, achieve mutual understanding between countries on a sub-regional level and foster ties between people in the spheres of business, culture and science as well as the intelligentsia and young people […]. In 2000, further to the Russian State Concept for Cross-Border Cooperation and in response to the European Union's Northern Dimension policy, we proposed that a Euroregion be established on the Karelian–Finnish part of the state border. The two-year existence of the Karelia Euroregion demonstrates that the idea has successfully become reality. Together with the regional councils of Kainuu, Northern Karelia and Northern Ostrobothnia, the Republic of Karelia has developed a new model for cross-border cooperation that is designed to make best use of the European Union's Interreg and Tacis cross-border cooperation programmes. The Russian and Finnish sides have planned a number of events for 2003 within the framework of the Euroregion:

1. A 'Train of Friendship' travelling on a circuitous route from Arkhangelsk to Petrozavodsk (capital of Karelia) via Kostomushka (Russia) and Oulu and Vartsila (in Finland);
2. A roller ski race along the Northern Transport Corridor (Oulu – Petrozavodsk – Arkhangelsk);
3. Karelian–Finnish events as part of the Petrozavodsk 300th anniversary celebrations;
4. A Karelian–Finnish youth forum to be held in Petrozavodsk in September 2003.[18]

Murmansk governor Yury Yevdokimov reported on his region's international contacts:

> Murmansk *oblast* entered into bilateral agreements with the northern provinces of Norway, Sweden and Finland in 1988. Five years later, we joined the Barents Regional Council. Active partnership within the framework of the Barents process not only gives us the opportunity to promote Russia's standing on an international level, but it also enables us to make social and economic headway and cope better with our own domestic problems [...]. In recent years the Barents Sea region has become a unique laboratory for the development of mutually beneficial activity and neighbourly cooperation between countries with different historical backgrounds, state structures, policies and economics as well as differing allegiances to modern-day economic, military and political organisations [...]. Today, there is not a single sphere of mutual interests where we do not work with our neighbours: small business and the environment, education and culture, transport and agriculture, energy saving and children's issues, the indigenous people of the North and twinning links, law enforcement and humanitarian aid for prisoners, border safety and fisheries, contacts between military structures and links between representatives of the Church [...]. Three years ago, Murmansk became the site of the first Norwegian industrial centre in Russia, followed by an analogous Swedish institution. Today, they both play a key role in developing business relations, promoting joint projects and attracting investment. We have opened a similar centre in the Swedish city of Luleå. The Finns have helped us to draw up an atlas of the *oblast's* natural resources and, with the assistance of Norway and Finland, a national cultural centre is being established in the village of Lovozero, where a teaching centre is being set up for Lapp children and deer-raising is being developed.[19]

The Republic of Komi is not lagging behind the neighbouring Russian regions. On 1 January 2000, it entered into cooperation agreements with four foreign states – Bulgaria, Czech Republic, Hungary and Slovakia – and six foreign regions: the province of Oulu in Finland; the Kaunas region in Lithuania; the Bratislava region in Slovakia; the province of Shani in China; and the provinces of Gilan and Mazandaran in Iran.[20]

As for international sub-regional organisations, the Republic of Karelia and Leningrad *oblast* are members of the Assembly of European Regions, together with the *oblasts* of Bashkortostan, Moscow, Ryazan, Samara and

Tatarstan. Kaliningrad and St Petersburg belong to the association of European cities known as Eurocities. A number of the North-west regions are involved in organisations in the area of the Baltic Sea, such as the Baltic Sea States Subregional Cooperation, the Conference of Peripheral Maritime Regions of Europe, the Northern Forum, and the Union of Baltic Cities. Arkhangelsk, the Republic of Karelia and Murmansk *oblasts* and the Nenets autonomous district are already permanent members of the Barents Regional Council, which unites the northern regions of Finland, Norway, Sweden and Russia, and other regions of the North-west are seeking to join, including the Republic of Komi and Leningrad and Vologda *oblasts*. In his speech cited above, Katanandov referred to the Karelia Euroregion that unites Karelia with eastern Finland, while cities and districts of Kaliningrad *oblast* participate in the Neman[21] and Baltika Euroregions.[22]

Intergovernmental visits

Visits by senior foreign dignitaries to the regions represent a special case of the direct impact of international relations on the political life of the regions. In recent years, the geography of such visits has changed significantly. Whereas until recently itineraries were often limited to Moscow and perhaps one showcase region (Nizhny Novgorod was particularly popular in the mid-1990s), today distinguished foreign guests are more likely to visit remoter places, particularly in the North-west (such as Arkhangelsk, Murmansk, Novgorod and Pskov). The North-west tour has become especially popular since Putin came to power in March 2000, as he likes to receive guests in his home city of St Petersburg. The pilgrimage of foreign heads of state to the northern capital reached its peak in 2003, when over 40 leaders came together to celebrate the tercentenary anniversary of Peter the Great's 'window onto Europe'. The Konstantinov Palace was restored in time for the event and new hotels were built. The question of permanently moving some offices situated in the capital to St Petersburg, such as the Federation Council or the Supreme Court, has been raised on numerous occasions.

The case of Belarus President Alexander Lukashenko provides an excellent example of the direct links between foreign leaders and the regions as well as of the potential problems they pose for the centre. In April 1997, shortly after signing the Russia–Belarus Union Treaty, Lukashenko announced that

> We spend too much time working with Russia's centre, with Moscow, with the government, with the president and the federal structures. We have signed a lot of agreements, but these, unfortunately, are not implemented in full. This is through no fault of our own. We have come to realise that we are not going to get anywhere by only knocking at Moscow's door. For this reason we have decided to work with the regions.[23]

The format for a visit from the Belarusian president, tried and tested in Krasnodar *krai* in June 1997, usually includes the signing of a set of agreements on economic, scientific, technical and cultural cooperation and on trade. Agreements on direct relations between the Russian regions and Belarus are often initialled at the same time. Lukashenko received numerous invitations from the heads of Russia's *oblasts* and *krais*. In the early days, he encountered certain difficulties: after one of the conflicts between Minsk and Moscow, for example, the governor of Kaliningrad *oblast* asked Lukashenko to cancel a planned visit, while the Belarusian president's trip to Lipetsk and Yaroslavl' was cut short when the Russian side refused to allow his plane to land (at the time, the Kremlin was demonstrating that, even within an emerging federal state, there would be no direct relations by the Russian regions without its consent). The situation soon changed, however, and Belarusian missions were opened in Kaliningrad, Krasnodar, Murmansk, St Petersburg and Tyumen. By 1999, the Russian regions had entered into 115 cooperation agreements with the government of Belarus and its individual regions and another 40 with its ministries and departments. In 1998–99, 13 official Belarusian delegations visited the regions of the Russian Federation, while Russian regional leaders made a total of 34 visits to Minsk.[24]

Foreign policy and domestic political life of the regions
Foreign-policy factors play an important part in the political life of many, if not all, of the country's regions. This influence can either remain in the background, determining the general nature of a political situation and the fears and expectations of the public, for instance, or it can be upfront and concrete, as when political powers use foreign-policy factors to achieve their own ends.

One of the main background elements in the border regions, particularly in Russia's North-west and Far East, is the clearly pronounced public mood of protest that is apparent during all elections, be they federal or local. This is illustrated in Table 7.1, which shows that more votes are systematically cast for protest candidates and parties, such as Vladimir Zhirinovsky in the presidential elections of 1991 and 1996, Alexander Lebed in 1996, and the Liberal Democratic Party of Russia (LDPR) (Zhirinovsky's bloc) in the State Duma elections of 1993, 1995 and 1999. Protest was also apparent in the gubernatorial polls of 1995–98 and 1999–2002 where votes for incumbent governors fell compared with the previous election. The heightened mood of protest in the western and eastern border regions can largely be attributed to the large presence of service personnel, who, together with their family members, represent up to one-third of the electorate, and a highly organised electorate at that.

Table 7.1 Protest behaviour of the electorate in Russia's North-western regions, 1991–2003

	Voting for 'protest' candidates/parties:						Voting 'against all':			Regional elections		
	Zhirinovsky (1991)	LDPR (1993)	LDPR (1995)	Lebed (1996)	Zhirinovsky (1996)	Zhirinovsky's bloc (1999)	Duma-1993 (party lists)	Presidential elections 1996 (second round)	Duma-1999 (party lists)	Defeat of regional governors, 1995–2002	Percentage of vote for incumbent, 1995–1998	Percentage of vote for incumbent, 1999–2002
Border regions												
Pskov	14.8	40.2	20.9	23.6	10.2	7	2.9	5.9	2.9	1	30.9	28
Leningrad	9	26.6	8	18.1	4.3	6.5	4	5.7	3.6	1	31.7	30.3
Kaliningrad	12.9	26.4	11.4	19.3	7.2	8.8	3.8	6.2	3.1	2	31.3	21.5
Karelia	8.1	18.3	13.6	12	8.5	8.6	3.8	6.6	4.2	1	35.1	53.5
Murmansk	9.8	21.4	12.4	25.4	7	11.2	5.4	7.4	4	1	31.1	86.7
Average	10.9	26.6	13.3	19.7	7.4	8.4	4.0	6.4	3.6	1.2	32.0	44.0
Other regions												
Komi	8.8	21.5	17.5	18.2	9.8	7.5	4.3	6.7	3.1	1	57.2	35
Arkhangelsk	6.6	19.4	10.8	17.3	6.6	9.2	3.8	7.5	3.9		34.5	49.7
Vologda	7.8	26.7	14.4	13.6	6.6	9.2	3.6	6.9	3.8		80.5	78.6
Novgorod	9.3	26.9	12.1	18.5	6.2	7	3.6	6.2	2.8		56.2	91.6
Nenets	8.5	15.9	16.8	12	9.9	10.7	7.6	8.5	6	1	40.6	68.1
Petersburg	5.6	16.4	3.4	14	2.1	4.2	3.5	4.7	4.1		29	72.7
Average	7.8	21.1	12.5	15.6	6.9	8.0	4.4	6.8	4.0	0.3	49.7	66.0
Russia overall	**7.8**	**21.4**	**11.2**	**14.5**	**5.7**	**6**	**3.9**	**4.8**	**3.3**	**0.4**	**45.2**	**45.8**

As regards the gubernatorial elections, the latest cycle of results is evidence of a mood of non-conformism rather than of pure protest. As Table 7.1 shows, in the first wave of elections, none of the governors were re-elected in any of the border regions. Whereas in the gubernatorial elections (1995–98) only 32% of the electorate in the North-west voted for the incumbent governor in contrast with the Russian average of 45.2%. In the second phase (1999–2002), though, North-west voters behaved like average Russians by voting for the regional heads elected four years previously (44% in the North-west compared with 45.8% nationally). By way of comparison, the table also highlights the voting patterns in North-west regions that are not border regions, some of which reveal slight evidence of behaviour akin to that of the border regions, while in others the voting behaviour is as for Russia as a whole.

The different influences of foreign-policy factors on the political development of the regions are best viewed in relation to specific examples.

Pskov and Novgorod It would be hard to find another two regions with such similar backgrounds but such different political fates. In many respects, Pskov and Novgorod *oblasts* are like twins: they have similar terrain and a shortage of natural resources, they have historical roots extending back to medieval quasi-democratic republics and Hansa cities, and they suffered almost complete ruin during the Second World War from which neither has fully recovered. Moreover, they are both situated in an economic crater between the two powerful metropolitan centres of Moscow and St Petersburg. Nonetheless, Novgorod *oblast* with its 'reformist' governor, Mikhail Prusak, is repeatedly touted as a classic success story,[25] while Pskov *oblast* with the only LDPR governor in the country,[26] Evgenii Mikhailov, represents a classic example of a failure story.

It is significant that the foreign-policy factor played an important part in both of the above cases. The authorities of Pskov and Novgorod alike relied on foreign contacts. Governor Vladislav Tumanov[27] of Pskov had hoped that Pskov *oblast* would benefit as a transit point for increased Russian–Latvian cooperation such as trade and had hoped the *oblast* would attract substantial federal funds in order to develop the border, inter alia. But these hopes were not realised. As a result, he lost miserably to a young and little-known LDPR candidate in the gubernatorial elections of 1996. Meanwhile, Prusak counted on attracting Western investment in the region's economy, helped considerably by his position as chairman of the Federation Council's Foreign Affairs Committee. His strategy was successful.

Tumanov started out in the federal power structure and is now deputy presidential representative for the Urals Federal District, which could be considered the one with the most central geographic location, furthest away from the periphery. In February 2002 Prusak was re-elected to the post of governor, leads the Democratic Party of Russia and, despite being in some opposition to the federal centre, has the potential to achieve a high position, such as prime minister or, perhaps, presidential representative for the North-west Federal District.

The winning economic strategy of the Novgorod élite has proved profitable to the élite itself, but not to ordinary citizens.

> Classic paternalistic relations have emerged in Novgorod between the community and the authorities: the people love the leaders, the leaders 'think of the people'. Occasionally (very rarely), the public shows its independence and acts against the will of the leadership [...]. As a rule, however, the authorities manage to come to an agreement with the most diverse social structures. Novgorod *oblast* has not witnessed a single serious social or political conflict for ten years. Pskov *oblast* shows a different and 'conflictual' mode of existence. Over the course of the last decade, the Pskov authorities have never once been strong enough to control all aspects of life. Clearly, this is a matter of objective weakness, rather than the conscious rejection of such endeavours. At first glance, conflict and competition seems more akin to classical democracy than paternalism does. Indeed, Pskov has 'islands of freedom', albeit small ones, whereas everything has been brought under control in Novgorod. From the point of view of the largest social groups in Novgorod and Pskov, however, the conflictual atmosphere is a nuisance in Pskov, while the Novgorod brand of paternalism is just the ticket. Over the last 10 years, the Novgorod model has proved effective from the point of view of both the development of the region and the psychological well-being of the people.[28]

Kaliningrad *oblast* There have been two changes of governor here since 1996: a professor of economics Yuri Matochkin was replaced by a business executive Leonid Gorbenko (the director of the fishing port), who, in turn, was supplanted by a military man Vladimir Egorov (the commander of the Baltic Fleet). It seems that, at the forthcoming elections in 2004, there will be yet another transfer of power. Meanwhile, the *oblast* has not lacked the attention of Moscow. In 1993–96, it was represented in the Federation Council by the Speaker, Vladimir Shumeiko. Furthermore, the Deputy Prime Minister and Minister for National and Regional Affairs, Sergei Shakhrai, showed a particular interest in the *oblast*. In January 1996, it was the first of the Russian regions to enter into a power-sharing agreement with the centre and it remains the subject of a federal programme of regional development.[29]

The situation changed abruptly in 2002, though, in the context of the enlargement of the EU and the North Atlantic Treaty Organisation (NATO). A special session of the Security Council was devoted to the issue of Kaliningrad *oblast*; the possibility of it becoming an independent federal district was discussed. However, matters were limited to the appointment of a special representative of the deputy president. In July

2002, Dmitry Rogozin, the chairman of the Duma International Relations Committee, became the special envoy of the Russian Federation charged with conducting negotiations with the EU on Kaliningrad (prior to that, Chechnya was the only Russian region to have such an envoy).

At present, the situation in regard to Kaliningrad *oblast* is one of stalemate. For understandable reasons, Moscow is afraid to relinquish its tight hold, yet, at the same time, it is unable to deal with the *oblast's* social and economic problems by installing a military governor.

Outlook

Foreign-policy factors, particularly relations with neighbouring countries that are members or prospective members of the EU, play an extremely important part in the North-west and in many ways define the political development of the regions. This influence, however, is more indirect than direct, with politics being affected via economics. As for the role of the leaders of the regions in shaping and implementing Russian foreign policy, it seems that the peak of their influence has long since passed. The MFA and other state or government offices now strictly control the regions' actions on the international stage. The influence of the governors at the federal level in general and in relation to matters of foreign policy in particular fell significantly with the reformation of the Federation Council in 2000-01. Telling evidence of this is the fact that the State Council (a consultative body chaired by the president and attended by the governors, which was established by way of compensation once the latter had left the Federation Council) only turned its attention to foreign-policy and cross-border cooperation in the third year of its existence.[30]

In recent years, there have been serious qualitative and quantitative changes in the nature of the regions' international contacts. They have lost some of their exoticism and become more routine as well as more pragmatic and better organised. Single ties have given way to complex webs of relations, which now make up a sturdy fabric. Relations have become institutionalised and subjectivism has become a much less significant factor. While great breakthroughs should not be anticipated, serious failures should not be expected either. The trends and forms of the regions' international contacts are constantly evolving and business partnerships are playing an increasingly significant role.

To a great extent, the regions appear to be hostages of the foreign policy of the centre, rather than policymakers themselves. In this sense, a change in the international situation could impact considerably on economic and political processes in the regions. The cases of Kaliningrad and Pskov *oblasts* examined above are good examples of this.

Foreign-policy issues played a part in the parliamentary elections in December 2003 and the presidential election in March 2004 for a number of reasons. First, foreign policy is the only sphere in which the extent of popular approval for the president's actions is commensurate with his high personal rating. Moreover, gestures, effective moves and proposed plans play a much greater role here than in relation to domestic policy. Regardless of their importance, neither Chechnya, nor housing, communal or other economic reforms, constitute winning issues for either the authorities or the main political powers.

Russia is a vast and extremely diverse country. One and the same foreign-policy factors can have a different and sometimes even contradictory effect in different parts of the country. The regional component should certainly be considered in any analysis of the mutual relationship between foreign and domestic policy. Both the nature and strength of a reaction is specific to a region. Foreign-policy impulses behind general and regionally specific behaviour can be determined according to the extent of their influence over the public. This applies, for example, to Kaliningrad, the problems faced by the North-west in conjunction with the Baltic States, and the 'Chinese factor' for the Far East.

As Russia becomes a normal democratic country with clear, open and relatively predictable domestic and foreign policies, the importance of analysing the foreign-policy component in terms of its applicability to domestic policy will inevitably increase. Evidently, like other major countries, the Russian Federation will go through phases of Jacksonism and Wilsonism, isolationism and globalism, but foreign policy will always play an important part in domestic policymaking and will, in turn, remain highly dependent on internal affairs. Essentially, no one doubts this. The problem is simply in making the transition from a general discussion about the relationship between foreign and domestic policy to a detailed instrumental analysis of the influences that they exert over one another.

Notes

1 The author would like to thank Alexei Titkov of the Carnegie Moscow Center for his comments on this chapter and assistance in drawing up the accompanying table.

2 Whereas in Soviet times, 12 of Russia's regions had land borders with other countries and ten had sea borders (not counting the Arctic), 43 can be considered border regions today. The number of regions with land borders has risen to 36 (including Krasnodar *krai*, Astrakhan *oblast* and Dagestan, which previously only had sea borders), while the number of regions with sea borders has dropped to seven.

3 Typically, in the early stages of the so-called Nizhny Novgorod miracle, Nemtsov drew upon his strong personal relations with Russian President Boris Yeltsin and the key figure of the liberal opposition, Grigory Yavlinsky, whereas Prusak and Titov, who entered the game later, relied upon the institutional base of the Federation Council, in which the former was chairman of the influential Foreign Affairs Committee and the latter was head of the Budget Committee.

4 'For many regions (not only border regions), stimulating international cooperation was a way of achieving self-identification and self-affirmation as subjects of the Federation.' Sergunin, A. and Rykhtik, M., 'Pravovoe regulirovanie mezhdunarodnoi deyatelnosti rossiiskikh regionov', in Makarychev, A. (ed.), *Rossiiskie regiony kak mezhdunarodnye aktory* (Nizhny Novgorod: Nizhnegorodski lingvisticheskii gosuniversitet imeni Dobrolyubova, 2000), pp. 44–45. The personal ambitions of regional heads who were keen to be seen as 'international leaders' were also a contributing factor.

5 See, for example, Sergunin and Rykhtik, 'Pravovoe regulirovanie', pp. 35–60.

6 From the MFA she joined the Russian presidential commission for drafting proposals for power sharing between the federal authorities and the subjects of the Russian Federation and the organs of local administration. Russian Federation Presidential Decree No. 1499 of 20 July 1994, cited in Guboglo, M., ed., *Federalizm vlasti i vlast' federalizma* (Moscow: TOO IntelTekh, 1997), pp. 244–246.

7 In the first such agreement, entered into with Tatarstan on 15 February 1994, the list of the republic's powers included: 'Article 11) to engage in international relations, establish relations with foreign states and enter into agreements therewith such as are in compliance with the Constitution and international agreements of the Russian Federation, the Constitution of the Republic of Tatarstan and the present

Agreement, and to participate in the activity of appropriate international organisations; […] Article 13) to implement foreign economic activity on an independent basis. The powers pertaining to the sphere of foreign economic activity shall be set forth in a separate Agreement.' A parallel agreement between the Russian government and that of the Republic of Tatarstan regarding powers in the sphere of foreign economic activity placed 'the conclusion of foreign economic agreements with subjects of foreign federations and the administrative units of other countries; the conclusion of trade and economic agreements between the Republic of Tatarstan and foreign states under the sole jurisdiction of the republic'. Guboglo, *Federalizm vlasti*, pp. 247–252, 437–438. Although it later became almost common practice for the centre to conclude intergovernmental agreements with the national republics regarding power sharing in the sphere of international and foreign economic relations, this was much less widespread in the case of the *oblasts* and *krais* (except for agreements with the *oblasts* of Nizhny Novgorod, Orenburg, Sakhalin and Sverdlovsk).

[8] Sergunin and Rykhtik, 'Pravovoe regulirovanie', p. 52.

[9] A. Novikov, in interview with the author.

[10] As regards the regions of the North-west, the agreements with Leningrad *oblast*, Kaliningrad *oblast*, Komi and St Petersburg were terminated in April–May 2002. The last to go was the agreement with Murmansk *oblast* in 2003. Of the 42 bilateral agreements concluded between 1994 and 1998, a total of eight were still in force as of December 2003. However, their days are numbered because the new rules state that such agreements will lapse if federal law does not approve them within two years.

[11] See Sovet po vneshnei i oboronnoi politike (Council for Foreign and Defence Policy), 'O vneshnepoliticheskikh resursakh RF', in *Rossiiskaya vneshnyaya politika pered vyzovami XXI veka*. In *Strategiya dlya Rossii: Povestka dnya dlya prezidenta-2000* (Moscow: Vagrius, 2000), pp. 88–89.

[12] The well-known Russian sociologist, Alexei Levinson, offers an interesting example regarding the self-identification of Russian citizens, which coincides with Gallup's 2002 Eurobarometer research into the extent of projective identification with European commonality in the countries of Central and Eastern Europe. A series of surveys conducted in recent years by the All-Russian Centre for Public Opinion Research has shown that one-quarter of the Russian population considers

itself European. The numbers are highest among Muscovites (57%) and inhabitants of the North-west (40%). In all other parts of the country, the number of individuals who believe that they are essentially European is higher than those who do not. Furthermore, in May and December 2002, the Central European Research Group organised a survey in the Czech Republic, Hungary, Poland and Russia along the lines of a referendum regarding accession to the European Union. In May 2002, the Russians proved the least inclined of all of the nations surveyed to take part in such a referendum (54%, compared to 76% in Hungary). In May, though, 75% of those who were prepared to participate voted in favour of joining the EU, putting Russia on a par with Hungary and Poland. In December, the number of Russians willing to take part in the referendum dropped to 46%, while the number of people in this bracket who were in favour of joining the EU rose to 79%, which was higher than in the other three countries. Levinson, A., *Evroz. Neprikosnovenny zapas*, No. 4, 2003, pp. 79–85.

[13] The office of the Russian MFA in St Petersburg serves Leningrad and Novgorod *oblasts* as well as the city of St Petersburg itself. In many cases, consular districts encompass a number of regions. As of October 2003, for example, the consular district of the Finnish Consulate General in St Petersburg extended to the Republic of Komi and the Vologda *oblast*. *Kommersant-Daily*, 2 October 2003.

[14] Petrov, N., 'Sovet Federatsii i predstavitelstvo interesov regionov v Tsentre', in Petrov, N., (ed.), *Regiony Rossii v 1998: Ezhegodnoe prilozhenie k 'Politicheskomu almanakhu Rossii'*, Carnegie Moscow Center, (Moscow: Gendalf, 1999), pp. 180–222.

[15] The speaker for Dagestan has been replaced as deputy chairperson by his representative. The governor of Stavropol and his colleagues from the Jewish autonomous *oblast* have likewise been replaced by their representatives. The new members include a representative of the Tomsk Legislative Assembly, the speaker of which sat on the previous committee.

[16] The most important of these include the Federal Law on International Agreements with the Russian Federation (15 July 1995), the Federal Law on State Regulation of Foreign Trade (13 October 1995), the Federal Law on the Principles and Procedure for the Demarcation of Jurisdiction and Powers between State Organs of the Russian Federation and State Organs of the Subjects of the Federation (24 June 1998) and the Federal Law on the Coordination of

International and Foreign Policy Relations of Subjects of the Russian Federation, which came into force in January 1999. While granting the regions significant powers, the law specifies a number of limitations, in particular preventing the *oblasts* and republics from acting as independent subjects of international law and obligating the regional authorities to give the MFA advance notice of the content of negotiations and to submit draft agreements with foreign partners for approval no less than one month prior to execution. 'Articles 3 and 4 of the Federal Law on the Coordination of Russian International and Foreign Economic Relations', *Sbornik dokumentov po voprosam mezhdunarodnykh i vneshnekonomicheskikh svyazei subektov Rossiiskoi Federatsii* (Moscow: Nauchnaya kniga, 1999).

[17] Until Putin launched his campaign in 2000 to harmonise regional and federal legislation, the constitutions and charters of a number of regions (Dagestan, Tatarstan, Bashkortostan, Tuva, Ingushetia, Komi republics, Krasnodar *krai* and Sverdlovsk and Novgorod *oblasts*) empowered them to regulate matters of foreign policy and international contacts and to conclude international agreements contrary to the Constitution of the Russian Federation. See Sovet po vneshnei i oboronnoi politike (collective authors), 'Perspektivy razvitiya federalizma v Rossii', in *Strategiya dlya Rossii: Povestka dnya dlya prezidenta-2000.* (Moscow: Vagrius, 2000), p. 246.

[18] See www.Regions.ru, 22 January 2003.

[19] Text of the speech given by Yury Yevdokimov, Governor of Murmansk *oblast*, at the session of the State Council of the Russian Federation on 22 January, 'Na styke tryekh granits', *Murmanskii Vestnik* (Murmansk), 23 January 2003.

[20] Shabaev, Y., 'Respublika Komi kak mezhdunarodny aktor: interesy bezopasnosti i sotrudnichestva', in Wenger, A., Perovich, I. and Makarychev, A. (eds), *Rossiya pered globalnymi vyzovami: panorama regionalnykh strategii. Materialy mezhdunarodnogo issledovatelskogo proekta,* (Nizhny Novgorod: Nizhnegorodski lingvisticheskii gosuniversitet imeni Dobrolyubova, 2002), p. 225.

[21] The authorities of the Polish province of Suwalki, the Mariampol and Olice districts of Lithuania, and the Grozdno region of Belarus signed a trilateral agreement on the creation of the Neman cross-border association (Euroregion) on 6 June 1997.

[22] For more detail about Russian regional involvement in international organisations, see Romanova, O., *Uchastie*

rossiiskikh regionov v deyatelnosti mezhdunarodnykh organizatsii. Mezhdunarodnye otnosheniya v XXI veke: regionalnoe v globalnom, globalnoe v regionalnom (Nizhny Novgorod: Nizhnegorodski lingvisticheskii gosuniversitet imeni Dobrolyubova, 2000), pp. 127–137.

[23] See Golubev, S., 'A. Lukashenko i rossiiskie regiony' in Petrov, N. (ed.), *Regiony Rossii v 1999. Ezhegodnoe prilozhenie k 'Politicheskomu almanakhu Rossii'*, Carnegie Moscow Center (Moscow: Gendalf, 2001), pp. 317–323.

[24] Ibid.

[25] Petrov, N., 'The Novgorod Region: A Russian Success Story', *Post Soviet Affairs*, 15(3), 1999, pp. 235–261; Ruble, B. and Popson, N., 'The Westernization of a Russian Province: The Case of Novgorod', *Post-Soviet Geography and Economics* 39(8), 1998, pp. 433–446; Zimine, D. and Bradshaw, M., 'Regional Adaptation to Economic Crisis in Russia: The Case of Novgorod Oblast', *Post-Soviet Geography and Economics* 40(5), 1999, pp. 335–353.

[26] In all fairness, it should be pointed out that Governor Evgenii Mikhailov, elected in 1996 with the active support of Zhirinovsky, only acted as an LDPR governor for a couple of years, which were marked by head-on confrontation with the centre. Having established better relations with the Kremlin and become head of the local branch of the United Russia party, he was re-elected, but not without a struggle.

[27] Appointed in May 1992, Tumanov replaced Anatolii Dobryakov, who was in power for just six months before being removed from office for his part in the illegal resale of non-ferrous metals and fuel to the Baltic States.

[28] Kovalskaya, G., Petrov, N. and Titkov, A., 'Pokoi i volya. Kazhdomu svoe', *Ezhenedelny zhurnal*, 26 February 2002, pp. 23–27.

[29] As Deputy Prime Minister Viktor Khristenko noted: 'Only four federal target programmes still stand in the government's work with the regions: Kaliningrad, the Kuril Islands, Southern Russia and the Far East.' Moreover, 'working with Kaliningrad and the Kuril Islands is more like working with a specific kind of territory with its own geopolitical significance than working with a subject of the Federation'. See the record of a meeting on social and economic development issues in the Far Eastern Federal District on 23 August 2002; at www.president.kremlin.ru.

[30] The State Council usually convenes three times a month in its full complement. In the periods between sessions, there are monthly meetings of a presidium at which one governor represents each of the

seven federal districts on a rotating basis. Once appointed to the presidium, the regional heads usually form a working group that examines the most important issues facing the country and the region. Notwithstanding, therefore, the special meeting of the presidium of the State Council held on the eve of the Russia–US Summit of May 2002 to discuss the effect of current international affairs on the country's policy, the governors did not get around to considering international issues until their tenth meeting. Only the tenth session of the State Council, held almost two-and-a-half years after its establishment, was dedicated to Russia's international activity. Prior to that, the issues that were discussed included: transport; housing and communal reforms; educational policy and medium-sized business; and the promotion of sport.

8. EU–Russia Security Relations and the Republic of Karelia

Derek Averre and Oleg Reut

Since 1990, the security environment in north-eastern Europe has changed fundamentally. At the regional level, Russia's participation in the NATO–Russia Council, the development of a regulatory and normative base for a 'strategic partnership' between Russia and the European Union (EU), reciprocal economic interests and ongoing demilitarisation and confidence-building attest to a far-reaching cooperative security agenda. The EU and Russia have established practical cooperation within the European Security and Defence Policy (ESDP) on crisis management, as well as across a range of non-military, 'soft' security issues such as intelligence-sharing on terrorism and organised crime, non-proliferation, drugs trafficking and migration. The EU–Russia summit in October 2001 initiated enhanced consultations on international security and crisis management. The May 2003 summit decided to strengthen the existing Cooperation Council as a Permanent Partnership Council aimed at closer policy coordination and streamlined structures for political dialogue.[1]

At the sub-regional level, Russia is involved in the EU's Northern Dimension (ND) initiative, the Council of the Baltic Sea States (CBSS) and the Barents Euro-Arctic Regional Council (BEARC). This has facilitated joint responses with neighbouring countries to a range of common 'soft' security challenges. Cross-border cooperation arrangements have promoted mutual understanding between Russia's north-western frontier regions and their neighbours, and provided an important alternative channel to state-level contacts. The federal government, attempting to cement stability on its borders and create the preconditions for economic and social modernisation, has largely welcomed the opportunities opened up by these sub-regional initiatives. The use of military force or coercive diplomacy to settle conflicts over resources or political influence is becoming inconceivable; some envisage a kind of nascent security community developing across Russia's north-western borders based on shared norms and values, reciprocity and common interests.

The limits of Russia's integration into a European political and economic community must be kept firmly in perspective, however. The institutionalisation of shared security interests with the EU and NATO is still confined to specific areas of cooperation. The Russian defence establishment is still unsettled by the military-technical capability gap with the Alliance and its enlargement into the Baltic states, while Nordic and Baltic countries in particular remain concerned about the slow pace of military reform and a possible return to a more aggressive outlook by their powerful eastern neighbour. Despite common strategic interests, relations between Russia and the EU have been soured by clashes over Chechnya, interpretations of human rights and freedom of the media. The as yet nebulous concept of a Common European Economic Space is beset by uncertainty over how far Russia is prepared to assimilate the EU's economic, social, political and legal models.[2] European concern over Russia's inability to deal effectively with security challenges originating on its territory or in the unstable region to its south has made it more likely that 'hard' borders will be imposed around the perimeter of an enlarged EU. While the new democracies of Central Europe and the Baltic states are being integrated into the euroatlantic community through the dual EU–NATO enlargement process, Moscow is offered only cooperative security arrangements. Europe's core institutions lack a clear strategic vision for future relations with Russia, while Moscow, preoccupied with the sovereignty and territorial integrity of the Federation, keeps regional security policies firmly subordinated to the federal agenda.

Perhaps as much as Kaliningrad, the Republic of Karelia, the Russian region with the most extensive border with an existing EU member state, has been a test-case for post-Cold War security relations between Russia and Europe. This article focuses on Karelia's experience of sub-regional initiatives, the achievements and limitations of cross-border cooperation programmes and the issues raised by the new border regime with Finland. It then analyses the roles of federal and regional bodies in security-related policy and the impact of centre–regional relations, and considers regional élites' changing perceptions of sub-regional security issues. Finally, the prospects for deeper cross-border security interaction against the background of the EU–Russia relationship are discussed. What are the political constraints and opportunities for Karelia stemming from, on the one hand, hard borders, and on the other, the common security agenda uniting Europe and Russia? Do Karelian élites – representatives from the regional administration, the legislative assembly, businesses, media and academia – believe that the lack of a clear federal policy on the ND has delayed implementation of projects? What is the division of responsibilities between federal and regional agencies? What do élites perceive as the key security challenges facing the region?

Do existing sub-regional/cross-border initiatives serve their interests? Finally, is there a need for a strategic 'push' from Moscow and Brussels to open up prospects for closer cooperation between sub-regional actors?

Sub-regional initiatives and cross-border cooperation

From the early post-Soviet years, Karelia was an active participant in sub-regional arrangements designed to promote 'soft' security cooperation. Uniquely among Russian regions, it acquired its own representative in the CBSS and the BEARC at the sub-regional level, although its involvement was sporadic, and Russia has mainly been represented at federal level.[3] At the bilateral state level, the 'Treaty on the Basis of Relations between Russia and Finland' and the 'Agreement on Border Cooperation between Russia and Finland', in which Karelia was one of the contracting parties, were signed in January 1992.[4] The Consultative Commission, consisting of Finnish and Karelian parliamentary and executive officials, has been operating since 1991, and ministerial-level workshops on cross-border cooperation have been held since 1992.

Sub-regional cooperation was subsequently intensified through project funding from the EU's Tacis and Interreg programmes, initiated in 1995.[5] Karelia has received Tacis funds for environmental purposes, public administration and capacity-building, as well as for infrastructure, energy and social programmes and public health.[6] The Interreg-IIA-Karelia programme, which operated up to 1999, had as its priorities supporting entrepreneurship, training specialists and environmental programmes. It generated funding to the value of FIM216.15m (around €35m). Interreg-IIIA-Karelia, over 2000-06, is providing €69m (€28m from the EU, €28m from national funds and €13m from other sources) for economic and scientific cooperation, education and culture, transport and infrastructure projects devised by Karelia and Finnish regional councils in Kainuu, North Karelia and North Ostrobothnia.[7]

The ND initiative added an important dimension to sub-regional cooperation. The scheme was devised by Finland in 1997 and funded primarily via Tacis and Interreg, as well as by Phare and Tempus, national governments and international financial institutions. Action plans setting out priorities and objectives have been drawn up, the first (adopted in June 2000 by the Feira European Council) for 2000–03 and the second (submitted to the Council in June 2003) covering the period 2004–06. The ND explicitly does not deal with traditional 'hard' security issues, but with those contributing to the stability and sustainable development of northern Europe – cross-border cooperation and regional development, infrastructure development, energy, natural resources and the environment (through the ND Environmental Programme), nuclear safety, science, education and training, public health and social administration, trade and investment, and combating cross-border crime. Projects include the Northern Dimension Action Plan incorporating Karelia, set up in 2001 to promote a knowledge-based regional economy and civil society via cross-border virtual learning environments. The Action Plan has attracted €12m of Tacis funding for 2002–03.[8] The second Northern Dimension Action Plan lays particular emphasis on the principle of subsidiarity and on involving regional and local authorities and civil society in its implementation; it states that the 'responsibility to initiate cooperation among bordering regions based on a genuine partnership lies mainly with the regions themselves'.[9]

The Euregio Karelia project, approved at the Assembly of Euroregions of Europe in September 1999, is closely tied to the ND concept. Through 'spatial planning', it aims to: match resources and infrastructure development on both sides of the border in joint projects financed on a parity basis; reduce the gap in living standards by creating production and service-sector businesses; nurture regional cultural uniqueness; foster the development of civil society and democratic institutions; and work towards environmental protection. In line with ND thinking on Tacis and Interreg funding,[10] it is intended to coordinate these programmes with Russian national and regional development programmes, though no clear model for coordination has emerged. Euregio Karelia thus constitutes a specific EU-assisted project for social and economic development in Karelia through deepening trans-border contacts. The head of the Karelian government sits on its Executive Committee, which examines and selects projects put forward under the auspices both of Interreg and the Karelia Border Cooperation Programme 2001–06.[11] A list of economic, social and cultural projects (nine priority joint projects and two priority areas of activity), underpinned by long-term objectives of supporting civil society and information-society development in Karelia, has been drawn up under an umbrella programme, 'Our common border 2001–06'. A key aim is to transfer decision-making powers on cross-border cooperation projects to the regional level.

The programmes described above have undoubtedly generated among Karelia's élites a sense of inclusion in the wider sub-region, and provided learning models in the areas of regional administration, local self-government and civil society. However, problems on the Russian side are widely recognised as limiting the effectiveness of the programmes. At the operational level, there is a relative paucity of financial, human and IT resources in Karelia to coordinate and manage programmes.[12] Coordination between federal, regional and municipal bodies in devising and funding projects is also poor; there have been cases where federal agencies have been prepared to co-finance projects, but regional bodies have failed to match them.[13] At the policy level, there has been local criticism about the lack of a federal strategy for the regions to engage with international organisations and financial institutions in regional projects which officially enjoy the support of the Russian government.[14] Moscow has failed to elaborate a coherent policy which would allow Karelia and other north-western regions the autonomy to deepen sub-regional integration through joint planning within the ND. This is seen as crucial for the success of the initiative.[15]

Shortcomings in European approaches have also been identified. The central role in formulating and funding the ND lies with the European Commission, but there has been limited inter-governmental agreement over the EU's priorities towards Russia and over levels of finance to promote more effective cross-border cooperation.[16] Russian partners have had limited say in funding; Tacis, which is in any case much less generous than EU funding for accession countries, is subject to bureaucratic delays and lack of programming capacity in Brussels,[17] while Interreg funds can only be used inside the EU. Proposals to allow Interreg funding to be subject to decisions made by the Euregio Karelia, lobbied by Finnish regional bodies, have not been approved. In this respect, the EU lacks effective models for cross-border cooperation in which external partners are granted decision-making functions.

Freedom of movement across borders for local populations, an important issue in cross-border cooperation, is affected by the imposition of 'hard' borders through the Schengen *acquis*. While much attention has been paid to the accession to the EU of the Baltic States and the new restrictions on movement for inhabitants of Russian regions bordering them – particularly Kaliningrad – the 'hard' but stable Karelian/Finnish border has often been seen as a model of a successful border regime. Indeed, interviews with Karelian élites (politicians/decision-makers) held in 2000 did not convey the impression that Schengen was then seen as erecting unbridgeable political and psychological dividing lines, though there was concern over potential difficulties in sub-regional relations.[18] However, interviews since suggest that perceptions are changing; in March 2001 Finland became a full member of the Schengen Agreement, spelling the end of the relatively liberal regime whereby local residents could apply for visas for Finland through the branch of the St Petersburg Finnish consulate in the Karelian capital, Petrozavodsk.[19] According to the Russian Ministry of Foreign Affairs, Finland is taking a harder line than other EU member states on the question of a single visa-free space between Russia and the EU.[20]

Compared to 'new' external borders in Russia's north-west arising from EU enlargement, the border between Karelia and Finland is relatively well equipped. However, the development programme overseen by a Karelian inter-ministerial commission has lapsed. The infrastructure is inadequate for more intensive cooperation, and the Karelian government is facing the problem of ensuring the development of interim border crossing-points to keep cross-border exchanges open. Thus, although cooperation on non-traditional security challenges is well established, easing concerns in Finland to do with threats emanating from Russia, restrictions on cross-border movement and the lack of border-infrastructure development are combining to block progress on cross-border cooperation.

Federal–regional relations and the Republic of Karelia

Despite successes in cross-border cooperation over the last decade, the legislative basis for relations between Karelia and Finland remains narrow and fragmentary. The draft law 'On the legal status of border territories' has been in the State Duma since 1996, but has not yet been enacted. The Concept of Border Cooperation in the Russian Federation, signed by the Russian prime minister Mikhail Kasyanov in February 2001, does not provide for more developed integration models which might permit greater interaction between Russia's north-western regions and the EU. The Concept does envisage more intensive cross-border cooperation, but only within a more centralised and unified federal structure. It is not accompanied by legislation granting additional powers to border regions; it appears that practically all decision-making remains with the federal authorities.[21]

This is in the context of the continuing paucity of laws regulating the division of powers between the federal centre and the regions, especially in areas subject to joint jurisdiction according to the Russian Constitution. The federal law 'On International Agreements of the Russian Federation' only permits the regions to present recommendations to the central government on issues under common federal–regional jurisdiction.[22] The Kozak commission, set up in 2001 to recommend changes in federal–regional relations and delineate respective powers, is yet to present firm conclusions. Regional governments in Russia still largely lack independent sources of financing, and remain heavily dependent on federal authorities; the Kozak commission's recommendations for greater centralisation of tax collection from 2003[23] have only exacerbated the situation, as regional authorities attempt to replace money taken by the federal government by extracting equivalent sums locally.

Some attempts have been made in Karelia to put in place a sounder legal framework for sub-regional interaction. In the early post-Soviet years, federal decrees granted permission to establish direct contacts and sign trade agreements with Finland and other Scandinavian neighbours.[24] Karelia subsequently adopted its own laws on foreign economic activity.[25] With the adoption in 1999 of the federal law 'On the Coordination of

International and Foreign Economic Activities of the Constituent Entities of the Russian Federation', which grants the regions rights to conduct economic relations with foreign states and their territorial entities, it would seem that a legislative framework has thus been created to develop foreign activities.[26] However, without more extensive political autonomy for the regions and more effective measures to implement Karelian laws on foreign trade and investment, it remains to be seen how far cross-border economic cooperation can provide a basis for sub-regional integration. The official Karelian government website itself has criticised flawed federal economic legislation and the absence of a cohesive foreign economic strategy.[27] The Karelian government, together with other regions, has lobbied the Russian Ministry of Foreign Affairs Consultative Council on International and Foreign Economic Relations on the status of border territories, but with little success.

The North-west Federal District is becoming an important channel of cooperation between the centre and the regions, ensuring the compliance of regional with federal legislation, coordinating the implementation of federal programmes, and reporting to central government on the security situation in the regions.[28] Federal inspectors, including one for Karelia, report directly to the President's plenipotentiary who heads the federal district. In this sense, Russian President Vladimir Putin's administrative reforms have proved successful in reversing the disintegrative trends of the first post-Soviet years. As well as helping to cement central control over regional administrations, the federal district governor-general has also given overt or tacit encouragement to regional governments to undertake similar measures within their own territories. This has fostered similar views at the level of both federal district and the Republic of Karelia on regional policy and economic development.[29] There has been some involvement at federal district level in sub-regional 'soft' security policy, but in terms of an effective regional strategy of engagement with neighbours, the federal district plenipotentiary lacks the constitutional status and resources to promote a wider regional agenda.[30]

The federal government and federal organs at the local level – the Federal Security Service (now with an expanded area of jurisdiction following the transfer of the responsibilities of the Federal Border Service to its remit), the Ministry of Internal Affairs, the customs and tax services, the voenkomat (military commissariat) which calls up conscripts to the army – have far greater weight than the Karelian government and legislative assembly in deciding security policy in the region. The latter deal mainly with internal social and economic matters (including civil defence) within their sphere of responsibility, but policy is coordinated with the federal centre and few major decisions are taken at regional level. This is not seen entirely negatively by regional élites; some approve of the federal government's attempt to 'claw back' some of the authority devolved in the early 'disintegrative' post-Soviet years. Others who hoped that the appearance of an okrug presidential envoy would help them in their struggle with the federal government have been largely disappointed, however.[31] There is little genuine federalism in the sense of devolution of decision-making authority to the local level; the balance in Karelia has tipped firmly in the direction of centralised top-down control.

Regional elites' perceptions of security challenges

Although in the aftermath of the Kosovo conflict in 1999 instability in Europe still excites concern, Karelian élites interviewed by the authors perceived no external threat to their territory.[32] While a few referred to Finland's ambivalent stance over NATO membership, the border question was not considered contentious.[33] Perceptions of security have changed; no longer defined as securing the state against external rivals, it is largely conceived in terms of threats to the individual and society represented by economic and social instability and, influenced by the events of 11 September 2001 and the hostage crisis in Moscow's Nord-Ost Theatre in October 2002, in a more generalised fashion by the inability of governments to protect their citizens from global threats.[34]

There is a strong sense that insecurity stems principally from flaws in political, economic and social governance in Russia. These lead to socio-economic stratification, the weakness of democratic institutions and civil society and the potential threat of a new authoritarianism. They manifest themselves in economic imbalances with neighbouring countries, technological stagnation, a fragmented society, poor health indicators and an inability to support the younger generation in terms of employment opportunities, social mobility and economic independence. Respondents stated that the region's problems were compounded by the loss of regional autonomy, the absence of clear political direction at both federal and regional level, and the emergence of informal élite networks which are difficult to penetrate.

Nevertheless, the security situation in Karelia is felt to compare favourably with many other regions across Russia. Commonly-defined 'soft' security challenges – environmental hazards (in particular the effects of deforestation and resource depletion), health, demographic factors, illegal migration, organised crime (including that originating outside the region), corruption and drugs trafficking – are considered to be manageable via normal political and legislative practices, rather than viewed as major threats necessitating extreme measures. It is felt that the media and some politicians – both in Russia and abroad – tend to securitise these issues, portraying Russia as in the throes of internal conflict and social disintegration.

There were conflicting views among Karelian élites on the extent to which national security priorities correspond to the challenges faced by their region. While some respondents perceived that national geopolitical interests dominate to the detriment of regional economic interests, others argued that the federal government's access to the 'bigger picture' justifies basing policy on national interests; in an unstable environment the state still has a key role as a provider of security. However, élites were virtually unanimous in stating that regional initiatives should take precedence over federal ones in cross-border cooperation, and that participation in sub-regional and bilateral Russian–Finnish initiatives have had a markedly positive influence on the security environment.[35] The virtual monopoly of the federal centre in making key decisions and the lack of clarity over the extent of local autonomy in the economic sphere is believed to limit the effectiveness of regional initiatives. Negative perceptions of Karelia among outsiders are reinforced by poor federal–regional (as well as regional–municipal) coordination over transborder security relations, so that the regions cannot 'offer a coherent message'.[36] Respondents, including those directly involved in Euregio Karelia, stated that there has been little real attempt to assess the impact of transborder initiatives. The lack of adequate human capital in the region is also felt to be hindering participation in sub-regional political and economic developments.[37]

The general perception was that other countries in the sub-region share key security concerns and recognise a common interest in sustaining economic development, preserving social and cultural identity and stemming the outflow of young qualified people from the more economically underdeveloped border districts. Increasing the economic and technological level in Karelia within a broader sub-regional framework for development is seen as vital. Alongside general principles of openness, mutual trust and partnership underpinning sub-regional security relations, Karelian élites suggested specific preconditions for improvement; the most important are transparency of borders to facilitate freedom of movement and trade (involving support by the EU), a 'common information space' and support for education. This is prompted by the perception that people in neighbouring countries still have difficulty understanding attitudes to change in Russia. In some respects, traditional fears about a threat from the powerful neighbour to the east persist.

The overall impression gained from the interviews is that Karelian élites recognise that rapid social and economic improvements are unlikely despite positive gains from sub-regional cooperation. With little prospect of economic and political integration into mainstream Europe, attention should be directed towards avoiding the creation of new dividing lines. A number of problems were highlighted: foreign businesses seeking to evade legal provisions and exploit local resources and markets; a substantial percentage of illegal or informal trade; the lack of firm investment legislation to attract foreign investors; the lack of an effective foreign economic strategy for border regions on the part of the federal authorities; and the inexperience of local actors in the market economy and trade. Several respondents expressed misgivings about economic actors taking the lead in sub-regional relations. This may be directed towards the informal economy, but may also indicate a deeper ambivalence about opening up the local economy to sub-regional cooperation.[38]

According to many respondents, political and administrative capacity in Karelia is weak, limiting the prospects for a successful external strategy. In May 2002, Sergei Katanandov, elected in 1998 as Chairman of the Karelian government and now in his second term, adopted the title of Head of the Karelian Republic. He abolished the Karelian Ministry for External Relations and transferred its responsibilities to the Administration of the Head of the Republic and to the Karelian Ministry for Economic Development. With external policy thus firmly under Katanandov's direct control, the current structure of executive power lacks a body with coordinating functions for Karelia's external affairs. Although his administration declares its support for sub-regional initiatives, its priorities appear to lie in consolidating political and economic structures in Karelia, rather than in developing external relations.[39] Unofficial channels of influence on the regional leadership are also underdeveloped; there is concern that pressure from the regional government has muted opposition in the Karelian media, creating a situation in which the former – in which political power and economic influence are already extensively entwined[40] – is able to exert extensive control over the latter. Although civil society is relatively well developed compared with some other regions, its influence over the regional bureaucracy is perceived to be very limited.

Conclusions
In many respects, Karelia's experiences in the post-Soviet period have been positive. The republic is in a more favourable situation than many border regions in terms of economic development and social cohesion, and – judging by the responses of its élites – is at less risk from non-traditional security challenges. It has benefited – psychologically if not so much materially – from participation in sub-regional and cross-border initiatives. One analyst has argued, in connection with the ND, that 'the key actors – Finland, the EU and Russia – have accepted the guiding principles of the new image policy: the distinction between "soft" and "hard" security issues and turning a blind eye to the latter as belonging to the Cold War past perfect tense; adherence to "EU jargon" like multi-level

governance, transboundary cooperation; building high expectations primarily on the "postmodern ground"'.[41]

However, with federal policies taking precedence over regional policies and with no cohesive strategy for wider sub-regional integration, there is little room for Karelian élites to influence the aims of cross-border cooperation programmes, to develop their institutional basis or to play a fuller role in implementing them. As noted above, the Second Northern Dimension Action Plan sees this as the regions' responsibility. It is by no means certain that, beyond rhetorical statements, key political and economic élites in Karelia – where external policy is closely coordinated with the federal government and conforms to the security aims of ensuring the sovereignty and integrity of the state – are committed to further integration into a broader political community. With little evidence of social mobilisation towards this goal, sub-regional cooperation has had a limited impact at the grass-roots level.[42]

Sub-regional political relations have to be placed in the wider context of Russia's relations with the EU, or more precisely, of Moscow's relations with Brussels. The ND has undoubtedly played an important role in allowing Russia's north-western regions to engage with the EU as well as with neighbouring countries, but its ambitious programme is not always matched by hard policy content and adequate resources. Moreover, the idea of a Dimension based on deepening sub-regional cooperation has always existed alongside an EU external policy, strictly separated from internal policy, which promotes the security of its environment within a 'traditional view of international relations controlled by a unified state system and prevailing hegemonic ideology of state control'.[43] There has been lack of clarity over the role of the ND, a 'policy without institutions and funding' based on multilateral interaction, vis-à-vis the EU's bilateral Partnership and Cooperation Agreement with Russia and the Common Strategy on Russia.[44] It is also uncertain how the ND fits into the EU's 'Wider Europe' policy, which set out an ambitious security-related agenda and aims to develop 'the political concept of a new neighbourhood policy' to create 'a zone of prosperity and a friendly neighbourhood or a ring of friends with whom the EU enjoys close, peaceful and co-operative relations'.[45] The EU, a 'centralised actor with the emphasis on centralised and/or intergovernmental co-operation', has often been reluctant to implement a multilevel policy which might allow sub-regional actors more of a role.[46] Enlargement may thus push borders – both political and psychological – eastwards, creating a normative fault-line which reinforces East–West divides.[47]

Particularly in the context of eastward enlargement, both Russia and the EU face major challenges in ensuring their respective security interests, while fostering more flexible cross-border cooperation so that sub-regional integration does not remain a rhetorical flourish. The experiences of Karelia suggest that, given the larger strategic interests of the two entities, initiatives confined to specific geographical areas such as Russia's north-west are likely to have a very limited impact. The ND provides a useful conceptual – and potentially operational – framework, but substantial progress requires a strategic 'push' from both sides, encompassing not just 'high' politics but also 'soft' security issues on the ground. This would involve a profound reassessment of their relationship – crucial at this juncture in view of impending EU enlargement[48] – and a more coherent reciprocal strategy. At the very least, a more flexible EU policy on resourcing cross-border cooperation and on border regimes – while recognising that a visa-free regime, opposed by several European national governments, is very much a long-term prospect – should be met with reciprocal moves by the Russian federal government to grant the regions greater autonomy and devise workable policies to allay EU concerns over uncontrolled migration. The economic and social 'welfare gap' also presents a shared policy challenge; measures to ensure trade and investment and support the formation of human capital – priorities in the Second ND Action Plan – are central to today's security agenda.

Notes

1. EU–Russian Summit Joint Statement, 31 May 2003, at http://europa.eu.int/comm/ext ernal_relations/russia/sum05_0 3/js.htm.
2. Ivanov, I. D., 'The Common European Economic Space: A View from Moscow', *Sovremennaya Evropa*, 1 (13), 2003, pp. 17–31.
3. Reut, O., *The Baltic and Barents Regions in Changing Europe: New Priorities for Security*, EFP Working Paper 2 (Groningen: Centre for European Security Studies, June 2000), p. 36. On these organisations and 'soft' security, see the chapters by Helmut Hubel and Stefan Ganzle and Carl-Einar Stalvant in Holger Moroff (ed.), *European Soft Security Policies: The Northern Dimension*, Programme on the Northern Dimension of the CFSP, Finnish Institute of International Affairs/Institut für Europäische Politik, 2002.
4. Around 400 projects have been completed and a further 200 are under way within the framework of the Agreement, targeted on energy, environment, modernisation of industry, infrastructure development, improving the border, developing tourism, training, education and culture, combating crime and strengthening democracy.
5. For information on cooperation programmes see the official Karelia government web site at www.gov.karelia.ru/gov/Power /Ministry/Relations/Boundary.
6. See local Tacis website at www.tacis-lso-rf.org/Petrozavodsk/projectf.as p and www.tacis-lso-rf.org/Petrozavodsk/projects.as p; see also Moroff, 'The EU's Northern Soft Security Policy: Emergence and Effectiveness', in Moroff (ed.), *European Soft Security Policies*.
7. *2002 Annual Progress Report on the Northern Dimension Action Plan*, SEC(2002) 1296, 26 November 2002, at http://europa.eu.int/comm/ext ernal_relations/north_dim/doc/ progrep02.pdf.
8. *The Second Northern Dimension Action Plan, 2004–06*, COM(2003) 343 final, 10 June 2003, pp. 7, 25 at http://europa.eu.int/comm/ external_relations/north_dim/n dap/com03_343.pdf; *2002 Annual Progress Report on the Northern Dimension Action Plan*, p. 13. Priorities are fast-speed networks (infrastructure), IT security, e-education, e-commerce and e-governance.
9. *The Second Northern Dimension Action Plan, 2004–06*, p. 11; see also pp. 2, 16.
10. *2002 Annual Progress Report on the Northern Dimension Action Plan*, p. 35.
11. Shlyamin, V., 'Cross-border Cooperation: The Experience of Karelia and Finland', *North-west Russia in the Baltic Sea Region*, IISS Russian Regional Perspectives Journal for Foreign

and Security Policy, issue 1, 2002, p. 25.

[12] Recent interviews with Karelian élites (see note 32 below) suggest, for example, that the eKarelia initiative is not being developed due to lack of attention and funding. Personnel changes in the Karelian government meant that the Euregio Executive Committee did not in fact meet between spring 2002 and May 2003.

[13] Comments made by Russian specialists based in Petrozavodsk at the Koli Border Forum 'Russian Borderlands', Koli, Finland, 17–19 May 2003. See also Haukkala, H., 'The Challenge of Russian Regionalism in the Implementation of the Northern Dimension', in The New North of Europe (policy memos from final conference in Helsinki, 8 October 2002), Programme on the Northern Dimension of the CFSP, Finnish Institute of International Affairs/Institut für Europäische Politik, 2002, pp. 31–34.

[14] Alexandrov, O., 'The Role of the Republic of Karelia in Russia's Foreign and Security Policy', Regionalization of Russian Foreign and Security Policy, Working Paper 5 (Zurich: Center for Security Studies and Conflict Research, Eidgenoessische Technische Hochschule, March 2001), p. 33; see also Analysis of the State of Border Cooperation at www.gov.karelia.ru/gov/ Power/Ministry/Relations/Boundary/02a4.html.

[15] Shlyamin, V., 'Euregio Karelia New Challenges and New Opportunities', in Euregio Karelia as a Tool for Civil Society, Information Bulletin, no. 1, February 2001, p. 3.

[16] Tarja Cronberg, A Europe Without Divides? The EU–Russia Partnership and the Case of Virtual Borders, COPRI Working Paper 37, 2002, p. 20.

[17] Moroff, 'The EU's Northern Soft Security Policy: Emergence and Effectiveness', in Moroff (ed.), European Soft Security Policies, pp. 173, 210–211. Russian Ministry of Foreign Affairs officials have complained that many ND projects 'have not been priorities for the Russian north-west'; see speech by Chizhov, V. A., at www.ln.mid.ru/brp_4.nsf, 21 April 2003.

[18] Averre, D. L., 'Security Perceptions Among Local Elites and Prospects for Cooperation across Russia's North-western Borders', Regionalization of Russian Foreign and Security Policy, Working Paper 16 (Zurich: Center for Security Studies and Conflict Research, Eidgenoessische Technische Hochschule, March 2002), pp. 39–40.

[19] Karelia residents must now follow the common application procedure used in all Schengen consulates and provide a hard copy of the invitation, medical insurance (since 1 April 2003 a

computerised or printer-typed insurance document), return tickets, hotel booking confirmation, a valid and all previous passports and a €25 visa fee for a single-entry trip (ending free visas formerly provided for some specific trips).

20 Press conference with foreign minister Igor Ivanov in Helsinki, 10 June 2003, at www.ln.mid.ru/ brp_4.nsf.

21 *North-west Russia in the Baltic Sea Region*, IISS Russian Regional Perspectives Journal for Foreign and Security Policy, issue 1, 2002, pp. 7, 8. A draft law 'On Border Cooperation of the Russian Federation' was in preparation in mid-2003. The European Framework Convention on Border Cooperation of Territorial Communities and Authorities came into force in Russia in January 2003, and Russia was preparing to sign protocols to it on the formation of joint organs of border cooperation such as Euroregions.

22 Alexandrov, 'The Role of the Republic of Karelia in Russia's Foreign and Security Policy', p. 40.

23 At the time of writing, the recommendations were before the regions' legislative bodies, which are due to present their opinions prior to the submission of draft laws to the State Duma.

24 Alexandrov, 'The Role of the Republic of Karelia', p. 41.

25 'On state guarantees for the implementation of foreign investments in the Republic of Karelia', 'On investment activity in the Republic of Karelia' and 'On republican taxes (taxation rates)', which would free investors from paying taxes into regional and *oblast* budgets until investments were fully recouped; Deryabin Y. , '*Severnoe izmerenie' politiki Evropeiskogo Soyuza i interesy Rossii*, Russian Academy of Sciences Institute of Europe Report, no. 68, 2000, pp. 59–60.

26 Alexandrov, 'The Role of the Republic of Karelia', pp. 41–42.

27 'Analysis of the State of Border Cooperation', at www.gov.karelia.ru/gov/Power /Ministry/Relations/Boundary/ 02a4.html. Karelian Prime Minister Pavel Chernov has also alluded to this; see www.kreml.org/decisions/1971 2692.19975078.

28 See the resoluton 'On the plenipotentiary representative of the Russian Federation President in the federal okrug', at http://www.gov.karelia.ru/gov/ Different/Federal/polojen.html.

29 Alexandrov, 'The Role of the Republic of Karelia', p. 45. The first head of the North-west Federal okrug, Viktor Cherkesov, generally seen as successful in implementing Putin's policies, was appointed chairman of the newly-created State Committee on Drugs Trafficking in March 2003; he was replaced by Valentina Matvienko.

30 Pursiainen, C., 'Soft Security

Problems of North-west Russia', in Moroff (ed.), *European Soft Security Policies*, p. 130.

31 In order to restore control over heads of the border regions, Cherkesov introduced three advisory councils: a Law Enforcement Agencies and Security Council; an Economy and Investment Council (incorporating representatives of federal agencies, regional authorities and business); and a Social Council (to study public opinion).

32 Averre, 'Security Perceptions Among Local Elites', pp. 27–28. Observations in this section draw on this source, written on the basis of interviews with élites in Petrozavodsk in September 2000 carried out by the authors of this chapter, with further analysis based on repeat interviews carried out by Oleg Reut in May–June 2003.

33 An experienced observer has concluded that 'there is neither dispute nor regional demands between Finland and Russia ... officially there is no Karelian issue'; L. Heininen, *Northern Dimension in EU–Russian Cooperation – the Finnish Perspective*, unpublished paper presented at the Koli Border Forum 'Russian Borderlands', Koli, Finland, 17–19 May 2003.

34 Some respondents in interviews held in May–June 2003 mentioned that the peripheral position of Karelia – distant from threats to civic life such as those

shown in the Nord-Ost crisis or the violence associated with Moscow and some other large centres – is in fact a positive factor, adding a new dimension to perceptions of sub-regional security.

35 As Holger Moroff has argued, 'much like hard security, soft security is a public good that needs to be provided by the state. But beyond that, providing soft security needs active participation on the regional and cross-border level and of civil society and the media ... different levels of security according to their stage of impact need to be analysed in order to understand how the various levels of security interrelate and whether there are possible trade-off relationships between them'; 'Introduction', in Moroff (ed.), *European Soft Security Policies*, p. 28.

36 Averre, 'Security Perceptions Among Local Elites', pp. 27–28.

37 This bears out Makarychev's description of regional governments' lack of experience of international relations, the lack of coordination between agencies and minimal interaction between authorities and the nascent third sector of non-governmental organisations, which is impeding sub-regional integration, including its economic dimension; Andrei Makarychev, 'Islands of Globalization: Regional Russia and the Outside World',

Regionalization of Russian Foreign and Security Policy, Working Paper 2 (Zurich: Center for Security Studies and Conflict Research, Eidgenoessische Technische Hochschule, August 2000), p. 38.

38 Some local élites are critical of the eKarelia initiative, arguing that it represents a continuation of attempts by European countries to obtain resources from Russia cheaply – today timber and other raw materials, tomorrow information technology and electronic data.

39 Katanandov's address to the Karelian Legislative Assembly on 18 March 2003 notably contained little on external relations; see www.gov.karelia.ru/gov/Leader /Document/030318.html.

40 Moroff argues that 'Russian regional elites themselves are not known for their cooperative political culture. Especially in Russia's north-west they are strongly connected to if not part of the business elite with strong monopolistic and protectionist tendencies ... they do not seem to be very susceptible to any new forms of interregional soft network governance as the EU's soft security agenda proposes'; 'The EU's Northern Soft Security Policy: Emergence and Effectiveness', in Moroff (ed.), *European Soft Security Policies*, p. 212. Further research on these matters is needed for a more detailed and authoritative assessment.

41 Kononenko, V., 'Evaluating the Northern Dimension as Finland's Image Policy Towards Russia', in *The New North of Europe*, p. 52.

42 See Reut, O., 'Asymmetry of the Euroregional Matrix', *Mirovaya ekonomika I mezhdunarodnye otnosheniya*, 9, 2002, pp. 76–82.

43 Heininen, L., 'Ideas and Outcomes: Finding a Concrete Form for the Northern Dimension Initiative', in Hanna Ojanen (ed.), *The Northern Dimension: Fuel for the EU?*, Programme on the Northern Dimension of the CFSP, Finnish Institute of International Affairs/Institut für Europäische Politik, 2001, p. 39.

44 See Hiski Haukkala, 'Comment: National Interests Versus Solidarity Towards Common Policies', in Ojanen (ed.), *The Northern Dimension: Fuel for the EU?*, pp. 107–115; Cronberg, *A Europe without Divides?*

45 The new policy promises better coordination of the existing instruments (Interreg and Tacis) for cross-border cooperation from 2004 to 2006 and, beyond 2006, a new 'Neighbourhood Instrument' (the details of which are yet to be elaborated) for cross-border and regional cooperation around the EU's external border, thereby 'combin[ing] external policy objectives and economic and social cohesion'. In the 2004–06 period the European

Commission is proposing €700 million funding from Interreg and €75m from Tacis. A preliminary assessment suggests that this appears only to constitute a status quo-plus policy from the Commission rather than the basis for the coherent reciprocal strategy called for below. See the initial Communication from the Commission to the Council and the European Parliament, *Wider Europe – Neighbourhood: A New Framework for Relations with Our Eastern and Southern Neighbours*, COM(2003) 104 final, Brussels, 11 March 2003, *Wider Europe: Commission To Strengthen Cross-Border Cooperation with New Neighbours*, IP/03/922, Brussels, 1 July 2003; and *Commission Decides on Further Steps To Develop Its 'Wider Europe' Policy*, IP/03/963, Brussels, 9 July 2003.

[46] Haukkala, 'Comment: National Interests Versus Solidarity Towards Common Policies', p. 111.

[47] Leshukov, I., 'Can the Northern Dimension Break the Vicious Circle of Russia–EU Relations?, in Ojanen (ed.), *The Northern Dimension: Fuel for the EU?*, pp. 127–128.

[48] See the recommendations of the report by the Committee 'Russia in a United Europe', *Russia in the European Union: Options for Deepening Strategic Partnership?*, (Moscow: Russia in a United Europe), 2002, pp. 56–59.

EU-Russia borders after Enlargement

Euroregions and neighbouring cities

Euroregions

- ⬭ Neighbouring cities
- —B— Euroregion Baltic
- —— Euroregion Karelia
- —— Euroregion Niemen
- —S— Euroregion Saule
- -PAV- Planned Euroregion Pskov-Aluksne-Võru (PAV)

- ▨ existing EU members
- ▦ new EU members
- ▨ non-EU members
- ▢ Russia

Kirkenes
Zapoliarnyi
Barents Sea
Murmansk
Murmansk oblast
Kola Peninsula

White Sea
Arkhangelsk

Euroregion Karelia
Kuhmo Kostomuksha
Republic of Karelia
Severodvinsk
Arkhangelsk oblast

FINLAND
Joensuu
NORTH-WESTERN FEDERAL DISTRICT
Petrozavodsk

Imatra
Lappeenranta Svetogorsk
Vyborg *Leningrad oblast*
Vologda oblast

Helsinki
Gulf of Finland
St Petersburg
Vologda

Stockholm
Tallinn
Narva Ivangorod

ESTONIA
Novgorod
Novgorod oblast

Pskov
PAV
R U S S I A

Ventspils
Riga
LATVIA
Pskov oblast

Euroregion Baltic
Moscow

N O R W A Y
S W E D E N
Gulf of Bothnia
Baltic Sea

DENMARK
S

LITHUANIA
S S
Bornholm
Kaliningrad
Gdansk
Euroregion Baltic
Euroregion Niemen

Vilnius
Minsk

CENTRAL FEDERAL DISTRICT

B E L A R U S

Warsaw
P O L A N D

IISS*maps*

50 miles
100km

—·— international boundary
—··— Russian Federal District
······· Russian administrative region
■ capital city

9. The Development of Pskov *oblast* in the Context of EU Enlargement

Lev Schlosberg[1]

The political and economic enlargement of the democratic European space has put the need for new approaches to state administration and regional government firmly on the agenda.[2] As the boundaries of practical interaction shift in Europe, new ideas and solutions for managing the economy and politics are required both at the centre and in the regions.

Cross-border cooperation should be part of a strategy for the stable development of the entire European community, since for the countries of Central and Eastern Europe this is one of the first steps in the process of European integration. The weakness of the strategic position of the federal and regional authorities is apparent from the absence of a concept for trans-border integration and cross-border cooperation at the regional and local levels.

Political problems (as a rule, national or inter-state) exist in the background due to the inertia in political thinking and the lack of understanding of the future prospects for, and the advantages of, international cooperation among a certain sector of the political élite, which includes the main decision-makers both in Russia and in neighbouring countries. Within politics, therefore, there is isolationism in the public sphere and protectionism in the economic sphere. These political problems mean that economic policy is not considered expedient; political issues limit economic actors in regard to the implementation of new projects, and they reduce the volume of investment and capital turnover. Consequently, markets have not been integrated effectively; countries are deprived of the resources that they need and opportunities to complete the transition and to foster further stable development are lost. This is the case in Pskov *oblast*, a border region of Russia that has limited basic resources for development and thus feels deeply the ramifications of political power measures, administrative barriers, and infrastructural restrictions. This is a serious problem, which, in effect, could make it impossible to implement a unified economic policy in

Europe. If the evident imbalance between the economies of Western and Eastern Europe becomes even more entrenched then social problems in Central and Eastern Europe, including for both new neighbour countries like Russia and new EU members, will be exacerbated, as social disparities and the gap in living standards increase and hamper all aspects of integration further. The problem does not lie in the standards of living as such, but in the growing disparity between neighbouring countries and the increase in the difference in standards of living between them. At the same time, it is political solutions that might create the conditions for fully fledged economic action and establish a favourable climate for cross-border cooperation.

Devising a strategy and a concept for regional development in pilot regions in terms of European cooperation should be put on the agenda of the national and regional authorities of the Russian Federation. Some of these pilot regions could be the areas along the Latvia–Russia and Estonia–Russia borders, for example, in Pskov *oblast*.

Characteristics of Pskov

Pskov *oblast* is situated in north-west Russia. It has a land area of 55,000 square kilometres (km), and the length of its border from north to south is 380km and from west to east is 260km. Pskov *oblast* borders Estonia and Latvia to the west and Belarus to the south. The length of its border with Estonia is 270km (including the sea border), with Latvia it is 214km, and with Belarus it is 305km. The climate is moderate: the average temperature in January is -7C, and in July it is +17C. The *oblast* is divided into 24 *raions* (administrative districts) and has 14 towns, the two relatively large economic centres being Pskov (with a population of 206,000) and Velikie Luki (with a population of 117,200). According to official statistics for 2002, 778,000 people live in the *oblast* (0.5% of Russia's total population), 59.3% are of working age; pensioners make up 23.8% of the population. The average age of the *oblast's* population is 38.8 years, and 18.7% has been through higher education. Pskov *oblast* is characterised by a homogenous ethnic group (94% ethnic Russian). As regards migration, in 1999, 62,000 people arrived in the *oblast*, while 59,900 people left. This includes migrants from countries other than Russia (5,800 immigrants and 4,500 emigrants).

Pskov's budget revenue in 2002 amounted to 5,948 million roubles (US$200 million) and its expenditure was 5,519m roubles (for the first 11 months of 2002). Revenues into the consolidated budget of Pskov *oblast* (i.e. all revenues from the budgets of the districts, towns and villages in Pskov *oblast*) amounted to 6,439m roubles in 2002 (2,814m roubles from the districts, towns and villages) and total expenditure was 6,241m roubles.

New research for future action

Interdisciplinary political, economic, sociological and legal research, both on the federal and regional levels, should be used to devise a strategy for regional development in some pilot regions of European cooperation. This research would reveal what resources regional cross-border cooperation currently has at its disposal and how they could be used to encourage regional and national development in the context of European integration. Practical recommendations could then be made to politicians at the national, regional and local levels, sidelining the present obstacles to effective political and economic cooperation in Europe and to stable development in its regions.

Under the project entitled 'The Influence of European Cross-border Cooperation on Regional Economic Development', the following work was carried out by the authors in Pskov between March and September 2003.

- An analysis of state statistics (from the Committee of State Statistics of the Russian Federation, and the State Customs Committee of the Russian Federation) for the period 1995–2002.
- Official and unofficial interviews with business representatives and the political élite of Pskov *oblast*.
- An assessment of international, Russian and regional legislation, and international and national legal acts.
- Analysis of special surveys of the state authorities and the organs of local self-government in Pskov *oblast*.
- A content analysis of media output in Pskov *oblast* in 2001–03.
- A survey of public opinion in Pskov *oblast* (1,600 respondents, August 2003).

This chapter presents and comments on the findings of the public-opinion survey and interviews on European Union (EU) enlargement, and then looks at the economic implications for Pskov *oblast* of EU enlargement.

In May–June 2003 the opinions of members of the Pskov élite were canvassed in discrete semi-structured interviews. Each interview focused on the results of preliminary research carried out by experts on the problems of cross-border cooperation and regional economic development. More than 30 individuals were questioned, including representatives of the political élite from across the ideological spectrum (ranging from national-patriots to communists to conservatives), as well as representatives of the business élite in Pskov *oblast*.

Pskov's political concerns about EU enlargement

The respondents were unanimous in their political evaluation of EU enlargement. The process per se does not provoke a feeling of alienation or negative sentiment among the Pskov regional élite. In the opinion of our experts, Russia does not oppose EU enlargement, but, to a large extent, desires economic and political cooperation with the EU, and, in some cases, military cooperation, too. Pskov has no overt objections to EU enlargement, perceiving it as an entirely objective process, and one that brings great advantages for Russia, rather than disadvantages.

Opinions on the accession to the EU of Estonia and Latvia, which border Pskov *oblast*, are more indicatory. Respondents were asked to evaluate the anticipated consequences of Estonia and Latvia joining the EU. While the survey results showed that there was more or less consensus in regard to attitudes towards EU enlargement in general, there were two dominating points of view – positive and neutral – on the consequences for Pskov of Estonia and Latvia becoming EU member states. Both positive and neutral attitudes were evident in all groups of respondents (politicians at the regional and local levels, business executives, and public figures). However, the experts consulted in this survey tended to adopt a neutral position; the positive perspective is less widely held than the neutral view: the ratio is 1:4. In other words, respondents were much more specific on the consequences of Estonia and Latvia joining the EU. Incidentally, opinions reflected differences of opinion in regard to the conduct of Russian foreign policy on the one hand, and of Estonia's and Latvia's on the other. Thus two sets of opinions prevail.

The first prevailing sentiment is that Estonia and Latvia have implemented discriminatory, nationalistic policies regarding Russia, Russians and Russian speakers in general; policies that have established barriers and an 'Iron Curtain'. People with strong opinions about the world might hold this view, for example, those who subscribe to communism, fascism or any other discourse that has a very rigid perspective of any object or subject. Such a discourse establishes a negative way of perceiving and categorising any phenomenon that does not fit into its framework as a negative occurrence, thereby creating the image of it as an enemy. People with completely different political slants also hold the view that Estonia and Latvia are anti-Russian; that said, sometimes people belonging to the nationalistic/patriotic school of thought do not think this at all. This attitude is quite abstract and has not been formed on the basis of personal experience but on the basis of the general context of Estonian–Russian and Latvian–Russian relations over the past ten-to-12 years. The entry of Estonia and Latvia into the EU is seen as extremely positive with the potential to solve the problem of poor relations with Russia. In the opinion of the respondents, with Estonia's and Latvia's accession to the EU it should no longer be possible for them to engage in discriminatory politics towards the Russian-speaking members of these countries because of European legal norms. That is, Estonia and Latvia will be forced by the EU to change their current policies towards their Russian-speaking minorities.

The second prevailing opinion is based on the view that neither Estonian–Russian nor Latvian–Russian relations began in 1917, 1940 or 1991, although these were key moments in their history. Estonians, Latvians and Russians have been neighbours for some 1,500 years and there were many other occasions when their interests did not coincide. Estonia, Latvia and Russia have a lot in common, but they also have their own interests. Estonia and Latvia have made their own choice regarding joining the EU and they had the right to do so. Respondents to our survey were neutral rather than negative on the fact that the Baltic States had made this decision to join the EU. This standpoint reflects attitudes to EU enlargement in general and is held by people of all political persuasions.

So, the dominant view in the results of the survey is a positive one in regard to EU enlargement and its benefits. This says something about an imminent improvement in inter-governmental relations between Estonia and Russia and Latvia and Russia on the eve of EU enlargement. When Estonia and Latvia join the Schengen arrangement there will be new opportunities for cooperation. The majority of expert respondents made no distinction between the concepts of the European Union and the Schengen zone; therefore, the accession of Estonia and Latvia to the EU is tantamount to them automatically joining the Schengen arrangement (although they are not likely to be admitted to Schengen before 2006). Incidentally, the residents of Pskov also have an incorrect perception as to when Estonia and Latvia will adopt the euro (the target date is in fact 2006–07). Inadequate information on the real state of affairs allows these erroneous views to take root. These beliefs are also generating cautious optimism that there will be a gradual and complete abolition of the visa regime between European nations and Russia and in some respects the full integration of Russia into the European space. This is attractive as an idea or prospect and, furthermore, has been discussed in the Russian media and mentioned in a positive way by Russian President Vladimir Putin, Italian Prime Minister Silvio Berlusconi and German Chancellor Gerhard Schröder.

At present, Russians need visas to visit Estonia and Latvia and vice versa. The usual procedure for obtaining a visa requires that a Russian applicant have a letter of invitation from an individual or organisation in Estonia or Latvia, complete a visa application form, pay a consular fee and be in possession of a medical insurance certificate. Tourist visas are a little different – no letter of invitation is required, but the visa is more expensive. Residents of Pskov *oblast*, particularly of Pskov city, are in a more privileged position than those of many other Russian regions in that

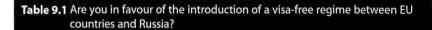

Table 9.1 Are you in favour of the introduction of a visa-free regime between EU countries and Russia?

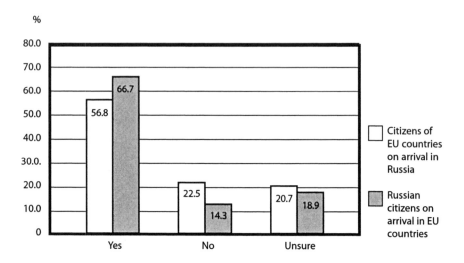

there are Estonian and Latvian consulates in Pskov. As for the border regime between Pskov *oblast* and Estonia and Latvia, it is already relatively strict. In Russia, in accordance with the Law on the State Border, there is a 5km zone within which visits are restricted; people who do not permanently reside in the border zone can only cross the border if they have special permission from the border administration service or if they have a relevant 'open' visa. Although getting permission to visit the border zone is not a complicated procedure and is more of a formality, it is, nevertheless, time-consuming.

To Pskov residents, it seems unnecessary for Estonia and Latvia to strengthen their borders further as part of the EU accession process. The borders should only be strengthened in the event of Russia changing its border regime, not because these countries have joined the EU. At present, the Russian federal authorities impose much stricter controls on crossing this border than do the Estonian or Latvian authorities. For example, when individuals cross the border, the Estonian and Latvian border authorities demand only to see their passports, whereas the Russian authorities also search their baggage. As for crime and illegal migration, again, it is the Russian side that has to deal with these problems, since the migration flow is primarily from East to West. These do not amount to a serious problem on this particular stretch of the Russian border; there are only isolated incidences of smuggling and attempts to cross the border illegally. Of most concern should be the lack of direct and constant information exchange between customs authorities, for it is this that creates opportunities for the shadow and criminal economies.

Practically all concerns regarding EU enlargement are centred on economics, while the political consequences of EU enlargement seem to concern the Pskov regional élite less. The one and only political concern is that Russia is being ignored in the European arena; sometimes, European institutions and the EU seem to resemble a 'gentleman's club' for the select few, which cannot and will not allow Russia to join. The Pskov élite views Russia (and thereby Pskov) as part of European civilisation and hence is offended by its exclusion.

It is important to note that these views of the political élite for the most part correspond with the results of a public-opinion survey of Pskov residents on questions concerning economic cooperation with EU countries, the likelihood of Russia joining the EU, and the possibility of the introduction of a visa-free regime between Russia and the EU. The age, education or income level of respondents did not appear to influence their views significantly. This is evidence that there is broad consensus among Pskov residents on relations with the EU and that the issue has not been politicised.

Regional cooperation with the neighbours
At the regional level people are talking about the need for a Euroregion (the Pskov–Aluksne–Voru Euroregion), in which Pskov *oblast*, Latvia and Estonia would participate. The Pskov administration and the heads of local administrations in Estonia and Latvia have all, in parallel, become more active in regard to this concept of a cross-border alliance. Yet, there is no consensus on its territorial area, its administration system and, most importantly, on the shared priorities of the participating regions. Everything is still at the drafting stage. It is important to understand that, at present, the current political direction of Estonia and Latvia is towards the West and not the East. Consequently, the active approach of the Pskov leadership has caused suspicion. It has also generated fear that the Pskov administration will try to dictate the terms and that would antagonise the Baltic partners, dampen their enthusiasm for the Euroregion and may lead them to suspend any intentions for cooperation through a Euroregion. A Euroregion would most likely be a good thing for Pskov for it would facilitate the resolution of cooperation problems, and this could have a positive impact on the regional economic development of Pskov *oblast*.

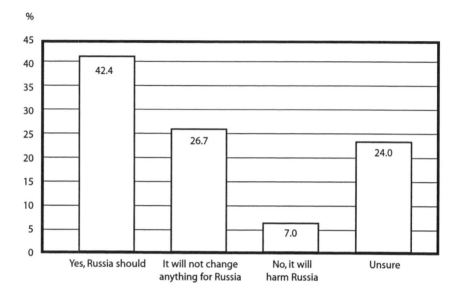

Table 9.2 Do you think Russia should join the EU?

The experts do not have a shared or accurate understanding of what such a Euroregion on the border of Pskov *oblast* with its western neighbours would look like, hence, the concept is still 'up in the air'. Pskov's political élite sees it as some kind of unclear symbol of an unknown type of cooperation with European countries to the west of the *oblast*. The term, Euroregion, in effect has been forcibly introduced into the regional élite's political vocabulary. It is a new, modern concept imported from elsewhere, which has been dictated by the general context of the European integration process and declared by the federal political élite (from the president downwards) but which in no way has found expression in the political practices of Russia at the regional level.

As for the Northern Dimension and the Wider Europe policies of the EU, there is not yet any understanding of them among the regional political élite of Pskov *oblast*. These concepts have only partially and episodically touched a very narrow circle of people within the élite, such as academics, diplomats and political managers, who have visited the regions in contiguous countries.

Economic implications of EU enlargement for Pskov *oblast*
Foreign trade
Even now, it is difficult to overestimate the impact of EU enlargement on the economy of Pskov *oblast*. Pskov enterprises are clearly oriented towards Europe in terms of their foreign economic activities (see Table 9.3).

Over the past ten years, the EU has become increasingly significant in regard to Pskov *oblast's* foreign-trade turnover: by 2002, it was its main market, accounting for over 85% of all foreign trade. For other countries, including the members of the Commonwealth of Independent States (CIS), aggregate trade is not more than 15%. This is due to the weakening or breakdown of economic ties with CIS markets. At the same time, there has been a significant increase in exports, in particular, supplies of electricity and timber to the Baltic States, and a rise in imports of machinery from the EU.

Estonia, Germany and Latvia are the main trading partners of Pskov *oblast*. Half of the foreign trade turnover of Pskov *oblast* is with these countries (see Table 9.4). In the mid-1990s, Germany – traditionally the most powerful economy in Europe– became the leading foreign economic partner of Pskov *oblast*. Estonia and Latvia are Germany's formal competitors only for the reason that they fulfil a transit function. Goods to and from Germany and Russia transit Pskov *oblast*, Estonia and Latvia. The end users of the goods exported from Russia through Estonia and Latvia are beyond the borders of these two states in economically developed Europe. The economies of Estonia and Latvia, to no less a degree than that of Pskov *oblast*, are oriented towards the economies of the more advanced and powerful countries.

The extent of cross-border cooperation is shown by the volume of foreign trade of the Pskov *oblast* in comparison to other countries (see Table 9.5).

In the mid-1990s, the Baltic States accounted for less than 20% of the foreign-trade turnover of Pskov *oblast*. However, in recent years, this figure has risen by 10%, despite the political disagreements between Russia and the Baltic States. In 2002, approximately one-third of the foreign trade of Pskov *oblast* was with the neighbouring Baltic countries.

The list of goods that Pskov imports from, and exports to, its trade partners is similar to Russian foreign trade in general, with raw materials dominating exports.

A significant proportion of exports (up to 30%) is not reprocessed goods but raw materials, natural resources and scrap metal. Consumer goods account for 10% of Pskov's exports. At the same time, the main features of the imported goods are that they are in the field of technology and that they are prone to a high level of re-distribution on the Russian

Table 9.3 Geographical spread of Pskov *oblast's* foreign-trade turnover

	1995	1996	1997	1998	1999	2000	2001	2002
Commonwealth of Independent States (CIS)	30.7%	22.4%	20.2%	13.9%	6.8%	5.7%	3.4%	2.8%
Abroad	69.3%	77.6%	79.8%	86.1%	93.2%	94.3%	96.6%	97.2%
Including:								
EU countries	34.1%	47.7%	36.7%	40.4%	44.8%	36.4%	42.9%	48.3%
Central and Eastern European countries	20.1%	20.9%	33.5%	35.2%	41.1%	47.3%	37.6%	37.5%
Total	100%	100%	100%	100%	100%	100%	100%	100%

Table 9.4 The dynamics of the foreign-trade turnover of Pskov *oblast*, 1995–2002 (as a percentage of the general volume of foreign trade)

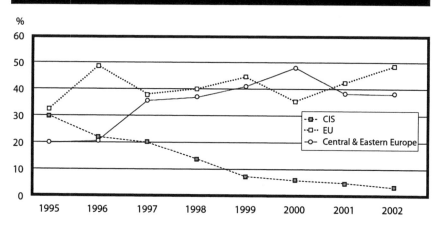

Table 9.5 Leading European foreign-trade partners of Pskov *oblast* (as a percentage of the general volume of foreign trade, 1999–2002, in comparison to 1996)

	1996	1999	2000	2001	2002
Baltic republics of the former Soviet Union	18.0%	38.0%	44.4%	34.4%	33.5%
Including:					
Latvia	7.1%	17.7%	15.1%	14.6%	11.7%
Estonia	6.8%	16,0%	25,9%	16,3%	19,9%
Germany	22.3%	27.0%	18.9%	17.1%	16.3%

Table 9.6 Products imported and exported by Pskov *oblast* (2000–2002)

	Export	Import
Food	8-10%	33-36%
Oil and energy	20-26%	0-1%
Petrochemicals	1-15%	10-12%
Ferrous and non-ferrous metals	8-9%	3-4%
Timber and goods made of wood	17-21%	4-8%
Mechanical engineering products	19-26%	32-36%
Leather, fur and related products	0-1%	0%
Clothes and shoes	8-11%	1%
Other goods	1-2%	9-10%

Table 9.7 Do you think it necessary for Russia to develop economic relations with EU countries?

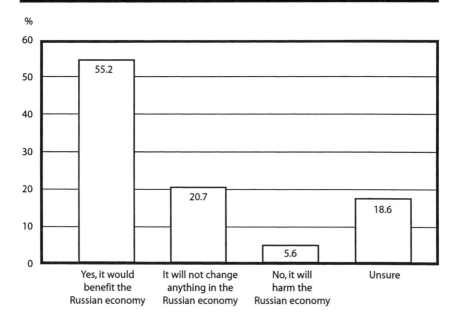

market. Only an insignificant proportion of imports are in competition with local industry (with local businesses losing out), for example, meat and other non-processed 'raw materials'.

At present, foreign-trade turnover does not meet the requirements for the strategic development of Pskov *oblast*. The nature of foreign-trade operations is not facilitating the qualitative development of the *oblast's* economy.

Pskov's economic concerns about EU enlargement

Unlike the political dimension of EU enlargement, representatives of the political élite are not unanimous in their views of the economic consequences of EU enlargement. People are concerned about the possible negative economic consequences. They are specifically concerned about the ramifications for Pskov *oblast*. However, there is also hope that EU enlargement will have a positive influence on: cross-border cooperation in the region; the prospects for economic development of Pskov *oblast*; the amount of foreign investment in the region's economy; and the amount of EU funds directed at developing cooperation. In particular, there will be changes regarding customs duties and the elimination of the existing double taxation rule (between Russia and Estonia) is anticipated. Also anticipated is a rise in the exchange of goods and, connected to this, the growth of businesses servicing the flow of transit goods through Pskov *oblast*. As a consequence, it is hoped that there will be parallel development of infrastructure on both sides of the border. Rhetoric about 'the existence of a rich neighbour' is heard widely. Those who engage in such rhetoric believe that a common border with the EU alone guarantees an influx of significant resources into the economy. This view is widely held among Pskov politicians.

Politicians and public figures on the one hand and business executives on the other have differing opinions about the impact of Estonia and Latvia's accession to the EU on the general economic situation in Pskov *oblast*. The politicians are very optimistic, but the business community is less so. Their opinions also diverge in regard to the impact on the investment climate, on employment levels in Pskov *oblast* and on the nature of cross-border trade. Politicians, for the most part, assume that economic cooperation with Estonia and Latvia will prevail over competition. Entrepreneurs are more cautious, pointing out that businesses will have to seek and foster new ways of making money in the new environment, since business executives from Pskov, Estonia and Latvia will all be looking to develop their own ventures. Some experts fear that investment from EU countries will be sunk into Estonia and Latvia and will not reach Pskov *oblast*. This will result in Estonian and Latvian (rather than Russian) businesses becoming more developed and

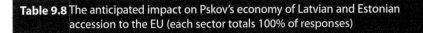

Table 9.8 The anticipated impact on Pskov's economy of Latvian and Estonian accession to the EU (each sector totals 100% of responses)

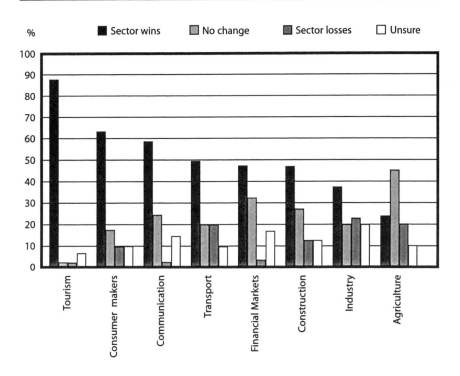

Note: The survey questioned experts including politicians, public figures and business people to assess the impact of EU accession on each sector.

competitive. Respondents pointed out that competition would intensify in the traditional sectors of the economy, such as agriculture and industrial production, as well as in the new financial and insurance markets. Experts assume that cooperation will develop only in sectors like energy and tourism, where collaborative projects might be proposed. This ties in with the commonly held assumption that not all branches of the economy will gain from EU enlargement. In particular, sectors that are not competitive now, including agriculture and industrial production, could lose out. For the most part, it will be businesses from other sectors of the economy, including tourism, the consumer goods market, communications, transport, the financial services market and construction, which will benefit.

Table 9.9 Ratings of 150 largest companies in north-west Russian regions (rated by volume of sales) in 2002

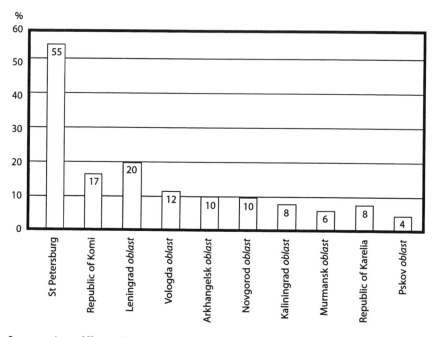

Source: *Journal Ekspert Severo-zapad* No. 39 (148) 20 October 2003

In the opinion of the majority of experts, the admission of the Baltic States to the EU will have a negative impact on agriculture in Pskov. The EU market protects the food-producing market, primarily through quotas. As experts have noted: 'Nobody in the EU is waiting for food produced in Russia.' At the same time, state subsidies for food production in the Baltic States enable Estonian and Latvian food businesses to expand into the Russian market.

Agriculture in Pskov *oblast* will not be able to compete with agriculture in neighbouring states if the new EU members receive agricultural subsidies, as anticipated. Experts in Pskov are very concerned about rising exports of European agricultural products to Pskov *oblast* after the current round of EU enlargement and also highlight the uncompetitiveness of Russian-made products on the European market (partly due to the EU's high import duty).

Table 9.10 Foreign direct investment in north-west Russia, January–September 2002: percentage received by each region

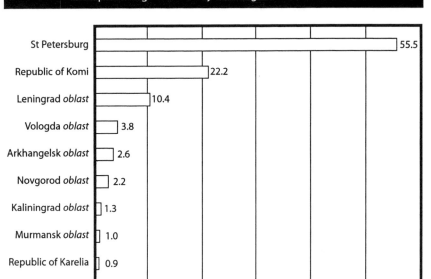

There is greater optimism in regard to industry. In the opinion of the majority of experts, Pskov's industry will benefit from EU enlargement as a result, it is believed, of the relocation of some labour-intensive enterprises from the Baltic States to the border regions of Russia. Furthermore, the increase in competition in Pskov *oblast* will spur the development of Russian business in general. Competition from Europe will accelerate the process of introducing new technologies and new production methods in Russia. The transition to European quality standards will also gather pace, although, in the opinion of the experts, the majority of Pskov companies will find it too expensive to make their products comply with EU standards. The barriers to foreign trade between Pskov *oblast*, Estonia and Latvia reflect the systemic barriers that exist between the transition economies (for example, Russia) and the countries that have accepted European standards (such as Estonia and Latvia).

Table 9.11 Ranking of the regions of north-west Russia according to average monthly wage (nominal value), 2002

Region	Ranking
Murmansk *oblast*	1
Republic of Komi	2
St Petersburg	3
Arkhangelsk *oblast*	4
Republic of Karelia	5
Vologda *oblast*	6
Leningrad *oblast*	7
Kaliningrad *oblast*	8
Novgorod *oblast*	9
Pskov *oblast*	10

Table 9.12 Consumer potential of Pskov *oblast* (as a percentage year-on-year)

	2000	2001	2002
Real disposable income of the population	112%	106%	114%
Average monthly real wages	119%	118%	125%
Retail turnover	116%	108%	113%

Increased competition will also lead some companies to change their line of business. Most experts believe that cooperation between producers of goods in Pskov *oblast* and the Baltic countries will prevail over rivalry, so long as the inevitable arrival of European companies in Estonia and Latvia forces businesses there to orientate themselves more closely towards the Russian market. It is believed in Pskov that Baltic businesses will strive to enter the Russian market as a consequence of being less assimilated into Europe and of the correspondingly low cost of doing so. (Some people think that this will not happen.) Only unitary Russian state enterprises will lose out, and they are inefficient even now. It has been proposed that they be transformed into joint-stock companies.

An opinion was expressed that, after the Baltic countries' accession to the EU, Estonia and Latvia's problems with Pskov *oblast* will be the least of their worries. Domestic challenges and integration with Europe will lead them to concentrate on their own concerns and to turn away from Russia. However, in the long term, the experts are optimistic: 'With time they will understand that they need Pskov.'

As for the problem of attracting investment for the region's industry, experts singled out lack of transparency in regard to the financial activities of Russian companies (primarily the book-keeping of accountants) as the primary obstacle. In our opinion, this could be overcome if Russian firms adopted the Generally Accepted Accounting Procedures (GAAP) applied by international companies. Additionally, Russian tax accounts should become more transparent and clearer to the Western business executive.

Specific hopes for change are pinned on the banking sector. At present, the quality of banking services leaves a lot to be desired. In Pskov *oblast*, there is not a single branch of a bank from the Baltic States. Moreover, in the opinion of one of our experts, it would not be to the advantage of Pskov banks to establish correspondent accounts (bank accounts used to process instructions on behalf of a bank that does not have a local presence) with banks from the Baltic States because of the insignificant volume of foreign-trade transactions in the region. Pskov banks, when providing a service to Pskov businesses that are active internationally, use intermediaries (for example, the Bank of New York for dollar transactions and Dresden Bank for euro transactions). One problem is the time difference between Russia and the US, which slows down bank transfers. Some Latvian companies have opened correspondent accounts with Alfa-bank of Russia. Since payments as a rule are made in dollars, roubles and euros (but not in Lat or Estonian kroons), it is problematic to deal directly with countries that use these currencies without the assistance of banks. So, there is room for vast improvement. Banking will become easier if and when the Baltic States join the euro zone for there will be fewer bank charges and transactions will be processed more quickly.

Some experts assume that having the EU on the doorstep of Pskov *oblast* might completely alter interaction between different sectors of the economy. In particular, it is said that the development of the tourism industry will guarantee the future economic prosperity of Pskov *oblast*. The service industry and related infrastructure would develop but industrial production would fall (see Table 9.8).

Pskov politicians and public figures are more pessimistic in their evaluation of the number of problems to be expected after Estonia and Latvia join the EU – believing that the number of problems will rise. This opinion is in contrast to their more optimistic assessment of the overall impact of EU enlargement on the economic situation.

Investment
Despite the discriminatory nature of foreign trade, Pskov *oblast* might derive definite advantages from EU enlargement in terms of its economic development. Pskov businesses are not in competition with Baltic businesses in Pskov *oblast* for any particular product or services. Other

regions of Russia, rather than the Baltic States, are Pskov's main competitors. On its own, the Pskov market is not of interest to Baltic businesses. The economic weakness of Pskov *oblast* is reflected, above all, in the fact that businesses in the Baltic States choose partners from the stronger regions of Russia. First and foremost, it is Pskov business itself that is interested in cooperation with the more developed business sector in the Baltic States in order to aid Pskov's own development. Pskov entrepreneurs, therefore, are interested in attracting business from those foreign entrepreneurs who currently bypass the region, not seeing any potential in it. The fact that Pskov businesses and businesses in the new EU member states are not currently in competition means that there could be opportunities for them to work in partnership to identify and exploit niches for products and services which are currently not found in Pskov.

However, cross-border cooperation in business is confronting real limitations. At the moment, Pskov business is too weak to implement large-scale projects. The main problem for Pskov *oblast's* economy is a shortage of local resources. Even by Russian standards, companies in the *oblast* are quite small. Only four enterprises from Pskov *oblast* made it onto the list of the 150 largest companies in north-west Russia in 2002 (Pskovenergo (74), the Velikolukinskii meat-processing plant (82), Pskovalko (130) and the Pskov power station (147, see Table 9.9).

Attempts to attract Russian capital from different regions have been made, but the reality is that there has been insufficient investment. In some branches of the economy, such as agriculture, there has been practically no capital investment. The explanation for this is to be found in the competitive nature of relations between Pskov business and companies in other regions of north-west Russia. Loans from banks are not an option due to high interest rates, the fact that the region's companies do not have a credit history, and the fact that local banks have insufficient capital to make available large-scale investment funds.

Foreign capital, then, is what the economy of Pskov *oblast* needs in order to give development a wide-scale boost. As a consequence of the accession of the Baltic States to the EU, Baltic companies will broaden their economic activities, and this might result in foreign capital being invested in Pskov *oblast*, thanks to the close trade relations between Pskov and Baltic businesses.

Attracting foreign capital through joint business ventures with European companies will give Pskov businesses a 'pass' to enter Europe. By being in partnership with foreign investors who know the 'rules of the game' in Europe, have the right connections, and, ultimately, face no political barriers, the political barrier to economic cooperation between Pskov *oblast* and the EU could be eliminated. By political barriers, businessmen and politicians are referring to non-tariff barriers such as the

2002 EU legislation on anti-dumping that they view as politically motivated (due to other aspects of the EU–Russia relationship).

Joint production projects established now will allow Pskov goods to be sold on the European market in future. Moreover, foreign trade partners in the Baltic countries might become a distinctive 'window to Europe' for producers in Pskov *oblast*. In this way, exports of products with high-added costs will become part of the foreign-trade turnover. And this will enable Pskov to rectify some of its economic problems: balancing the budget, creating jobs, raising home-grown capital for investment on a large scale, and boosting the economic development of the region in general.

Right now, the investment process in Pskov *oblast* is developing at a slow pace. Of the ten regions in north-west Russia, Pskov *oblast* has attracted the least amount of foreign direct investment (FDI). Investors are deterred by the region's poor economic progress and undeveloped infrastructure. Pskov *oblast* received only 0.1% of the total FDI into north-west Russia in 2002 (see Table 9.10).

The 2001 regional law on 'State Support for Investment Activities in Pskov *Oblast*' could not end the stagnation in the investment process. The law benefits first of all large enterprises, which are burdened with a lot of property. But the key characteristic of the economy of Pskov *oblast* is that small and medium-sized enterprises are in the majority. Thus, they do not benefit from this law.

A different but significant limitation on investment is the high cost of energy, which is preventing technological processes that consume large quantities of energy from being established in the *oblast*. There is low power consumption in the *oblast* at present, because there is no large-scale concentrated production; as noted above, small and medium-sized companies are the main feature of the economy. Hence, the introduction of power-conserving technologies is seen as a logical step for the economic development of the *oblast*. Europe has accumulated rich experience of devising and using energy-efficient technology. Some in Pskov believe that, thanks to the fact that the majority of foreign investment in the economy of Pskov *oblast* is European capital, it is reasonable to expect that foreign direct investors will use energy-efficient technology when they enter into a project to reorganise production in Pskov's companies. This is an optimistic assumption. In fact, it is unlikely that, in the near term, any such projects will be established in Pskov *oblast*.

The geographical position of the region (on the periphery of Europe) gives it the status of being situated in the 'Russia–Europe' transport corridor, but, at the same time, Pskov suffers from being a long distance from the main consumer markets, such as Moscow and St Petersburg. Production of consumer goods on a large-scale occurs in Leningrad *oblast*, circumventing Pskov *oblast*. Pskov *oblast's* consumer potential is not very high due to the low income of the population (see Table 9.11). In 2002, the level of income in Pskov *oblast* was 40% lower than the Russian average.

However, consumer demand is growing in Pskov *oblast* at a fast rate (see Table 9.12). Residents' purchasing power is greater than one might think. The real disposable income of the population of Pskov *oblast* rose by 113.8% in 2002. Pskov *oblast* has one of the cheapest baskets of basic goods in the whole of north-west Russia, providing the population with greater disposable income. The region's geographical location provides opportunities for people to work in the shadow economy (undeclared income for example from cross-border shuttle trade), which also affects their spending power positively. Pskov *oblast* is in second place of the regions of north-west Russia in regard to the rate of increase in residents' incomes. If this trend continues, by 2006, incomes of the population of Pskov *oblast* could potentially catch up with those of Leningrad and Novgorod *oblasts* – its direct competitors for investment. As a consequence of these projected increases in disposable income, production of consumer goods, in particular the development of the food industry, could, in time, become a priority in relation to the *oblast's* economic development.

The priorities
Two conceptual factors (the population's low level of income and the high cost of energy resources) significantly reduce the opportunities for foreign direct investment in Pskov *oblast*. At present, the basic competitive advantage of the *oblast's* economy is the organisation of production, which, because of its technological cycle, is dependent on low power consumption or high labour costs (such as in the textile industry). Investment capital will have the most impact in precisely these sectors. Investment into the food industry would also be logical, considering the *oblast's* growing consumer potential.

The task of the regional administration is to support the investment process. A dialogue with Pskov businesses is required so as to understand the region's competitive advantages. But, at the present time, the regional authorities' economic policy has a rather unsystematic, chaotic character. A comprehensive programme to attract foreign investment is needed. The low consumer potential is a factor here inhibiting Pskov from attracting investors. After all, consumer potential is a good indicator of the success (or otherwise) of the regional authorities in developing the *oblast's* economy. Until the domestic problems in Pskov are resolved, attracting foreign investment will be an inert process. By resolving the current economic challenges, the authorities will thus automatically be capable of widening the investment process, and thereby able to facilitate the general development of the economy of Pskov *oblast*.

It follows that a regional strategy for the economic development of Pskov *oblast* should be drawn up that takes all of these factors into account. The strategy should define the direction of development (the points of economic growth), which could pull the whole regional economy along behind it. Only after this will steps to attract European capital investment in Pskov *oblast* be systematic and bring about a qualitative outcome.

Conclusion

The general public, the business community and representatives of the regional élite appear to want Pskov *oblast* to develop in a European direction. But, at present, the conditions are not right to allow the *oblast* to become a competitive region in Europe. Serious problems of a political, economic and judicial nature need to be resolved in Russia itself before cooperation with EU countries can advance and the conditions for economic prosperity in Pskov *oblast* can improve. Decisions on these problems usually lie with the federal authorities. However, change in Russian regional politics is necessary so that the regions can address these problems themselves. The regions should be granted greater independence and Russian customs and tax legislation should be amended. In addition, there need to be guarantees that laws will be implemented and a comprehensive programme for the development of the regional economy needs to be drawn up.

Top of the agenda in both Russia and Pskov *oblast* should be the drafting of a long-term strategy for Pskov's development that takes cognisance of new political and economic realities. Only if political and economic practice is changed at the regional and local levels – on the basis of federal legislation, establishing the division of responsibilities to allow this – will Russia and its regions experience political and economic development together with European regions.

Notes

1. Valentin Chesnokov, Andrei Gavrilov, Maksim Golikov, Maksim Kopytov, Vasilii Kosterkin, Alexei Malov and Aleksandr Mashkarin contributed to the research and writing of this chapter.

2. This chapter is based on materials derived from the interdisciplinary academic research project, 'The Influence of European Cross-border Co-operation on Regional Economic Development', which was carried out with the support of the government of Sweden in March–September 2003.

10. Poland's Accession to the EU and Its Impact on the Movement of People and Goods over the Kaliningrad–Poland Border

Bartosz Cichocki

Poland's accession to the European Union (EU) is sure to have an impact on the movement of people and goods over the Polish–Kaliningrad border. Predictions of how current trends will change when the new visa regime is introduced are being made. Many of them assume that trade dynamics in particular will alter fundamentally, and for the worse, after EU enlargement. This chapter examines regional trade with Kaliningrad; the character of cross-border trade between Kaliningrad and Poland; who is trading; and how many people are involved. It also offers some conclusions on the impact of Poland's accession to the EU.

Characteristics of the border

The Polish–Russian border is 230 kilometres long, and constitutes slightly more than 6% of Poland's entire frontier.[1] Its shape was established shortly after the Second World War, and it divides the former territory of German Eastern Prussia.[2] The border does not follow a water system or land contours, and is therefore relatively difficult to police. There are five regular border crossing points open for the movement of people. Two of them are rail crossings (Braniewo–Mamonovo and Skandawa–Zheleznodorozhnyi); and three are road (Gronowo–Mamonovo, Bezledy–Bagrationovsk and Goldap–Gusev).

Border movements over the Polish–Russian frontier reached their peak in 1995–97, when they exceeded 4.5 million annually.[3] Since then, border movement has decreased year by year (4,427,189 crossings in 2000,[4] 3,957,102 in 2001 and 3,946,134 in 2002).[5] The proportion of crossings that are made by Russians is also decreasing, from 53.16% (2,353,478 crossings) in 2000 to 50.85% (2,012,162) in 2001. In 2002, the proportion dropped sharply, to 32.39% (1,669,159). The tendency continued in the first half of 2003 (603,239 crossings by Russians, compared to 849,052 in the first half of 2002). Poland is the main travel destination for Kaliningraders crossing the Polish frontier (i.e. most do not then travel on to a third country) – in the first nine months of 2002, only 11.2% declared a destination other than Poland (most often to Germany).[6]

These figures only go part of the way towards answering the fundamental question of how many individuals cross the Polish–Russian border, since many do so regularly and frequently every year. The answer needs to be known before any forecasts can be made of future border crossing patterns, as a consequence of EU enlargement. Research by Andrzej Janicki-Rola,[7] a former Polish consul-general in Kaliningrad, gives an indication of the scope for multiple crossings, and offers some possible reasons why people make them.

According to information gathered by Janicki-Rola in passport offices in Warmia-Mazury voivodship (province), a group of people registered in the Braniewo, Bartoszyce and Goldap districts (bordering Kaliningrad) regularly apply for a new passport every six months. A Polish passport allows for up to 70 visits (this limit stems from the limited number of pages – 27 – for border stamps). This means that people from this group can visit Kaliningrad 140 times a year. They could therefore cross the border 280 times (entry and exit): four or five times a week on average. Although estimates of the number of people who do this vary widely (from 6,000 to 20,000),[8] there is consensus that this group accounts for up to 90% of total border crossings, and that it is made up of shuttle traders and smugglers. Other border crossings from Poland into Kaliningrad involve officials of the state administration visiting the exclave for professional reasons, entrepreneurs visiting their counterparts in the *oblast*, and people visiting the *oblast* incidentally every year (scholars, tourists, etc.). There is no reason to believe that the pattern is any different the other way.[9] The fact that only one in four Kaliningraders has a passport indicates that the majority of the *oblast's* population is either not interested in travel abroad, or cannot afford it.

Smuggling

Annual reports by the Polish Border Guard indicate that smuggling of goods liable to a high rate of excise tax is rife over the Polish–Russian border. In 2002, most of the smuggled cigarettes seized on the borders of Poland were captured on the Kaliningrad section, even though this frontier accounts for little more than 6% of the entire border, and the number of crossings does not exceed 2.5% of the total. The value of smuggled goods seized on the Polish–Russian border was estimated at over €5m in 2002, or 164% of the value of smuggled goods seized in 2001.

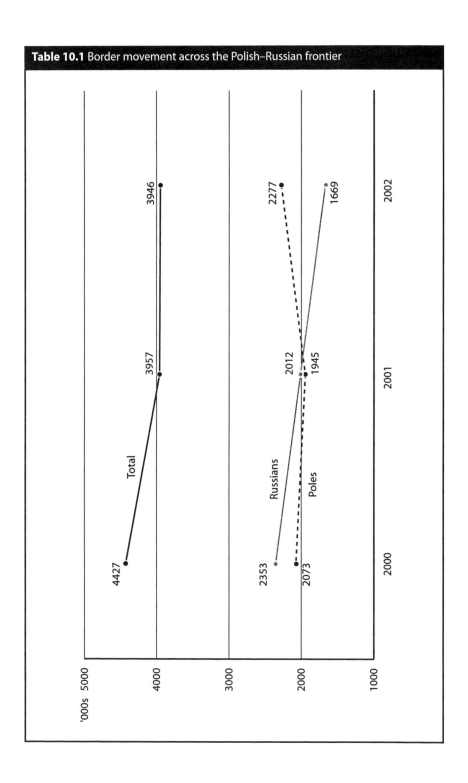

Table 10.1 Border movement across the Polish–Russian frontier

'000s

	2000	2001	2002

Total: 4427, 3957, 3946

Russians: 2353, 2012, 2277

Poles: 2073, 1945, 1669

Since it is not likely that smuggling itself can have increased so significantly in such a short period of time, this growth should rather be considered as proof of negligence and/or corruption among officers working at the border before 2002. Border guards have been undergoing training, and measures to tackle corruption have intensified.[10] This might mean that more criminal activity is being thwarted at border checkpoints, and thus that more goods are being seized. It is difficult to estimate the real amount of tobacco, alcohol or petrol smuggled, though the fact that there are 18 buses between Bartoszyce and Bagrationovsk every day, and that the main roads between Bezledy and Bagrationovsk and between Gronowo and Mamonovo are blocked by queues several hundreds of metres long, provides some indication of the scale of this activity. It can safely be assumed that there is an international criminal structure behind individual smugglers and shuttle traders. Combating smuggling is the most serious challenge that border guards on both sides of the border are now facing.

The impact of Poland's EU accession on border movement
How the visa regime will change
Contrary to popular belief, visas have been in force for years for reciprocal travel between Poland and Russia, and between Lithuania and Russia. However, there were many exceptions to these visa regimes. In the case of travel between Poland and Russia, an 'AB' stamp in a passport could be presented to the border guards instead of a visa for business trips. To obtain such a stamp, a Pole had to apply to a Passport Office (in Poland), or to a Registration Office (OVIR) or the Ministry of Foreign Affairs (in Russia). The application had to be confirmed by the company or other institution sending the person abroad. Holders of an invitation (from friends or relatives) or so-called vouchers (for tourist travel) also did not need a visa. These vouchers, which were especially popular on the Polish–Russian border, confirmed formally that a person had booked a room in a hotel – but in fact nobody checked their validity. They were readily available and cost next to nothing. The only strictly required document on the Polish–Russian border was a Polish, Russian or Soviet international passport. Poland has had a unified visa policy for Russians, regardless of whether they came from Kaliningrad or other parts of Russia. Lithuania's visa policy towards Russians exempted residents of Kaliningrad from needing visas to enter Lithuania for stays that did not exceed 30 days. Poland made it a requirement for Russians from outside Kaliningrad to have a visa in 2001.

As a result of its EU negotiations, Poland is obliged to cancel exemptions in its visa regime towards Russia. Originally, Warsaw scheduled the introduction of a visa regime for 1 July 2003, but then postponed this to 1 October 2003. Lithuania complied with the EU's requirements on 1 July 2003, when the Kaliningrad exemption was revoked, though special arrangements for Russian rail transit were put in place according to the EU–Russia Joint Statement on Transit, signed in Brussels on 11 November 2002.

The annulment of exemptions does not amount to the introduction of the full Schengen visa regime by the new EU members, and these states will not become Schengen zone members until at least 2006.[11] New members will not, for example, have access to the Schengen Information System (SIS) until its capabilities are developed to include the enlarged EU. Until then, Poland and Lithuania will impose national visa policies. Although there are only a small number of differences between Schengen visa policy and the national visa policies of the accession countries, these differences are important. From 1 October 2003, Polish consulates have issued visas valid for more than three months; issued visas at a low price or free of charge; and arranged visa procedures in the most simple way possible (for example, they will accept visa applications by e-mail as well as post).

These elements are of great importance to all non-EU countries, including Kaliningrad *oblast*. An agreement on reciprocal travel between Poland and Russia was signed on 18 September 2003, three months later than originally planned. According to the agreement Poles and Russians can apply for one-year multiple visas, which can reduce significantly unpleasant, but necessary contacts with consulates. Prices are close to symmetric for both nationalities: €50 for the Russians and US$50 for the Poles. So far, it is the only case where the Russian Federation has agreed to lower the cost of visas significantly. There are also single and double entry visas (€10 and €16). An important exemption has been put into force for Kaliningrad. Neither Kaliningraders visiting Poland, nor Poles visiting the exclave pay for visas; Poles do not need an invitation either. Both arrangements look set to significantly reduce the consequences of introducing the visa regime. Paying €/$50 for a visa would reduce the profit margin from shuttle trading. The procedure for registering invitations in Russia is lengthy and can be costly but, unfortunately, Poles travelling to mainland Russia still have to ask their Russian counterparts to fulfil the procedure.

The rules will, however, change significantly when checks on the internal borders of the enlarged EU are lifted and the new EU member states are included in SIS II. Poland and the other new members will only be allowed to issue three-month visas, just as current Schengen zone members do. The price for visas is also subject to common policy within the Schengen group. Currently, Schengen visas cost €20–50. Furthermore, the first visa application would have to be submitted personally – the next application could be submitted via post or through a travel agency, but only in the case of people with a bona fide reason for travelling. Requirements concerning the documents necessary to substantiate the visa application will be much stricter. Only a document complying with international standards will be accepted, which obviously excludes Soviet international/internal passports and Russian internal passports. In the case of business trips, the applicant would have to present a contract he/she has signed with a foreign company or hold an invitation from one. The applicant will also have to prove that he/she has enough money to cover accommodation when abroad. Finally, health insurance (issued by a reliable insurance company) will be requested. The advantage of these regulations is that the visa would be valid across the entire territory of the Schengen group, rather than only in Poland or Lithuania. On the other hand, it is clear that fewer people – and especially those most active on the Kaliningrad borders – will be able to comply with these stricter regulations.

The Schengen *acquis* also provides for a limited-territory visa, which allows its holder a stay exceeding three months. It is valid only on the territory of the country issuing such a visa. These types of visa are designed for specific categories of people: university students; and holders of documents not recognised in Schengen countries, or people who are not allowed to enter Schengen territory, but where one of the Schengen members has special reasons to host them (a witness in a court case, for example). Visas with territorially limited validity account for only 0.5% of all visas issued by the Schengen group members.[12] If Poland or Lithuania issued them on a large scale for people engaged in cross-border shuttle trade, this would certainly provoke a negative political reaction or even counter-steps (for example, checks on internal borders might be restored) from the other members of the Schengen group. It would be extremely difficult to guarantee that the holder of a limited-territory visa would not move into Schengen territory from the host country.

In this context, ideas circulating among senior EU authorities on local border movement are relevant. On 9 September 2002, the European Commission delivered to the Council a working document entitled 'Developing the Acquis on Local Border Traffic'. The Council sent it to a Working Party, and on 1 September 2003 the Commission presented the Council with two proposals for Resolutions on local border traffic.[13] One attempts to facilitate movement across the future external borders of the EU. It proposes that residents of border areas travelling frequently to a Member State for legitimate reasons could obtain special visas. The territorial validity of such a special visa would be limited to the border area of the Member State that issues it. This special type of multiple-visa would be valid for one year from the date of issue, but there are limits on the amount of time the holder could spend in the country which issued the visa. The holder could spend a maximum of seven consecutive days each visit up to a maximum total of 90 days in each half year of the visa's validity. It might be issued free of charge. It is also foreseen that special channels at crossing points could be established for border residents.

Crossings made over the Kaliningrad border and other frontiers between the new members and the new neighbours (Russia, Belarus, Ukraine) have, in most cases, illegitimate purposes. Therefore, there will not be a high demand for such 'local' visas. Furthermore, the introduction of the proposed rules in Poland or Lithuania would make combating illegal migration and smuggling even more difficult. It would not be possible to prevent holders of 'local' visas from leaving the border areas and travelling deeper into EU territory. Furthermore, Poland has not signed readmission agreements with Belarus or Russia, and there is no evidence so far that Russia, Belarus or Ukraine are considering reciprocal arrangements.

Russian visa policy

Russia changed its visa policy for Poland on 1 October 2003. From that date all Poles wishing to visit Russia have had to apply for a visa. Those travelling to mainland Russia have to present an invitation confirmed by a local OVIR, which may be the hardest element of the visa procedure. Another difficulty is that Russia has only two consulates in Poland which are convenient for travel to Kaliningrad: in Gdansk and in Warsaw (though the Polish capital is 300km from the exclave's border). The Russian Ministry of Foreign Affairs might open a new consulate in Olsztyn. This would be a very convenient location, since traffic heading for the crossings at Bagrationovsk and Mamonovo could pass through the town. More than 80% of border crossings between Poland and Kaliningrad are via these two routes.

The new visa regime and shuttle trade

Low prices for visas or facilitated consular procedures bring limited if any advantages for shuttle traders and smugglers. They cannot prove legitimate reasons to travel abroad. At present, they do not have contracts with their counterparts on the other side of the border, and they do not pay taxes. Unless they legalise their activity, they will be refused visas. And since they account for the majority of border crossings, there will be a significant drop in the number of crossings once the visa regime is implemented. That said, many factors other than visas affect flows of people across the Kaliningrad frontier. The most important include the costs of travel; the general economic and social situation in Russia, Lithuania and Poland; and the levels of excise tax.[14] The dynamic changes in border movement over the Polish–Russian frontier in recent years are evidence of these constraints.

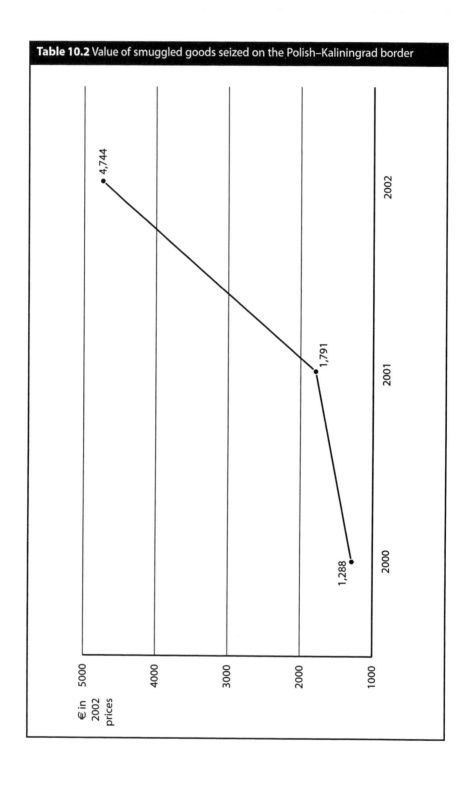

Table 10.2 Value of smuggled goods seized on the Polish–Kaliningrad border

The impact on cross-border dynamics

The immediate impact of the introduction of the visa regime prior to EU accession depends on the date of its introduction, and the nationality of the traveller. A dramatic decrease in border crossings by Kaliningrad residents who are not traders was not anticipated after 1 October 2003. Immediately after this date, numbers dropped, as they did with Russian transit through Lithuania just after 1 July 2003. But neither Polish nor Lithuanian national visa policies will present significant barriers for Russians: the low cost of the visa, the well-developed consular infrastructure in Kaliningrad and the simplified visa procedures militate against major changes in current patterns. Furthermore, Lithuania will accept Russian internal passports as valid for travel by Kaliningraders until the end of 2004, and Poland recognised German visas for transit through Poland after 1 October 2003. At the same time, there are political factors which should not be underestimated. Warsaw and Vilnius wish to avoid tensions in their relations with Moscow, and are likely to push for a liberalisation of their visa policy. On the other hand, the new members are strongly committed to proving to the EU that they are able to comply with the *acquis communautaire* in order not to postpone lifting of the checks on internal EU borders. One obstacle to the smooth operation of the new visa policy will be the small number of Russian consulates in Poland, and the lack of modern practices for the prompt and efficient issuing of visas.

The number of people who crossed the Polish–Kaliningrad frontier in the first week of October 2003 was four times lower than the same period of September 2003.[15] But during the rest of the month, the number of border crossings increased steadily and in the last week of the month had reached 80% of the level of border crossings registered in the last week of September (when there was a large number of crossings prior to the introduction of the visa regime).

The introduction of visas has not changed the general trends which characterise crossings over the Polish–Russian border into and out of Kaliningrad. These are: first, that the movement of persons across the Polish–Kaliningrad border has been consistently decreasing for the last four years; second, the number of Polish citizens as a proportion of the total number of persons crossing the border is increasing despite the introduction of the visa regime; and third, that the number of passenger cars crossing the border is decreasing while at the same time the number of trucks and buses is increasing. This is explained in part by the positive upward trend in trade and tourism between the northern provinces of Poland and Kaliningrad *oblast*; and in part by new smuggling practices: smugglers have found their activities are less likely to be detected if they travel by bus or truck rather than by private car.

The Polish Consulate General in Kaliningrad experienced significant demand for visas in the very first months of the new border regime as is shown in data on visas issued on randomly selected days in subsequent months: 773 visas were issued on 10 October 2003 (including 770 visas issued to Russian citizens); 843 visas issued on 24 November 2003 (788 to Russians); 643 visas issued on 12 December 2003 (570 to Russians); 279 visas issued on 26 January 2004 (276 to Russians); and 383 visas issued on 12 February 2004 (382 to Russian citizens). According to the Consul General in Kaliningrad, Jaroslaw Czubinski, there were only a few cases of visa applications being rejected in the first six months of the visa regime. Despite the fact that an additional building for consular services was opened at the Polish Consulate General, queues did form in the first weeks of October. High demand for Polish visas can be partially explained by the fact that they were issued free of charge. Many Kaliningraders wished to obtain a visa 'just in case' or for curiosity – they did not have firm plans to travel to Poland. Visas to Kaliningrad were issued free of charge in the first months of the visa regime, and within five working days, although sometimes it takes eight working days which contravenes the intergovernmental visa agreement. On the Polish side, visas are issued by Russian consulates in Gdansk, Poznan, Kraków and Warsaw. There is no Russian consular facility in Warmia-Mazury voivodship – the region of Poland contiguous with Kaliningrad – even though demand there is high. Nevertheless, dissatisfaction with procedures for obtaining a Russian visa has not been discernible in Poland since October 2003.

The accession of Poland and Lithuania to the Schengen group in 2006 or thereabouts will undoubtedly have a greater impact on Russia than the changes in 2003. Both Poland and Lithuania will have to fully implement the Schengen *acquis*, which does not allow visas for people who cannot demonstrate a legitimate reason for travelling abroad. Prices for visas will rise, and visa procedures will be stricter. However, even now it is not easy to cross a former Soviet border, especially the Kaliningrad border, which is blocked for hours by shuttle traders or freight trucks. Even in reciprocal travel between mainland Russia and Poland (for travel between Lithuania and mainland Russia, a visa regime was introduced in 1993), there are many administrative barriers, as described above. The introduction of the visa regime has not stopped illegal activities on the border. These activities continue mainly due to the tolerance of Polish Customs officers, who rarely order a smuggler to go back to the Russian side with his or her contraband; they usually let the smugglers proceed after merely cautioning them on the illegality of their actions.

It is not the probable decrease in border movement that should be the key issue when considering the consequences of EU enlargement. There is a real need to change the nature of these crossings – supporting legal trade exchange and tourism on the one hand, and combating the shadow economy and smuggling on the other. Today, movement across Kaliningrad's frontiers (especially the Polish part) has a profoundly criminal character. Its scale, involving state officials and local government personnel, extends beyond the border regions themselves. Shuttle trading, although formally not a crime, results in economic losses for local communities, since state budgets do not benefit from tax revenues from the trade. The new visa regime can at least partly address this problem, since some shuttle traders will conclude that it is worth registering their economic activity and paying taxes rather than losing their incomes.

It is popularly believed that shuttle trading and smuggling keep the border regions alive in the face of the structural unemployment there. Yet a relatively small group of people dominates border movement, so on this account the economic effects must be small. Even if 15,000 people are directly involved in shuttle trading/smuggling on each side of the borders (making 45,000 in all), and even if we add in their families, this would not allow for the conclusion that this activity keeps the Russian, Polish and Lithuanian borderlands, inhabited by up to 3m people, alive. On the contrary, the shadow economy, murky ties between politics and business and organised criminal structures hamper economic development and deter foreign investment.

All the parties involved in the Kaliningrad issue should step up social and economic reform and the modernisation of the whole region. Measures are needed immediately in the following areas: retraining programmes for inhabitants of the borderlands; agricultural development projects; an international scholarship programme for young people; a new credit system for economically active individuals; and state guarantees for investors. A promising sector for the whole region could be tourism. Paradoxically, tourism to Kaliningrad has benefited from the introduction of visa regimes for Russians by the Czech Republic, Slovakia and Bulgaria in 2001, and Kaliningrad has attracted increased numbers of Russians living on the mainland. Other potentially promising sectors include transport and the building industry.

EU enlargement – more than visas

The pattern of movement of people and goods across borders cannot only be explained by visa policies. EU enlargement has already brought major changes in the economy, security and social development of the Polish–Russian border regions. EU requirements have significantly accelerated reforms undertaken by the new member states. Polish–Russian border regions, with their economic backwardness inherited from their communist past, are also benefiting from European integration. The need to comply with EU requirements has encouraged interest in the Polish government, the voivodships and the local authorities in developing road networks and taking steps to protect the natural environment. Through the Phare programme, the EU has made a significant financial contribution to the development of the region's transport infrastructure, the modernisation of the equipment used by Border Guards and personnel training. Support for the Polish Border Guard has amounted to nearly €90m since 1997. EU funds cover up to 20% of the Border Guard budget.[16] As a result, the Polish–Russian border (and the whole eastern frontier of Poland) is becoming safer and its management is improving. A modernised transport network and new or improved roads contribute to the development of regional trade. On the Russian side of the border, however, conditions are not as advanced. Further assistance (i.e. investment) is required if the disparity in socio-economic conditions on the two sides of the border is to be reduced.

Poland sees its EU membership as a way to increase its economic and political resources. Border regions should profit from this. Shuttle trading should disappear and visas (in a way by accident) will accelerate this process. Poland and Russia need to develop other forms of bilateral social contacts and trade. Kaliningrad *oblast* is still unknown in Poland as a tourist destination, and to some extent also as an investment destination – despite more than a decade as a Special Economic Zone.

There is already evidence that Poland has become a victim of its own success. The country is an increasingly attractive destination for illegal migrants from Central and South-east Asia, and Kaliningrad is a busy transit corridor on this route. It is relatively easy to reach Kaliningrad from Moscow by air, and then Poland by sea – all without a visa. The current visa regime is barely a 'paper curtain'. From Poland, just one border separates migrants from Western Europe. The fight against illegal migration and drug trafficking in the Baltic Sea region will remain a major concern for both the Polish and the Russian authorities. If the fight is to succeed, it will require close cooperation between EU and non-EU parties.

For all the negative consequences of the new visa regime for the current structure of trade in the region, Poland's EU membership should have a major positive impact on Kaliningrad. The European area of stability and prosperity will move closer to this Russian region, which should result in increased interest from investors. The EU's strict regulations on production, labour and the environment will not embrace Kaliningrad, but the EU market will be right next door.

Notes

1. Polish Border Guard statistics; see www.sg.gov.pl/granice/index.asp.
2. For more details on the post-war territorial divisions of the former Eastern Prussia and the legal status of Kaliningrad *oblast* see Krickus, R., *The Kaliningrad Question* (Lanham, Maryland: Rowman and Littlefield, 2002), pp. 1–2, 34–35, 67–68; Hreczuk, A., 'Polish–Russian Relations and Kaliningrad', in Holtom, P. and Tassinari, F. (eds), *Russian Participation in Baltic Sea Region-Building: A Case Study of Kaliningrad* (Berlin: Gdansk University Press/Nordeuropa-Institut der Humboldt Universitaet zu Berlin, 2002), pp. 72–73; Sergounin, A., 'Kaliningrad', in Lieven, A. and Trenin, D. (eds), *Ambivalent Neighbors: The EU, NATO, and the Price of Membership* (Washington, DC: Carnegie, 2003), pp. 147–148.
3. Janicki-Rola, A.,'Stosunki spoleczne miedzy Polakami a mieszkancami Kaliningradu' [Social relations between Poles and Kaliningraders], speech given at the conference 'The Future of Kaliningrad *Oblast* in the Integrating Europe', Krakow, 28 November 2002.
4. *Sytuacja na granicy panstwowej RP w 2001 roku* [Current situation at the state border of Poland in 2001], Straz Graniczna, Warszawa styczen 2002.
5. *Sytuacja na granicy panstwowej RP w 2002 roku* [Current situation at the state border of Poland in 2002], Straz Graniczna, Warszawa styczen 2003. All border statistics concerning the Polish–Russian frontier for 2001–02 are based on this report; statistics for 2000 are based on *Sytuacja na granicy panstwowej RP w 2001 roku*, unless indicated otherwise. According to another report by the Border Guards, movement of people over the Kaliningrad–Polish frontier in the first half of 2003 reached 1,598,482 crossings which was a drop of 17.3% on the first half of 2002: *Sytuacja na granicy panstwowej w I pólroczu 2003 roku* [Current situation at the state border of Poland in the first half of 2003].
6. Data presented by Wojciech Kalamarz, Ministry of Foreign Affairs of the Republic of Poland, at the conference 'Kaliningrad – Border Movement and the Enclave's Future', Centre for International Relations, Warsaw, 7 November 2002.
7. Janicki-Rola, 'Stosunki spoleczne miedzy'.
8. The Kaliningrad administration estimates that 6,500 households on the Russian side are directly involved in cross-border trade with Poland and Lithuania.
9. In November 2002, Polish Border Guards at the Bezledy–Bagrationovsk crossing opened a green channel for people with nothing to declare.

Over four days, only 45 drivers used it despite the fact that about 1,500 cars and 50 buses crossed every day. *Na pogranichnom punkte propuska Bezledy–Bagrationovsk prokhodit ekperiment* [An experiment is under way on Bezledy–Bagrationovsk BCP], Lenta-kaliningrad.ru, 3 December 2002.

10 For example, on the Bezledy–Bagrationovsk crossing point six Polish officers were arrested for alleged bribery on 20 November 2002, and 12 more two weeks later. According to a District Prosecutor in Olsztyn, one officer could 'earn' €750 in one shift. *Arestovany shest' sotrudnikov propuskonogo punkta na rossiisko-polskoy granitse* [Six officers arrested on the Russian–Polish border], Lenta-kaliningrad.ru, 20 November 2002; *Dvenadtsat' pol'skih pogranichnikov zaderzhany na vzyatki* [Twelve Polish Border Guards officers arrested for taking bribes], Lenta-kaliningrad.ru, 6 December 2002.

11 For example, it took Sweden five years to become a Schengen zone member after it became an EU member.

12 Data presented by Wojciech Kalamarz.

13 *The Commission Proposes Concrete Measures for Facilitating Local Traffic at the Land Borders of the Union*, IP/03/1186, 1 September 2003; at www.europa.eu.int.

14 Excise tax on alcohol was significantly reduced in Poland in 2002. The immediate result was a sharp fall of over 67% in alcohol contraband seized on Poland's eastern frontier in the first half of 2003, compared to the first half of 2002 (a 56.8% drop on the Kaliningrad border, a 92% drop on the Lithuanian border, a 48.7% drop on the Belarusian border and a 77.7% drop on the Ukrainian border), according to Polish Border Guard figures.

15 *Funkcjonowanie ruchu granicznego miedzy Polska i Obwodem Kaliningradzkim po wejsciu w zycie obowiazku wizowego* [Border movement across the Polish–Kaliningrad border after introduction of the visa regime] (Warsaw: Border Guards of the Republic of Poland, 2003).

16 See www.sg.gov.pl.

11. Estonian–Russian Relations in the Context of EU Enlargement

Piret Ehin and Andres Kasekamp

Having completed its return to the West, through membership of the European Union (EU) and the North Atlantic Treaty Organisation (NATO), Estonia has not been able to formulate a clear and convincing collective vision regarding its goals and priorities as an EU member. The former front-runner candidate in the accession process is now a member state whose inter-governmental official rhetoric is accompanied by high levels of popular Euroscepticism.[1] This reactive position is also evident in regard to its relations with Russia. Seemingly unsure about the prospects for its relations with Russia under the EU umbrella, Estonia continues to view EU strategies towards Russia with mixed feelings. In the long term, however, EU enlargement is likely to have a positive impact on Estonia–Russia relations.

The guiding principles of Estonia's European policies are clearly apparent from the cautious inter-governmentalist stance of Estonian representatives in the European Convention and at the Intergovernmental Conference.[2] In addition to the natural anxieties of small states, the historical experience of the Baltic countries has made them particularly wary of supranational institutions and grand blueprints for 'ever closer union'.[3] Estonia has insisted on sovereign equality for EU member states, prioritising symbolic aspects of the EU's institutional framework, such as retaining the rotating presidency and every member state being allowed to have a commissioner.[4] Siding with the Republic of Ireland and the UK, Estonia has strongly opposed expanding integration to areas like social policy, taxation, and foreign policy.[5] This favouring of an inter-governmental stance applies specifically to the Common Foreign and Security Policy (CFSP) and the European Security and Defence Policy (ESDP), where there is strong reluctance to countenance any further extension of integration.[6] Underlying this position is the explicit concern that NATO could be weakened and the tacit fear that the original EU members might somehow force the Baltic States into some kind of unacceptable accommodation of Russia.

Estonia is acutely aware of its role as a border state on the eastern periphery of the EU. In many areas, such as the control of external borders, Estonia's interests coincide with those of the EU. In other regards, such as the possibility of visa-free relations with Russia, Estonians remain wary of excessive rapprochement between the EU and Russia and great-power politics that may yield results detrimental to the interests of the country. While several politicians and commentators have remarked that Estonia could develop its own niche in the EU by actively contributing to the Northern Dimension – or, potentially, a new Eastern Dimension – Estonia has not assumed a proactive role in shaping Europe's Russia policy. Indeed, the Estonian government's EU Action Plan for 2004–06 devotes only one paragraph to relations with Russia, calling attention to the 'development of democracy and the rule of law in Russia, guaranteeing human rights (including in the Northern Caucasus), and the securing of the EU's external border and the related issues of immigration and asylum policy'.[7] Evidently, the call to 'Europeanise' Russia, implied by the conditionality associated with the concept of Wider Europe, has not found many backers in Estonia, where historical experience has bred pessimism about Russia's commitment to democracy and fair play.

Baltic–Russian relations on the eve of enlargement

Baltic membership of the EU will undoubtedly influence EU–Russia relations, as was amply demonstrated by negotiations over transit rights for Kaliningrad in 2002. More fundamentally, however, EU enlargement has the potential to renew and restructure dramatically the historically burdened relationship between the Baltic States and Russia. It is hoped that subsuming Baltic–Russian relations within the wider EU–Russia relationship will force Russia to abandon its post-imperial attitude and instead treat the Balts as 'normal' countries and not as part of its 'near abroad' or sphere of influence.

The foreign policies of the Baltic States vis-à-vis Russia have been primarily conditioned by their historical experience. All three countries emphasise that they are not 'newly independent' nations, but restored states. The principle of restitution was central to their state-building efforts. The withdrawal of the last Russian troops from Baltic territory in 1994 completed the rupture of the Soviet Union. By 1995, the majority of Estonian trade was no longer conducted with Russia but, rather, with the 15 members of the EU.[8]

Relations between the Baltic States and Russia remained frosty throughout the 1990s. The main source of tension between Estonia and

Russia has been the status of the Russian-speakers who settled in the country during the Soviet occupation.[9] Reacting to uncontrolled immigration from the East in the Soviet period, the Law on Citizenship of February 1992 granted citizenship only to the original citizens of the inter-war Republic of Estonia and their descendants. Consequently, the Soviet-era immigrants who wished to become citizens were subject to naturalisation. Although the citizenship and minority policies of Estonia are now regarded as being in line with international standards, Russia continues to regard the 'discrimination of the Russian-speaking population' as the main impediment to the improvement of bilateral relations.

Different security agendas have also complicated relations. Committed to regional hegemony in the former Soviet Union, throughout the 1990s, Russian officials regarded the Baltic States as part of the near abroad – a position fundamentally incompatible with the NATO aspirations of the Baltic countries. The accession of Estonia, Latvia and Lithuania to the Alliance in April 2004 triggered stern reactions from Russian politicians, although the rhetoric has been less bullish than throughout most of the 1990s.[10] The large gap between Russia's foreign-policy ambitions and its power capabilities has forced it to acknowledge reluctantly the new geopolitical realities.

Economic relations remain underdeveloped due to politically motivated barriers to free trade. Russia imposed double tariffs on Estonian products in 1995, which effectively prevent many Estonian enterprises from gaining access to the Russian market. These punitive tariffs have hindered economic and trade links and, subsequently, accelerated the reorientation of Estonian foreign trade towards the West. In 2002, Russia accounted for a mere 3% of Estonia's exports and 7% of its imports.[11] Russian direct investment (totalling €40.6 million) constitutes a negligible 1.3% of aggregate foreign investment in Estonia.[12]

Finally, the dearth of basic treaties regulating economic and political interaction has become a key factor hindering closer cooperation and contacts. Absent are vital accords like a border treaty and an agreement on trade and economic cooperation.[13]

The expected positive impact of Estonian membership of the EU and NATO on Baltic–Russian relations was not evident in the accession period. To the contrary, on the eve of EU and NATO enlargement, Russia stepped up its rhetoric and took several alarming steps. A prominent example of this was Russian bargaining over the extension of the EU–Russia Partnership and Cooperation Agreement (PCA) to the new members. Although it was assumed that the PCA would automatically include all of the new EU member states as of 1 May 2004, Russian President Vladimir Putin claimed that this was not necessarily the case.

In early 2004, Russia presented the EU with 14 demands that had to be met before the PCA could be extended. Most of these were connected to trade, but worryingly for Estonia and Latvia, the treatment of the Russian minority in their countries was once again raised as an issue. After a couple of months of uncertainty, the EU and Russia reached an agreement in April, after the EU addressed some of Russia's concerns about trade. This agreement is important to Estonia because, under the PCA, Russia will have to abolish the double tariffs and open up its markets to Estonian products on equal terms.

While Estonia welcomes the opportunity to solve long-standing policy stalemates through the broader EU–Russia framework, it remains wary of possible great-power deals that could neglect the interests of smaller members. One of the most sensitive issues for Estonia is that of visa freedom for Russians, a matter that Russia has repeatedly tried to place on the EU agenda. The Estonian government's EU Action Plan states that third countries must unconditionally fulfil all of the general requirements for obtaining visa freedom with the EU, including 'effective control of external borders, secure travel documents, existence of a repatriation agreement, and control over illegal immigration'.[14]

The Estonian–Russian border as the EU external frontier

The Baltic States have always been the gateway between the East and the West. After joining the EU on 1 May 2004, important new functions were added to this role. As a gatekeeper of the Schengen zone, Estonia must ensure adequate control over its 339-kilometre (km) border with the Russian Federation.

The policies of the Estonian government in relation to control of its eastern border have been consistent with the principles underlying the Schengen *acquis*. Establishing tight control of the eastern frontier immediately after the restoration of independence in 1991 was linked to the vital interests of the Republic of Estonia. These include: de facto separation from Russia; establishing control over Estonian territory; ending the massive influx of Russian-speaking migrants; and keeping out organised crime and preventing drug trafficking and smuggling. The complementary nature of Estonian and European interests distinguishes Estonia from many other accession countries that have been reluctant to introduce visa regimes with their Eastern neighbours and which regard the requirement to upgrade border controls as an undesirable aspect of the accession criteria.[15]

The length of the current Estonian–Russian demarcation line is 338.6 km, 76.4km of which runs along the Narva River and 124.2km along Lake Peipsi. The border has been demarcated, the control regime functions effectively, and the government has invested heavily in surveillance systems, the training of border guards, and border facilities.[16] Although Estonia argues that guarding external borders should remain the sole prerogative of member states, it is nevertheless interested in sharing the financial burden and has gladly accepted EU financial assistance for upgrading the border.[17]

While the 'closing' of the border and the introduction of the visa regime for Russians in early 1992 disrupted trade, travel and tourism, recent statistics show that cross-border traffic is increasing. The number of border crossings at the three international crossing points, at Koidula, Luhamaa and Narva, approached 3.5m in 2002, compared to approximately 2.5m in 1997–98.[18] The number of vehicles crossing the border has risen consistently, from 380,000 in 1996 to 870,000 in 2002.[19] The number of Russian tourists visiting Estonia has also increased in recent years. Although Finns constitute by far the largest group of visitors, Russians now make up the third largest group of foreign tourists.

A visa regime between Estonia and Russia has been in place since 1992, although, until 2000, certain categories of residents of the border regions were allowed to cross the border without a visa.[20] This visa waiver was established under a 1991 government directive and was set to last for one year. It was 'semi-legally' extended by the municipal governments, which confronted pressure from local residents with 'urgent needs' to travel to Russia on a regular basis. The reasons for establishing such a procedure were largely 'humanitarian': the simplified regime was designed to allow residents to visit close relatives on the other side of the border, attend church, and visit cemeteries. The regime was of particular importance to members of the Seto ethnic group in south-east Estonia and adjacent areas of Russia, whose historical homeland is dissected by the border. In total, 17–20,000 local residents were on lists of exempt persons or were issued with special permits.

Because the procedure was implemented largely by local governments, there were regional differences in border-crossing regulations. These are important. In north-east Estonia, local governments issued special permits to those border-region residents who had close relatives on the other side of the frontier or who owned land or real estate on the other side. In south-east Estonia, local residents were allowed to cross the border freely, without a visa, on certain holy days of the Orthodox Church, allowing members of divided congregations to visit places of worship and cemeteries. It should be noted that the border-crossing regime turned into a source of additional income for many local residents.[21] The Russian financial crisis of 1998 and the concurrent devaluation of the rouble turned small-scale cross-border trading into a profitable enterprise. This is reflected in the rapid rise in the number of people crossing the frontier in 1999–2000 under the simplified regime.

Abolishing the simplified border-crossing regime was a major step towards implementing the Schengen *acquis*. This was highlighted repeatedly in progress reports prepared by the European Commission in the late 1990s.[22] While a position paper from Brussels requested that the simplified arrangement be abolished by the time of accession, Estonia beat this deadline by introducing a full visa regime with Russia in September 2000 and closing local crossing points, such as at Kulje, Lüübnitsa, Meremäe and Võmmorski. To compensate for the loss of previous privileges for local residents, a new agreement between Estonia and Russia stipulates that both sides can issue up to 4,000 multiple-entry visas per year to those border-region residents who have a compelling need to cross the frontier on a regular basis. These visas are issued free of charge and are valid for one year. The specifics of this agreement were based on an analysis by the Estonian Foreign Ministry, which found that, in many cases, residents using the simplified regime did not have vital interests on the other side that would justify visa-free crossing. In issuing free multiple-entry visas, priority is given to residents: a) who wish to visit close relatives; b) who wish to visit the graves of close relatives; c) who wish to visit distant relatives; d) who wish to visit the graves of distant relatives; or e) who own real estate on the other side. All residents of border regions can apply for these visas; the final selection is made by so-called visa coordinators in the towns of Narva and Võru (the regional centres in north-east and south-east Estonia, respectively). Interviews conducted in summer 2002 with visa coordinators, members of local authorities and residents suggest that the quota is sufficient and meets demand.[23]

Overall, EU accession will not bring about major changes in the Estonia–Russia border regime. The long-term complementary nature of national and European interests with regard to the safeguarding of external borders ensures a high degree of policy consistency. While the closing of the border and the introduction of the visa regime exacerbated the socio-economic problems of the border regions, this damage is the result of national policies that predate Schengen. While the European and national emphasis on security issues occasionally conflicts with local preferences for unrestricted trade and travel, it is clear that national interests will continue to prevail over local ones.

Border negotiations: between international law and realpolitik

One indicator of the inadequate state of the Estonia–Russia relationship is the absence of a border treaty, despite the fact that all territorial and technical questions have been resolved and the accord has been ready for signing since 1996. This has produced a curious situation: the de jure and de facto borders do not coincide. Legally, Estonia defines its land border with Russia according to the Tartu Peace Treaty of 2 February 1920 and refuses to recognise the legality of arbitrary changes made to the border by Joseph Stalin after Estonia's annexation by the Soviet Union.[24] The de facto international border, however, corresponds to the Soviet-era administrative boundary. It is demarcated and has been controlled since 1991. This line has also served as an EU external border since 1 May 2004, although the State Borders Act of 1994 regards the present frontier merely as a temporary demarcation line – defined as a boundary that separates those Estonian territories that are currently under the jurisdiction of the Estonian government from those that are not. In order to comprehend the complexities of the situation, a brief overview of the border negotiations is required.

The border issue was one of the four main themes of the general negotiations between the Republic of Estonia and the Russian Federation from 1992 to 1995. Estonia insisted on recognition of the Tartu Peace Treaty as the legal basis for any border negotiations, while the Russian side refused to attribute anything more than historical significance to it.[25] As the discussions were dominated by other pressing concerns, such as the withdrawal of Russian troops, they ended in 1995 with the border issue left unresolved. In January 1996, a separate delegation was formed to negotiate a border treaty.[26]

Significant changes occurred in relation to the position of Estonia between 1994 and 1996. As the border stalemate was seen as an impediment to the achievement of Estonia's foreign-policy goals, including EU and NATO membership, the government altered its policy line. In December 1994, Prime Minister Andres Tarand announced that Estonia was ready to drop the territorial claims emanating from the Tartu Peace Treaty. Under the new strategy of 'positive engagement' with Russia, restitutive principles were gradually replaced by a more pragmatic methodology.[27] From autumn 1996, Estonia sought to conclude a so-called technical border treaty that makes no reference to any previous inter-state treaties. This approach proved productive. Experts from both sides drew up the text of the treaty and its annexes, agreeing to a frontier that, for the most part, coincided with the administrative boundary of the Soviet period. At a meeting in Petrozavodsk, Russia, on 5 November 1996, the work of the expert groups was approved by the foreign ministers of both countries.

Although technically, the treaty was ready for signing, Russia backed away from its initial promise to finalise the agreement quickly in the hope that it could link it to the status of Russian-speakers in Estonia. In an attempt to delay the process, it demanded that technical aspects be clarified. As a result, the negotiating delegations started the work that had been designated for the demarcation commission – a move that delayed the process for an additional two years.[28]

Changes in the international context, notably the EU's decision to invite Estonia to start accession talks, seemed to increase Russian willingness to proceed with the treaty in 1997–98. In spring 1998, the appointment of Ambassador Ludvig Chizhov as the new head of the Russian delegation signalled a 'new beginning' and facilitated agreement on the technical details.[29] The border treaty between Estonia and the Russian Federation was initialled by the foreign ministers of the two states in St Petersburg on 5 March 1999.

Signing and ratification depend on Russia generating the necessary level of political will. According to the Estonian Foreign Ministry, the issue 'has become linked to internal institutional dynamics and continues to be exploited for domestic political profit. There is an apparent intention by the Russian Duma to use the treaty as a bargaining chip that supposedly gives Russia increased leverage over issues such as the status of the Russian-speaking population in Estonia and Estonia's aspirations to join NATO.'[30]

This bargaining strategy seems increasingly outdated in light of the changed regional and international political context. However reluctantly, Russia will have to adapt to Estonian membership of NATO. Furthermore, Estonian membership of the EU serves to certify that its policies towards the Russian-speaking minority are in line with international standards. Indeed, Russian accusations in this area seem increasingly untenable in view of the brutal policies that it has pursued in Chechnya and the erosion of democratic institutions and rights at home. Internal political dynamics in Russia have changed as well. While the administration of former Russian President Boris Yeltsin could cite the Duma's unwillingness to ratify the treaty as a reason for delaying the process, Putin has effectively co-opted the Duma and should be able to count on its cooperation. Indeed, there is some indication of a new pragmatism in regard to Russia's approach to the issue. During a meeting with former Estonian Prime Minister Mart Laar in April 2004, Putin promised to proceed with the treaty.[31] While this is not the first time that such a promise has been uttered, the time may be ripe for abandoning obscure and ultimately unproductive linkage tactics.

Improved bilateral relations under the EU umbrella?
While Estonia's accession to the EU will not change the border regime, it is likely to have a significant long-term impact on the country's relations with Russia. Pessimists fear that the Baltic States and the other Central and Eastern European candidate countries will bring their negative historical experiences with Russia into the EU, which will impact negatively on EU–Russia relations. Former Estonian Foreign Minister Toomas Hendrik Ilves has warned that the new members will employ a much more 'realistic' and 'less naive' approach towards Russia than the current member states.[32]

However, the fear appears to be greatly exaggerated. Baltic anxieties and suspicions of Russia stem from their acute sense of insecurity. Once this root cause of distrust is removed (through membership), bilateral relations have the potential to improve markedly. In fact, many of the outstanding problems in Baltic–Russian relations could be dealt with within the broader framework of EU–Russia relations. Given the importance of the EU as a regional powerhouse and trade partner, Russia will have new incentives to cooperate with its Baltic neighbours.

Turning to the list of specific problem areas, the issue of Russian-speaking minorities in the Baltic States is likely to lose relevance gradually. European institutions – the EU, the Council of Europe, and the Organisation for Security and Co-operation in Europe (OSCE) – have already used their leverage to pressure the Balts into liberalising their minority policies. Successive Estonian governments were persuaded to take decisions – unpopular among the electorate – to relax language and citizenship laws.[33] Recognition of their success in meeting the international community's demands was confirmed by the closure of the OSCE mission in Estonia at the end of 2001. Accordingly, Estonian accession to the EU constitutes proof that minority rights in the country continue to be protected, and it will also act as a guarantee. Moreover, the hypothesis about EU/NATO 'stability projection' can be corroborated: a situation of potential conflict has been diffused due to the EU/NATO 'shadow of the future'.

Second, the accession of the Baltic States to the EU will facilitate economic contacts with Russia. With the extension of the PCA to the new members, the punitive double tariffs that Russia imposed on Estonian products in 1995, and which Estonian producers sought in vain to eradicate for nearly a decade, will have to be abolished. Russian markets will then become considerably more open. In addition, rising trade between the EU and Russia is likely to increase transit flows through the Baltic States. This will be all the more true if Russia joins the World Trade Organisation – a goal that Estonia strongly supports.

Third, the opportunity to regard Estonia–Russia relations as a subcategory of EU–Russia relations should allow both sides to transcend old stalemates and deeply ingrained suspicions. The undeveloped treaty base of Estonia–Russia relations will be complemented by a number of agreements that exist between the EU and Russia, including the PCA, as well as various sectoral accords. As an EU member state, Estonia is now represented in institutional frameworks that focus on cooperation with Russia (summits, cooperation councils and committees). While Estonia remains a small state with limited influence, EU membership gives it increased leverage, allowing it to become a more equal partner in the 'same weight category'. In areas regulated by existing agreements, Russia has to treat member states equally and will have to end discriminatory practices. This refers, in particular, to the abolition of the double import tariffs. Furthermore, there are hopes that the EU could use its influence to convince Russia to sign and ratify the pending border treaty.

Fourth, support from programmes run by the EU and other international bodies will provide concrete incentives to engage in cooperation projects. There are already strong institutional actors with significant experience of managing international projects and the EU and its various instruments play an important role in supporting cross-border initiatives in the region.[34] The accession of Estonia and Latvia opens up more opportunities for promoting mutually beneficial cultural and economic relationships, and for involving local and regional actors at higher political levels. The opportunities associated with EU membership, then, may strengthen existing cooperation networks (such as the Pskov–Livonia project) and provide the impetus needed to jump-start cooperation in areas (like the north-east) where conflicting interests have so far overshadowed the benefits of cooperation.

Finally, the Baltic States have sought opportunities to play a constructive role in disseminating European and transatlantic values. Participation in peacekeeping missions in Bosnia-Herzegovina and Kosovo and in the US-led 'coalition of the willing' in Afghanistan and Iraq has enabled the Balts to demonstrate that they are not simply security 'consumers' but also security 'providers'.[35] A new area where the Baltic States have started to carve out a niche for themselves relates to the export of their experience of transition and reform to the countries of the Commonwealth of Independent States (CIS). It is clearly in the direct interest of the Baltic States to support democratic reforms in, and to bolster the statehood of, neighbouring countries, such as Belarus and Ukraine, but also the more distant nations of Georgia and Moldova. The EU's European Neighbourhood Policy initiative is expected to give the Baltic States a more active role in this regard.

Overall, therefore, there are good reasons to be hopeful that Estonia's membership of the EU will lead to an improvement in bilateral relations. The reduction of tension will enable, inter alia, a shift in emphasis from 'high politics' concerns to 'low politics' issues. Integration with the West has meant that Estonia has had to distance itself from Russia. Yet, paradoxically, the process will contribute to the normalisation of relations, which has long been the desired objective.

Notes

1 Eurobarometer Surveys on Attitudes of Europeans show that Estonia consistently demonstrated the lowest levels of popular support for the EU of any candidate country. In the accession referendum of 14 September 2003, one-third of participants voted against joining the EU.

2 For the most recent positions, see *Valituse Euroopa Liidu poliitika 2004–2006* (the Estonian government's EU Action Plan for 2004–06), draft bill, 13 February 2004. Of the Estonian political parties, only the opposition Social Democrats, led by former Foreign Minister Toomas Hendrik Ilves, have criticised this approach. See Ilves, T.H., 'Kobamine pimeduses', *Postimees*, 6 April 2004.

3 It was easy to score emotional points in the debate on EU membership by drawing superficial parallels between some of the bureaucratic excesses of the EU and the absurdities of the Soviet Union.

4 Lobjakas, A., 'Estonia Adrift: Caught in the Crosswinds of the EU's Constitutional Debate', in Kasekamp, A. (ed.), *Estonian Foreign Policy Yearbook 2004* (Tallinn: Estonian Foreign Policy Institute, 2004).

5 UK Prime Minister Tony Blair and his Estonian counterpart Juhan Parts even co-authored an article in *The Financial Times* on 3 October 2003, entitled 'The enlarged EU must be free to compete'.

6 Raik, K., 'Does the European Union Still Matter for Estonia's Security? Positioning Estonia in CFSP and ESDP', in Kasekamp, A. (ed.), *Estonian Foreign Policy Yearbook 2003* (Tallinn: Estonian Foreign Policy Institute, 2003).

7 *Valitsuse Euroopa Liidu poliitika 2004–2006.*

8 By 1995, Russia accounted for 17.7% of Estonia's exports and 16.1% of its imports. *Statistical Yearbook of Estonia 1998* (Tallinn: Statistical Office of Estonia, 1998), p. 291.

9 The percentage of ethnic Estonians declined between the end of the Second World War and 1989, from 90% to 65%.

10 See Ivanov, S., 'As NATO Grows, So Do Russia's Worries', *The New York Times*, 7 April 2004.

11 Estonian Ministry of Foreign Affairs, 'Economy at a Glance'; at www.vm.ee/estonia/kat_172/281.html (6 August 2003)

12 Estonian Ministry of Foreign Affairs, 'Bilateral relations: Estonia and Russia', www.vm.ee/eng/kat_176/1430.html (24 October 2003).

13 Estonian Ministry of Foreign Affairs, 'Bilateral relations'.

14 *Valitsuse Euroopa Liidu poliitika 2004–2006.*

15 In fact, many analyses contend that Schengen conflicts with the vital economic or political interests of accession countries,

disrupting established patterns of cross-border movement, as well as economic and political ties and kinship links, and causing economic problems in border regions. See 'Seventeenth Report: Enlargement and EU External Frontier Controls', European Union Committee (British parliament), 24 October 2000; at www.parliament.the-stationery-office.co.uk/pa/ld199900/ldselect/ldeucom/ldeucom.htm. For analyses portraying accession countries as reluctant implementers of Schengen, see Favell, A. and Hansen, R., 'Markets against politics: migration, EU enlargement and the idea of Europe', *Journal of Ethnic and Migration Studies*, Vol. 28, No. 4, pp. 581–601, and Mitsilegas, V., 'The implementation of the EU acquis on illegal immigration by the candidate countries of Central and Eastern Europe: challenges and contradictions', *Journal of Ethnic and Migration Studies*, Vol. 28, No. 4, pp. 665–682.

[16] In August 1998, the government purchased a radar surveillance system from the French military technology producer, Thompson-CSF. In 1999, heat-sensing cameras procured with the support of the Phare programme were integrated into the system.

[17] *Valitsuse Euroopa Liidu poliitika 2004–2006.*

[18] Travel to and from Russia constituted a quarter of all crossings of the Estonian border in 2002. Border Guard of the Republic of Estonia, 'Statistics 1996–2002'; at www.pv.ee.

[19] Ibid.

[20] For a more detailed account of the simplified border-crossing regime and its impact on the regions' residents, see the reports prepared by Eiki Berg and Piret Ehin under the framework of the project 'Impact of EU enlargement and the Schengen treaty in the CEE region', coordinated by the Institute of Public Affairs, Warsaw, Poland; see www.isp.org.pl/libr/pobierz/pmEN.htm.

[21] The simplified border-crossing regime was an important medium for informal small-scale trading, which emerged because of the incentives provided by cross-border differences in prices, wages and pensions. Wages and pensions are about four times higher on the Estonian side, while foodstuffs, alcohol and tobacco are two or three times cheaper on the Russian side.

[22] 'Estonian visa policy is aligned with that of the EU, except for the facilitated border crossing formalities for Russian nationals living in border areas (Narva–Ivangorod). Estonia should continue progressive alignment of visa legislation and practice with that of the EU.' See the European Commission's

1999 Regular Report from the Commission on Estonia's Progress towards Accession. Available at www.europa.eu.int/comm/enla rgement/report_10_99/pdf/en/ estonia_en.pdf.

23 A series of interviews with key actors in the border regions was conducted in 2002–03 by Eiki Berg and Piret Ehin, 'Impact of EU enlargement'.

24 As a result of these changes, Estonia lost 2,334 square kilometres (5%) of its territory.

25 For Estonia, the significance of the Tartu Peace Treaty, which concluded the Estonian War of Independence (1918–20), is far greater than just the definition of borders. By signing the treaty, Soviet Russia recognised the independence of Estonia unconditionally and in perpetuity. This accord remains the cornerstone of Estonia–Russia relations today.

26 The Estonian delegation was headed by Deputy Under-Secretary Raul Mälk, who continued to lead the delegation even after assuming the post of foreign minister in 1998. Ambassador Vassili Svirin led the Russian delegation.

27 Eiki Berg and Saima Oras, 'Kümme Aastat Eesti-Vene piiriläbirääkimisi', in Kasekamp, (ed.), Estonian Foreign Policy Yearbook 2003.

28 Ministry of Foreign Affairs of the Republic of Estonia, 'Estonia and Russia: Border negotiations completed', 29 March 1999; at www.vm.ee/eng/kat_176/1180. html.

29 Ibid.

30 Ibid.

31 'Laar pidas Putiniga sõnasõda', SL-Õhtuleht, 12 April 2004.

32 Comments by former Estonian Foreign Minister Toomas Hendrik Ilves at the conference, 'The New North of Europe', Finnish Institute of International Affairs, Helsinki, Finland, 8 October 2002.

33 Jurado, E., 'Complying with European standards of minority education: Estonia's relations with the European Union, OSCE and Council of Europe', Journal of Baltic Studies, 34(4), Winter 2003, pp. 399–431.

34 The Council for Cross-border Cooperation – a voluntary association for local and regional governments in the border regions of Estonia, Latvia and Russia, founded in 1996 – has received support from a variety of EU instruments, including the Phare CBC and Credo programmes. The activities of a major regional non-governmental organisation (NGO), the Peipsi Centre for Transboundary Cooperation, have been supported by the European Commission, the EU 5th RTD Framework Programme, and the Phare LIEN programme, among others.

35 Jaaks, P., 'Hanson: Iraagi-missioon pole läinud ohtlikumaks', Postimees, 7 August 2003.

12. Sub-Regional Organisations in Action in North-west Russia

Kathryn Pinnick

Northern Europe is host to a number of organisations engaged in cooperation with Russia in general, and with the north-west regions of Russia in particular. The substantial increase in international and inter-regional cooperation in Northern Europe throughout the 1990s was largely due to the parts played by four inter-governmental organisations: the Arctic Council (AC); the Barents Euro-Arctic Council (BEAC); the Council of Baltic Sea States (CBSS); and the Nordic Council of Ministers (NCM). The activities of these sub-regional bodies overlap with the European Union (EU)'s various policy initiatives, such as the Northern Dimension, and assistance programmes (Interreg and Tacis) covering a plethora of policy issues in north-west Russia. They share the broad objective of wanting to build a stable, secure and economically developed region (Northern Europe) based on interdependencies between its constituent states, including Russia.

The remits, strategies and operating mechanisms of the four organisations vary. Their geographic boundaries do not coincide, nor is the composition of their membership uniform (see Table 12.1). Russia is considered part of all four sub-regions because of its contiguous location and through its membership of the AC, the BEAC and the CBSS. These bodies, and the Nordic Council of Ministers, are involved in activities in the Russian Federation, particularly in the north-west border regions of the country.

The Russian border regions in question (the Republic of Karelia, St Petersburg city, and Arkhangelsk, Kaliningrad, Leningrad, Murmansk and Pskov *oblasts*) all had greater strategic and military significance in the Soviet period, hosting nuclear submarines, military technology and military personnel. The north of Europe and the ice-free areas of the Barents Sea were heavily militarised by the Soviet Union's Cold War adversaries, too. Traditional security concerns dominated relations

Table 12.1 Membership of sub-regional organisations working in Russia's north-west

Founded	Arctic Council 1996[1]	Barents Euro-Arctic Council 1993	Council of Baltic Sea States 1992	Nordic Council 1971 (1994)[2]
Canada	●			
Denmark	●	●	●	●
Estonia			●	
European Commission		●	●	
Finland	●	●	●	●
Germany			●	
Iceland	●	●	●	●
Latvia			●	
Lithuania			●	
Norway	●	●	●	●
Poland			●	
Russia	●	●	●	
Sweden	●	●	●	●
US	●			

1. The formation of the Council institutionalised the Arctic Environmental Protection Strategy (AEPS), which had been launched by the same eight states in 1991. 2. It has only encompassed external affairs since 1994

between the Soviet Union and neighbouring states in Northern Europe. There were, however, some cultural and scientific exchanges between Russia and its North European neighbours during the Cold War, but at times, such activities were held hostage due to a deterioration in inter-governmental relations. Since the collapse of the Soviet Union in 1991, cross-border cooperation between the border regions of Russia and communities in neighbouring states has increased significantly. Many of the projects fostering human contact and training in the arts, education and science have taken place under the auspices of the four sub-regional organisations.

From the start of the post-Cold War era, these organisations have adopted an inclusive approach towards Russia, and have aimed to normalise relations in the wider region by 'building bridges' between communities over the border. This strategy reflects the new approach to Russia that North European governments have pursued since the collapse of the Soviet Union; the rationale behind cooperation with Russia remained the meeting of national security goals, but through friendly interaction rather than adversarial militarisation. The new strategy shifted policy from high politics on the inter-state level, as had been the case when relations with Soviet Russia and control of the border were politically sensitive, to the level of low politics. The sub-regional organisations now engage directly with regional administrations, non-governmental organisations (NGOs), educational establishments, and businesses.

Sub-regional cooperation has focused on dealing with the legacy of militarisation, for example, the cleaning up of radioactive waste from nuclear-powered submarines in Murmansk *oblast*. Not only are military and environmental issues closely linked in this part of the world, but also the interrelation between economic growth and new security challenges is a key area of concern. The new challenges are instability, unpredictability, and negative social and economic factors; one of the objectives of the sub-regional organisations is to keep these trends in check.[1] Russia's border regions are characterised by low standards of living: a consequence of the loss of state incentives for workers to live and work there and the closure of industrial enterprises. Hand in hand with poverty go socio-economic and health problems, such as crime, disease and pollution. These 'soft security threats' often have a transnational character and for this reason they have captured the interest of, and attracted resources from, actors in the wider region (not only participating states like Norway, but also the EU and the US). Cooperation at the sub-regional level is of a functional nature: it addresses common interests or challenges that require international solutions. Russia has largely welcomed these initiatives and financial injections from its richer neighbours. But, after approximately a decade in existence, the achievements of, and the prospects for, the sub-regional organisations are the subject of debate, including by residents of the border regions, especially those in Russia. A review of activities shows how Russia has benefited from the cooperation projects, but it also raises questions about the effectiveness of the sub-regional organisations and their readiness to engage with Russia following enlargement of the EU on 1 May 2004.

Policy areas of interaction
Soft security
Projects aimed at dealing with soft security challenges are high on the agenda of the inter-governmental organisations in Northern Europe. The AC mainly runs projects that deal with environmental and sustainable-development issues.[2] Many of the AC's projects in Russia are concerned with clearing up nuclear waste, such as those run by the Arctic Monitoring and Assessment Programme (AMAP). It works with the Nordic Environment Finance Corporation (NEFCO), a risk-capital institution financing environmental projects in Central and Eastern Europe.[3] Projects in the neighbouring region (mainly in Russia) are deemed to be of benefit to the ecology of the Nordic region as a whole. AMAP and NEFCO released a joint report in 1995 on international cooperation on nuclear safety, which had a number of significant outcomes.[4] It led to the establishment of the EU's Northern Dimension Environmental Partnership and an EU contribution of €150 million to resolve nuclear-waste problems in north-west Russia and encouraged Russia to sign the Multilateral Nuclear Environmental Programme for Russia (MNEPR) in May 1995, along with its main backers and financial sponsors – Belgium, Denmark, the European Commission, Finland, France, Sweden, Netherlands, Norway, the UK and the US.[5] Funds have been directed at handling and storing spent nuclear fuel and radioactive waste from decommissioned nuclear submarines in north-west Russia. The BEAC also runs projects that concentrate on treating Russian nuclear waste and spent fuel (on the Kola Peninsula).

Steps have been taken to improve safety at nuclear power plants. For instance, the EU, Finland, Norway and the US have contributed $10m to the AC project at the Kola nuclear power station in Polyarny Zory. The CBSS Working Group on Nuclear and Radiation Safety assesses safety at nuclear power plants in Russia. Guided by the working group, all CBSS member states signed an Agreement for the Exchange of Radiation Monitoring Data in 2003. Radioactive contamination of the Barents Sea caused by discharges from the Atomflot liquid radioactive waste treatment plant in Murmansk *oblast* is being monitored, but the intention is to expand significantly environmental monitoring of releases of radioactive material from civilian and military sources.[6]

The four councils also address environmental issues of a non-nuclear nature, which affect the entire region. There is a particular focus on pollution, for example, the cleaning up of contaminated areas (landfills or illegal disposal sites) in north-west Russia. Thanks to funding from the Nordic Council, Canada, Denmark and Russia, a joint AMAP–Russia station to monitor contaminants is in operation at Amderma (Nenets autonomous region). A total of $11.2m has been pledged by NEFCO, Denmark, Sweden and the US for the Arctic Council Action Plan to phase out the use of PCB (polychlorinated biphenyl) toxic pollutants in Russia. Arkhangelsk, Komi and Murmansk have been designated priority regions. The sub-regional organisations have attracted some criticism for weak programme management. Different AC working groups have run almost identical programmes on the environment in Russia and have sought funding from the same source simultaneously. For instance, projects on pollution and the elimination of contaminants in north-west Russia have been run by AMAP, the Arctic Council Action Plan to Eliminate Pollution in the Arctic and the Arctic Council Protection of the Marine Environment.[7] The AC has recognised this problem and is addressing it.

If the projects initiated over the past 12 years are to be sustained, and if new ones are to be launched, greater injections of investment will be required – in addition to coordination of assistance programmes. Projects in Russia often suffer from a lack of commitment by the Russians in relation to the provision of financial resources or the taking of appropriate action. For some projects, Russia has advocated making payments in kind rather than providing financial capital, but, in the end, foreign partners are often left without a contribution from Russia. There are administrative obstacles on the Russian side, too; the Russian regional authorities sometimes fail to put pressure on the businesses and factories that emit the pollutants and Russian ministries have not been efficient at compiling inventories of obsolete pesticides. While the foreign partners would admit that it is a challenge to understand the vagaries associated with political realities in Russia, they do perceive a lack of commitment by Russia in regard to international cooperation on the environment. The councils work with Russian ecological NGOs to help them to put pressure on regional governments and polluting companies.

Russian project partners comprise a diverse set of entities: national governments, regional administrations, civil-society actors, including indigenous communities and NGOs, the Ministry for Atomic Energy (until it was incorporated into the Ministry of Industry and Energy in March 2004), the Ministry for Economic Development, research institutes and private companies like Norilsk Nickel.

The sub-regional organisations strive to reach out to local-level actors to resolve soft security problems, for example, practitioners from the border guards services, police forces, and emergency and rescue services. During the accession period for the new EU members, the councils became increasingly active in relation to non-environmental trans-border threats. The CBSS Civil Security Programme has established a special Task Force on Organised Crime and is coordinating the efforts of its member states to enhance surveillance at sea. The Nordic Council of Ministers places more emphasis on public health issues and on trafficking in human beings, especially women. Activities in the field of security, justice and home affairs are now being integrated into the EU's Second Northern Dimension Action Plan (2004–06) (see below). The starting point for these projects is the assumption that sustainable development is key to security. For this reason, the sub-regional bodies run programmes that target Russia's economic integration into the wider region.

Economic integration and sustainability
The BEAC, the CBSS and the Nordic Council of Ministers have grand aspirations for sub-regionalism in the sphere of economic development. The goals of the BEAC are industrial renewal and the promotion of regional policy through trade, economic cooperation and business. Through cooperation with the north-west region of Russia and other adjacent areas (Estonia, Faroe Islands, Greenland, Latvia and Lithuania), the Nordic Council is seeking to encourage stable development and to contribute to the creation of a functioning market economy in Northern Europe. One of the three main policy goals of the CBSS is to boost economic integration in the Baltic region through transport, energy and business projects. A regional policy or regional spatial planning, however, remains a distant dream due to economic disparities between Russia, the new EU members in the region, and their richer Scandinavian neighbours. The business and economics-oriented projects of the councils support economic reforms and regulatory convergence in Russia. Trade restrictions on the EU/European Economic Area (EEA) and Russia are also an impediment to economic integration.

The councils are trying to reduce the barriers to trade that exist across the border between the EU/EEA and Russia. The CBSS Working Group on Economic Cooperation and the CBSS Customs Liaison Committee have brought together customs authorities and border guards from the different states in order to coordinate border management. The EuroRussia Customs Programme (involving Finnish, Russian and Swedish customs committees, and occurring under the umbrella of the EU Northern Dimension initiative) and Chambers of Commerce from the Baltic States, including Russia, have made a contribution to this objective.

The BEAC also has a border-management programme and works with customs authorities and businesses from the border regions to facilitate cross-border trade. As a result of these meetings and seminars, pledges have been made to cut the waiting time to cross the border between Russia and Finland or Norway.

Cross-border trade and commercial cooperation – which the councils are seeking to foster – between the Baltic, Barents and Nordic countries and Russia are on the rise.[8] Norwegian trawlers have been built at the Zvezdochka shipyard in Severodvinsk, and joint projects are taking place in the fields of agriculture and energy. The positive role played by the BEAC in promoting the development of Russia's north-west regions was acknowledged by the Russian Ministry of Foreign Affairs delegation at a meeting of the BEAC in 2003. A spokesperson pointed to the modernisation of the Pechenganickel plant, the opening of the Sturskug–Borisoglebsk crossing point on the Norwegian–Russian border, and commercial use of the Arctic Sea Route.[9]

Nevertheless, then Russian Foreign Minister Igor Ivanov berated the sub-regional organisation for its lack of assistance in relation to the economic development of north-west Russia. He stated that Russia's neighbours were not paying due attention to Russia's proposals, such as: upgrading airports in north-west Russia through a joint investment programme; regular cargo shipments by neighbouring states on the northern sea route between Europe and the Asia–Pacific region; investment in infrastructure to extract oil and gas from the continental shelf in the Barents Sea;[10] and deeper involvement in trade and investment cooperation in general. Ivanov is right that economic cooperation within the BEAC and the other sub-regional organisations has not yet led to massive investment (and certainly little direct foreign investment) in the underdeveloped parts of the region.[11] Of all the policy areas, cooperation in the economic sphere has been the least successful.

Political development and civil–society contacts
Sub-regional cooperation has, on the whole, been apolitical. By keeping issues of high politics, such as security and territorial integrity, off the agenda, the sub-regional organisations have been able to foster cooperation between Russia and its neighbouring states during a period of political tension – due to enlargement of the EU and the North Atlantic Treaty Organisation (NATO). The CBSS, which comprises old and new EU members, as well as Russia, believes that it has played an important role in bringing all parties together in a dialogue on politically neutral policy areas and getting them involved in associated activities. The application of the Baltic States to join NATO was not discussed within the CBSS, nor did the CBSS make a contribution to the resolution of the dispute between the

EU and Russia over Kaliningrad transit, citing the lack of a mandate to discuss matters pertinent to Russia's territorial integrity.

The CBSS assumed a political dimension between 1994 and 2003 in the form of its Commissioner for Democratic Institutions and Human Rights. The Commissioner produced reports on democratic practices in the Baltic region, for example, on obstacles to travel between member states, but sought to avoid the contentious issue of the human rights of Russian minorities in Estonia and Latvia. The commissioner did highlight individual cases of alleged human-rights abuses but most of them were not controversial; over half of the cases in 2001 concerned families separated by national borders. It is alleged that Estonia put pressure on the CBSS to wind down this aspect of the council's work.[12] Yet the decision taken by the CBSS to abolish the post of commissioner from the end of 2003 was consistent with the seal of approval given to the Baltic States for their treatment of minorities by the Council of Europe and the Organisation for Security and Co-operation in Europe (OSCE) and because 'democratic institutions in the region have reached a level of maturity allowing the CBSS to scale down its work in this area'.[13] The functions of the commissioner have been integrated into the CBSS Working Group on Democratic Institutions.

All of the sub-regional organisations promote the development of civil society and the spread of democratic values across their member states. This is a priority area for the Nordic Council of Ministers, which devotes the majority of its resources to its Democracy and Welfare Programme. With the long-term aim of fostering a regional identity, the Nordic Council of Ministers' approach to the strengthening of democracy involves promoting shared values and informing Russia about the Nordic welfare model. Funding is directed at achieving gender equality, improving access to healthcare, and bettering the position of young people, as well as at supporting NGOs and the media and encouraging cultural exchange.[14] There is also a para-diplomatic component: a study tour programme, whereby Russian regional politicians and civil servants meet their peers from the Nordic states. All four organisations are engaged in cross-border cooperation projects that facilitate contact between people and between NGOs and that encourage the advancement of education and culture. The CBSS provides support for curriculum development in the fields of law and economics at the Eurofaculty, Kaliningrad University – an initiative that was set up with the financial assistance of Denmark, Germany, Lithuania, Norway, Poland, Sweden and the UK.

Cross-border cooperation in the human-interest areas of education and culture is considered to be the policy sphere in which most success has been achieved. Apolitical in nature, it has been possible to establish people-to-people contacts on different levels (with national, regional and municipal administrations) and with a variety of non-state actors. However, the councils all bemoan the challenge of operating at the sub-national level.

Participation by sub-national actors

The introduction of new border regimes by Estonia, Latvia, Lithuania and Poland could create new impediments to cooperation projects between the sub-regional organisations and Russia. Russian participants in cross-border cooperation projects will require Schengen visas from 2006 in order to meet with their peers in these states. The CBSS has commissioned research studies on relations between Pskov *oblast* and the regional authorities in neighbouring Estonia and Latvia, with the aim of identifying obstacles to cross-border cooperation and their causes. Norway has much experience of cross-border cooperation with Russia as an EEA (but not EU) member; a Schengen regime has been in place there since 2001. Consequently, there is optimism that BEAC and Nordic cooperation projects could serve as an example of best practice in relation to the new external borders of the EU in the Baltic States and Poland.[15] The evidence so far supports the conclusion that a Russian region with foreign consulates, such as Murmansk, which hosts those of Finland and Norway, has a greater capacity to engage in cross-border cooperation than a region without foreign consulates. Such regions suffer disproportionately and local and regional contacts with neighbouring states are prone to disruption as a result of the time and cost associated with travelling to a consulate.[16] Russians wishing to travel to Finland and Norway have become used to the extra paperwork required to obtain a Schengen visa, but complain about the fact that it has become more difficult to obtain multiple-entry visas.

Sub-regional organisations increasingly prefer the partner in a given project in Russia to come from the sub-national level, from a regional authority or civil society. Since 2002, the CBSS has been pursuing greater interaction at the local level, partly spurred on by a call to do so from Ivanov when Russia held the CBSS presidency in 2001–02.[17] The CBSS identified Kaliningrad, Leningrad and Pskov *oblasts*, as well as the city of St Petersburg, as target areas for increased cooperation and the promotion of local government development projects on both sides of the new EU–Russia border. The Baltic Sea States Sub-regional Cooperation (BSSSC) Council within the CBSS encourages contact between regions and municipalities. Its Secretariat aims to represent the regions in national, European and international organisations. Similarly, a key component of the BEAC is the Barents Euro-Arctic Regional Council (BEARC), which operates on the sub-national level.[18] The BEARC not only runs an array of programmes, but it also seeks to balance the national objectives of member states with political priorities on the regional and local levels. The BEARC, which has a Secretariat in the Norwegian town of Kirkenes on the border with Murmansk *oblast*, grants regions (sub-national entities) the same degree of representation as national governments enjoy at the inter-governmental level of the BEAC. Of the four sub-regional organisations in Russia's north-west, the BEAC has arguably been the most effective on the sub-national level.

The Nordic Council made north-west Russia the primary target of its Adjacent Areas Programme in 2000 and planned to launch a special action plan in the area before the end of 2004.[19] Less expenditure is foreseen for Nordic Council projects in the three Baltic States due to the assumption that they will benefit from EU-funded projects. One-fifth of the total budget for 2004 (almost €20m) of the Nordic Council of Ministers has been earmarked for existing and new projects that involve Russia.[20] The programme's goal is to promote stability and democracy in areas adjacent to the Nordic countries, particularly in Kaliningrad, Leningrad and Pskov *oblasts*.

The capacity of the sub-national bodies

Governance in participating states is one of the primary obstacles to implementation of the programmes of the sub-regional organisations. Norway, in particular, has expressed frustration at structural imbalances or discrepancies in the political capacity of the BEARC's constituent regions and judges this to be the main hindrance to effective cross-border cooperation at the sub-national level. While the three regions of Norway have enough political and financial power to engage effectively in cross-border cooperation, power is more centralised in Finland and Sweden, while the Russian regions have an unclear political mandate. Within Russia, the predominance of the vertical structure of executive power raises three main problems. First, the capacity of the Russian regions to act is limited and it is not always clear to the foreign actor looking for a Russian partner how much authority a regional or municipal administration has to interact internationally. Second, horizontal links between the Russian regions are weak, so that they are more likely to be in competition for funding and projects than partners in cooperation ventures. Third, the state (ministries) or the federal government may interfere in the work of experts or practitioners on the ground. Russia's regional administrations and municipalities know this; they argue that cross-border cooperation would benefit if they had greater authority to manage external relations.

Russian President Vladimir Putin's federal reforms and the future of the federal districts are seen as a source of unpredictability, and are a cause of concern for the sub-regional organisations. The creation of the federal districts has not meant that the border regions have less opportunity to pursue cross-border cooperation projects with foreign partners. The presidential plenipotentiaries, however, do check that the regions engage only in foreign economic activity and do not interact directly with any national government (the prerogative of the Russian federal administration). If the federal districts become a permanent feature of the Russian political hierarchy, bodies like the BEAC and the CBSS might be more effective if they had contact with the North-west Federal District (NWFD), particularly if there was a coordinated policy within the district that all of the constituent regions contributed to, as well as availability of federal funds for implementing programmes. This would address the current problem of a lack of 'a clear and distinct policy [in Russia] towards the Barents region. Russian northern regions included in the Barents region are not involved in joint action and this also prevents them from formulating a single policy within [the] BEARC.'[21] This is true of Russia's participation in Arctic, Baltic and Nordic sub-regional structures, too.

Coordination between the organisations and the EU

Typically, one factor contributing to the failure of transnational organisations is competition between member states. In Northern Europe, the competition is between the international organisations themselves and with EU programmes like the Northern Dimension. The result is overlapping programmes in Russia, due to the lack of information exchange between actors. The councils are pursuing similar objectives and activities. Overlap is clearly a waste of financial and human resources. A report commissioned by the Norwegian Ministry of Foreign Affairs in 2000 proposed better coordination to enable the sub-regional organisations to identify best practice and to transfer this to other entities. Synergies would then be achieved and duplication avoided. It is possible that these shortcomings will be allayed as a result of EU enlargement; the accession process has given the councils and the EU an impetus to work more closely together. The EU wants the sub-regional organisations to play a greater role in implementing its Second Northern Dimension Action Plan (2004–06).[22] Regarding cross-border cooperation, the plan states that 'better results will be achieved by building on existing examples of tri-partite [local actors, communities and administrations] cooperation and by using the expertise of regional and sub-regional bodies such as … the Barents Regional Council'.[23] Project networking is now being advocated to encourage the interlocking of working groups from each council and from EU-funded projects. The sub-regional organisations will support the EU in its efforts to implement projects with Russia in the five priority areas of the Second Northern Dimension Action Plan.

- **Economy, Business and Infrastructure** Engaging in efforts to tackle trade barriers through the CBSS Business Advisory Council, increasing the involvement of regional business actors through the Barents Working Group on Economic Cooperation, and networking between regulatory bodies and consumers through the Nordic Council of Ministers.
- **Human Resources, Education, Culture and Public Health** The BEARC's regional network plan linking national and regional project leaders and the Nordic Council's Partnership for Health and Well-being, which involves the other three councils, the World Health Organisation and the United Nations Programme on HIV/AIDS.
- **Environment, Nuclear Safety and Natural Resources** Monitoring of pollutants by the AC and the exchange of data on radiation monitoring between CBSS members.
- **Cross-Border Cooperation** Exchange of information on best practice in regard to cross-border cooperation with Russia, organised by the Nordic Council of Ministers.
- **Justice and Home Affairs** The CBSS Task Force on Organised Crime will work more closely with other multilateral bodies to address issues concerning law enforcement, while the Nordic Council will encourage networking between courts and prosecutors in the Baltic and Nordic countries to combat organised crime and illegal migration.

This all sounds well and good, but, without a special unit in the European Commission to implement the Northern Dimension and the anticipated new EU strategy towards Russia, comprehensive coordination is unlikely. And nor will sub-regionalism, or the establishment of a dense network of sub-regional linkages (one of the objectives of the Northern Dimension), become a reality.

Funding constraints
Closer coordination between the councils might also be restricted by their access to funding. Only the Nordic Council has an operational budget and can therefore plan for the long term. Coordination would be easier (and the effect on the Russian regions more positive) if all of the councils were able to make long-term project plans. The Secretariats of the AC, the BEAC and the CBSS are funded through annual contributions from stakeholder states, but these contributions do not include resources for projects. They raise finance from a variety of sources on a project basis. The EU contributes to the whole range of projects, often through the Interreg and Tacis mechanisms, while the European Council and the Council of Europe fund youth programmes. Projects dealing with environmental challenges have been prioritised as a result of the supply

of national funding from Russia's neighbours, the EU and the US. A mixture of public and private finance is available for business and trade projects; for example, the BEAC border-management project, costing €0.5m, was funded by the EU, regional and municipal authorities in the regions of Finland that border Russia, Finnish and Russian Chambers of Commerce, and individual businesses. Private-sector investment has not been significant, however, and the lion's share of funds from Russia's rich neighbours has come from governments and international financial institutions, such as the European Bank for Reconstruction and Development and the Nordic Investment Bank. Project partners in Finland and Norway have been successful in their bids to obtain share capital or loans and guarantees, whereas Russian project partners and companies find it very difficult to acquire such funding. Some loans from the North-west Savings Bank (part of Sberbank) and the federal government have been forthcoming. Foreign partners often voice frustration that Russian participants are unable to find their own sources of finance.

On the whole, though, the councils believe that there is enough finance for their projects but that the funds need to be better managed. This is a challenge, since financiers have different rules on how their funds should be spent. Co-funding of related activities by the four councils and the EU would ensure more effective project outcomes. The new Northern Dimension Action Plan states that a new Neighbourhood Instrument might also come into being for the funding of cross-border cooperation initiatives; the councils are calling for the EU to provide adequate financing through a permanent funding instrument for the Northern Dimension.

No political conditionality is tied to assistance from the sub-regional organisations and decision-making practices appear equitable in principle. However, since the funding comes from rich neighbours, the donors, in effect, have a large degree of control. In fact, the sub-regional organisations can be seen to be reinforcing the uneven distribution of economic and political power. To counter the view of sceptics that the rich countries of Northern Europe and the four sub-regional organisations are more interested in market access than in the sustainable development of the Russian border regions per se, the sub-regional organisations and the EU are endeavouring to increase 'ownership' of cross-border cooperation projects by the Russian recipients. An objective of the Nordic Council is to ensure that activities 'correspond more closely with the wishes of the host countries' by giving Russian partners a say in the choice of projects. The lack of Russian funds – public or private – will, however, restrict the prospects for subsidiarity now advocated by the EU and the sub-regional entities. To apply the principle that action should take place at the lowest and most prudent level is not straightforward in Russia, where the financial and political capacity of the regions to act remains restricted.

For the most part, the programmes run and funded by regional bodies, together with the projects of the EU, are welcomed in Russia as a local-level mechanism to facilitate human contact and, more broadly, to bring the country further into Europe. It is for this reason that the councils are seen as an essential external resource in Russia's development (in terms of finance, knowledge, advice and technology). At the same time, the level of development in Russia's border regions is a barrier to real engagement – they lack modern infrastructure, particularly in the areas of transport and technology, including information and communications technology. Increased interaction has revealed the extent of this disparity between north-west Russia and neighbouring regions across the border. Meanwhile, the accession of the Baltic States to the EU is generating a greater flow of resources on the wealthier side of the frontier. The stated aim of the projects run by the Nordic Council of Ministers in north-west Russia is to reduce this socio-economic asymmetry.

Prospects for sub-regionalism

Following enlargement, the border regions of north-west Russia have contiguous frontiers with either EU or EEA member states. The four sub-regional councils still preside over a divided economic area. On the whole, and despite the shortcomings, the sub-regional bodies are having a positive impact on Russia's integration into Europe by building links across the borders between the EU and Russia. These organisations have achieved most success in their programmes on the environment and in regard to human contact in the spheres of research and higher education. Despite setbacks in the area of economic cooperation, the Russian border regions have received a boost to their development from the sub-regional bodies and this is facilitating the integration of the Russian border regions into Northern Europe. The sub-regional organisations have fostered an increase in political, social and economic interaction between Russia and Northern European states and mutual dependencies exist. However, the space cannot yet be considered a 'regionalised international area'.[24] Real sub-regional processes have not taken root; although there is plenty of talk about bottom-up initiatives, it is often mere rhetoric in official declarations.[25] Critics say that the CBSS has too full a diary of seminars and conferences, which have sometimes been judged to be lacking in focus and that no concrete results have emerged from numerous BEAC meetings and visits by delegations.[26] Most Russians in the north-west have not been touched by the array of programmes.

The lack of resources and power has served to limit action, yet the overarching problem is that there is not an inclusive cooperation strategy, or an overall mechanism to guide sub-regional cooperation, providing direction to all of the participating actors. This is now being addressed. The EU is claiming the leading role, with the sub-regional organisations contributing to the process. It is to be hoped that the EU will expand, not restrict, the capacity of the councils. However, expertise and resources need to be consolidated; cross-border interaction will then move on to a new, more effective level and Russia will reap more benefits from it.[27]

The institutional network in the Baltic and Nordic area has the potential to become a tighter-knit (rather than loose) operational arrangement based on alliances involving EU members (original and new), EEA members, and non-EU members like Russia.[28] In the context of an enlarged European Union, the four sub-regional bodies are more likely to expand than contract and the dense network of interdependency will grow. The centre of interaction as a result of the accession of the Baltic States to the EU will shift eastwards, to north-west Russia. Increased cooperation with Russia through the sub-regional organisations (particularly in cases where the new members – Poland and the Baltic States – are involved) is essential so that the impact of EU enlargement is positive for Russia. The sub-regional organisations challenged the division of Europe after the Cold War and will continue to do so following EU enlargement in order to prevent Russia from being isolated from processes in the rest of Europe. Europe is more than the EU and the four sub-regional bodies reflect this fact.

Notes

1 Joenniemi, P., 'The Barents Euro-Arctic Council', in Cottey, A. (ed.), *Subregional Cooperation in the New Europe* (Basingstoke: Macmillan Press, 1999), p. 41.

2 See the website of the Arctic Council: www.arctic-council.org.

3 It was established in 1990 by the five Nordic countries (Denmark, Finland, Iceland, Norway and Sweden).

4 The report, *Environmentally Sound Investment projects in the Russian part of the Barents Region*, was followed up in 2003 by another, *Updating of Environmental Hot Spots List in Russian Part of the Barents Region*; see www.amap.no.

5 The Arctic Council helped to resolve the disputes between Russia and European officials concerning liability for any accidents and the initial insistence of the Russian authorities on taxing the financial assistance of the donors.

6 'Progress Report on Barents Region Environmental Hot Spot Projects' (Oslo: Nordic Environment Finance Corporation (NEFCO), 1998), available online at www.nefco.org/progr.htm.

7 Palosaari, T., 'The Northern Dimension – The Arctic Component', paper delivered at a seminar on The Future of the Barents Region and the Northern Dimension, Kiruna, Sweden, 14–17 June 2001; at www.bd.lst.se/dimensionen/rapport/11.pdf.

8 Norwegian exports to Russia increased from NOK 1.7 billion in 2000 to NOK 2.4bn in 2001 ($231m in 2000 to $327m in 2001). The greatest increase has been in relation to exports of fish and seafood, according to data from the Norwegian Ministry of Foreign Affairs; see http://odin.dep.no.

9 Alexander Yakovenko, a spokesperson for the Russian Ministry of Foreign Affairs, speaking prior to the opening of the BEARC meeting in Umea, Sweden, on 2 October 2003. Interfax, 2 October 2003.

10 For exploitation of the reserves to become part of a sub-regional development strategy, a territorial dispute between Norway and Russia over the underwater zone where the deposits lie has to be resolved.

11 'International Perspectives on the Future of the Barents Euro-Arctic Region and the Northern Dimension (Part 1)', Report 4 from a think-tank seminar in Bjorkliden, Sweden, 14–17 June 2001 (Lulea: Swedish Initiative of the BEAC and the Northern Dimension, 2002), p. 87.

12 Birkenbach, H.M., 'Strengthening dialogue and coordination between the multitude of actors: the role of international organisations', in Birkenbach, H.M. and Wellmann, C. (eds), *The Kaliningrad Challenge: Options and*

Recommendations (Munster: Lit Verlag, 2003), p. 66.

[13] See the commissioner's website at www.cbss-commissioner.org.

[14] See the website of the Nordic Council and Council of Ministers at www.norden.org.

[15] Rafaelsen, R., 'Concrete Results of Cooperation in the Barents Region', paper presented at the conference entitled 'EU Enlargement and Russia's Border Regions: Borders without Dividing Lines', Kaliningrad State University, 21–22 February 2003, and *Barents Journal*, BEAC, No. 1, 2002, p. 6

[16] Since Finland and Norway joined Schengen, Russians wishing to visit have had to provide more documentation than was required under the previous visa regime (such as return travel tickets and insurance papers).

[17] See the CBSS website at www.cbss.st.

[18] The Regional Council consists of representatives from the member regions which are Lapland in Finland, Finmark, Nordland and Troms in Norway, Arkhangelsk, Karelia and Murmansk *oblasts* and the Nenets autonomous region in the Russian Federation and Norrbotten and Vasterbotten in Sweden.

[19] Jan-Erik Enestam, Minister for Nordic Cooperation, Finland, in a speech to the meeting of the Nordic Council of Ministers, Helsinki, 14–15 April 2004; at www.norden.org.

[20] Ibid.

[21] Ibid.

[22] The Second Northern Dimension Action Plan (2004–2006); at www.europa.eu.int/comm/exter nal_relations/north_dim/ndap/ ap2.htm. p.26.

[23] Ibid. p. 13.

[24] Heininen, L., 'The regional dynamics of the European North in the 1990s – a case study of different actors', in *International Perspectives on the Future of the Barents Euro-Arctic Region and the Northern Dimension* (Part 2), Report 5 from a think-tank seminar (Lulea: Swedish Initiative of the BEAC and the Northern Dimension, 2002), p. 36.

[25] Shklar, N., 'Russian regions in subregional cooperation', in Dwan, R. and Pavliuk, O. (eds), *Building Security in the New States of Eurasia: Subregional Cooperation in the Former Soviet Space* (Armonk: M. E. Sharpe, 2000), p.111.

[26] Goldin, V., 'BEAR – uroki istorii, sovremennost, budushchee' ('BEAR – The Lessons of History, the Present and the Future'), *Barents Journal*, BEAC, No. 1, 2002, p. 58.

[27] See a comment on the EU forcing regional actors to 'play by the rules defined by this supranational body'. Godzimirski, J., ' Russian and Norwegian Interests in the North: Parallels and Gaps', in *Focal Point North-West Russia: the Future of the Barents Euro-Arctic*

*Region and the Northern
Dimension*, Report 3 (Lulea:
Swedish Initiative of the BEAC
and the Northern Dimension,
2002), p. 86.
[28] Heininen, L. *International
Perspectives* (Part 2), Report 5,
p. 34.

PART THREE

13. A Regional Strategy for Kaliningrad

Andrey Klemeshev and Gennady Fedorov

The Baltic region is an area of intense cooperation between the European Union (EU) and Russia. The region is gradually becoming not only a geographical concept, but also an economic, social and even political entity. Integration processes are especially active, since they are supported by the federal government, as well as by the Kaliningrad *oblast* administration, the business community and non-governmental organisations.

Kaliningrad has become a prominent centre of international cooperation – it is home to numerous pilot projects and programmes in which Russian and Western experts play an active role. Following EU enlargement, Kaliningrad *oblast* became an enclave within the EU, and may face a number of economic, social and political problems as a result. How these problems are tackled will depend on the state of the EU–Russia partnership as a whole.

The regional strategy

At the regional level, the key policy initiative is the 'Strategy for the social-economic development of Kaliningrad *oblast* as a region of cooperation for the period until 2010', ratified by the Kaliningrad Duma on 19 April 2003. A declaration affirming a strategic partnership to implement this strategy has been signed by Kaliningrad's administration, the regional Duma (parliament), the Municipality of Kaliningrad and non-governmental organisations, such as the regional association of municipalities.

The strategy is based on research organised by the Kaliningrad administration, and conducted by academics from Kaliningrad State University. It assesses several important Tacis projects for the region, and incorporates indicative planning, a 'SWOT' (strengths/weaknesses/opportunities/threats) analysis (see Table 13.1), and forecasting. It has been discussed in business, public and political circles. Municipalities were involved in proposals and discussions at working groups. The federal government in Moscow also influenced the process: there is a federal programme for Kaliningrad, and the Russian government provides subsidies to the *oblast* and sets the rules of its Special Economic Zone (SEZ).

The experience of the 1990s demonstrated that external factors by themselves cannot guarantee the dynamic development of the Kaliningrad *oblast*. Neither the Free Economic Zone (FEZ), designed to attract investors, nor the federal programme for the development of the SEZ, which relied on the support of the federal government in Moscow, gave the necessary impetus or laid the foundation for the development of Kaliningrad *oblast*. Qualitative changes are needed in the region itself, in those sectors where there are prospects for economic growth.

At the same time, however, it is also clear that the kind of self-reliance attempted by the regional administration in the second half of the 1990s, which took no account of external factors and which yielded no positive results, is also without promise. The region is small both in size and economic potential, which means that all the main stimuli for development are outside, within Russia proper and international markets. Striving for autonomy will only be damaging.

Three core elements of the regional strategy

The regional development strategy must have three dimensions: regional, federal and international.

The regional component consists of developing market conditions in the *oblast*. This might proceed faster in Kaliningrad than elsewhere in Russia given the proximity of EU countries and their developed market economies. Kaliningrad's enclave status should allow it to incorporate essential elements of a market economy, which can later be utilised by other Russian regions.

The federal component means that Kaliningrad develops in the interests of the Russian Federation as a whole; in this respect, the significance for Russia of Kaliningrad's external relations is considerable. The Russian federal government should pay particular attention to this, as well as to Kaliningrad's extra-territorial location. It cannot be ruled out that Moscow might favour direct control over key sectors of Kaliningrad's economy.

The international aspect of the regional strategy requires Russia and Western Europe to acknowledge Kaliningrad's special place in their relations, and to intensify cooperation between the region and the EU.

Table 13.1 Strengths, weaknesses, opportunities and threats in Kaliningrad *oblast*

Strengths

1. Proximity to well-developed regions of Russia.
2. Proximity to well-developed countries in Europe.
3. Mild climate (compared to most of Russia).
4. Access to the sea.
5. Availability of mineral resources (amber, oil).
6. Intense land use.
7. Dense transport network.
8. Well-developed market environment (by Russian standards).
9. High education levels.
10. Scientific potential.
11. SEZ and federal programme of regional development.
12. Russia's evolving partnership with NATO.

Weaknesses

1. Isolation.
2. Differences in land-use conditions.
3. Cold climate (compared to most of Europe).
4. Lack of deep-water ports.
5. Poor energy supply.
6. High power load.
7. Poor-quality transport.
8. Poorly-developed market environment (by European standards).
9. Labour training poorly matched to needs of the economy.
10. Weak demand for science.
11. Unstable conditions for economic activity.
12. Uncertain geopolitical environment.

Opportunities

1. Access to the Russian market.
2. Development of external relations.
3. Low salaries.
4. Use of cheap marine transport.
5. Exploitation of local raw materials.
6. Intensification of social and economic relations in the region.
7. Gateways to European transport network.
8. High rate of development.
9. Integration with European education system.
10. International scientific projects.
11. Relations with neighbouring states.
12. Baltic Sea as a 'sea of peace'.

Threats

1. Autarky.
2. Difficult entry to the EU market.
3. Rising costs.
4. Competition from Baltic countries' ports.
5. Potential deficiencies in delivery of energy.
6. Mounting ecological problems.
7. Exclusion from European transport network.
8. Decreasing rate of development.
9. High unemployment rate and low labour productivity.
10. Degradation of scientific potential.
11. Economic stagnation.
12. Potential threat of conflict.

The regional component

It is in Kaliningrad's interests for its economy to be rapidly restructured, to adapt swiftly to the new economic and geopolitical situation post-EU enlargement and to orient itself towards both domestic and international markets. Some of the *oblast's* large and medium-sized enterprises are beyond revival; others are unable to restore their former capacity. Thus, as well as attracting domestic and foreign investment to the industrial sectors which in the past were the most dynamic, it is also necessary to create new industrial projects and to develop new specialised sectors of the economy in areas such as transport, information technology, tourism and the service industry. All this must be done together with neighbouring regions and other Russian regions.

On a regional level, the strategy calls for improved information and publicity; capital investment in basic infrastructure; regional legislation to stimulate capital investment; a new version of the regional law on the SEZ; the creation of a system of small-business centres; a thorough study of the effects of previously adopted regional laws; and new regional programmes to promote a favourable business climate.

In June 2002, the law 'On state support for organisations making capital investments on the territory of the Kaliningrad *oblast*' was passed. This aims to increase the volume and efficiency of investment. It guarantees protection of investors' rights.

To stimulate the growth of a functioning market economy, the strategy proposes that an international Investment and Finance Corporation (IFC), a Guarantee Fund and an Information and Consultation Centre should be set up. The purpose of this move would be to guarantee the conditions essential for the stable functioning of the financial market in Kaliningrad *oblast* – above all, of the capital market. Such a market does not currently exist, for three main reasons: first, there is insufficient information about the region's investment potential; second, investment carries a high level of risk; and third, the financial-market infrastructure is insufficient.

The IFC would promote the timely identification of projects worthy of investors' attention; second, it would make these projects less risky (through thorough prior examination, the increased financial transparency of Russian companies involved in the project, and by strict monitoring of the investment process); and third, it would further develop the financial infrastructure, including the creation of powerful investment companies and the generation of information for the market (telecommunications, the press, a rating agency).

The IFC's tasks are to seek out attractive investment projects, while support services would draw up business plans, help arrange financing, monitor project implementation and provide assurance that investors' profits can be repatriated. It is assumed that the IFC will become an effective financial and economic mechanism contributing to Kaliningrad's overall development strategy. At the same time, the IFC will be protected from political interference. It will become a powerful element in Kaliningrad's market structures: it will make a profit, pay taxes and support the development of financial markets, both in Kaliningrad and in the rest of Russia.

Setting up an IFC will be useful even if no agreement is reached between the Russian Federation and the EU on Kaliningrad as a pilot region. However, EU participation in the project would undoubtedly increase its visibility and standing in Western Europe, and would help to attract private investment, in particular through international investment banks. In addition, the IFC would become a founder of the Guarantee Fund and the Information and Consultation Centre. The active participation of local enterprises in the IFC can thus be expected. These enterprises and their professional associations and consortia might also become founders of the IFC.

The federal component
Kaliningrad should have a more prominent position than it currently does in the regional policy of Russia's federal government. The *oblast* should be turned into a nucleus of growth and integration. For this to occur, the Russian approach, as elaborated in the 'Main Principles and Guidelines of Federal Policy' for Kaliningrad, should be based on the following concepts:

1. The sovereignty of Russia over Kaliningrad *oblast* is beyond doubt.
2. Kaliningrad *oblast* is to become a Russian pilot region of cooperation, the connecting link in the integration of, and convergence between, Russia and the enlarging EU. Russia considers Kaliningrad to be a distinctive area, and creates special economic conditions for it.
3. The region will continue to function in accordance with the defence doctrine of the Russian Federation, and will implement the state's objectives within the Russia–NATO partnership in the Baltic Sea region.
4. The possibility of Kaliningrad's economic and political isolation from mainland Russia must be removed, and the region should remain part of Russian cultural space.
5. At the same time, it is necessary to ensure that Kaliningrad will not be isolated from the territories of neighbouring countries, and cross-border cooperation and cultural links with the countries of the Baltic Sea region should be supported.
6. The living standard of Kaliningrad's residents needs to be higher, and should not be lower than the Russian average.

Financial support for Kaliningrad is provided through a special federal programme, 'The Development of Kaliningrad *oblast* for the period until the year 2010'. This programme should be adjusted in accordance with the changing conditions of regional development. In addition, there is a federal law 'On the Special Economic Zone in the Kaliningrad region', which aims to address the drawbacks of the region's exclave position and encourage a favourable business climate.

The federal government's concerns about Kaliningrad's future were expressed at the Russia–EU summit on 11 November 2002. Many are shared in the region itself, where there is a strong interest in how cooperation between Russia and the EU will develop. Both parties view Kaliningrad as a special pilot region of active cooperation, with benefits for each. Kaliningrad should become a testing-ground for new mechanisms of cooperation between the EU and Russia. At issue here is the development of new forms of economic integration and cross-border cooperation, and the unimpeded movement of people and goods.

The international component
At both the federal and regional levels, Russia's position coincides with the EU's on two main issues: first, the economic isolation of Kaliningrad is unacceptable; and second, Kaliningrad has great potential for economic cooperation.

Economic cooperation between the EU and Russia is not starting from scratch. In fact, first as an FEZ and then as an SEZ, Kaliningrad has become a testing-ground for economic cooperation, where new integration patterns are tried out.

Cross-border cooperation plays a similar role. The last decade has seen a number of significant joint projects in areas such as environmental protection, energy, education (including the training of military personnel for civilian life), health care (including AIDS and drug abuse), transport and social issues. There are also a number of international research projects on transport, telecommunications and energy. Another important area for international cooperation is the development of industrial infrastructure – an indispensable foundation for attracting investment and developing specialised regional industries. These projects are sponsored mainly by the EU through its Tacis programme; Denmark (ecological projects) and Sweden (the AIDS-prevention programme) are also active bilaterally.

These projects do not exhaust Kaliningrad's significant potential for international cooperation. Besides, most are still in the feasibility-study, pre-investment phase. Kaliningrad shares a general Russian frustration with many EU projects: the lion's share of EU project funds is spent on European experts and advisors, who are sent to Russia rather than directly in the Russian region which is the project's object. Finally, the lack of a unified steering body is a hindrance to international projects. Although the Regional Development Agency is trying to do this, it is still a 'virtual body', and no clear-cut powers have been delegated to it.

The creation of a favourable external environment to support the region's development has been the main objective of the international activities of the *oblast* administration. Given Kaliningrad's geographic location, adequate visa-handling arrangements for the region's residents are critical. Lithuania, Poland, Denmark and Sweden have consular facilities in the *oblast*, and Latvia is set to open a consulate.

The legal basis for international cooperation between Kaliningrad and international partners has been developed, and cooperation agreements with local and regional authorities in Poland and Denmark have been signed.

Finally, cross-border transport networks have been expanded. A new ferry line connecting St Petersburg, Kaliningrad and German ports was opened in November 2001. Regular flights to Warsaw began operating in June 2002, and an air connection to Copenhagen is to be restored after a two-year break. The very useful rail link between Kaliningrad and Berlin has also reopened.

As Kaliningrad *oblast* is part of the Russian Federation, it is governed by the federal constitution and federal legislation, and Kaliningrad's external contacts derive from the foreign policy of Russia as a whole. Regional bodies are obliged to 'coordinate' external relations with foreign partners with the federal centre. For instance, the *oblast* draws up proposals for bilateral agreements, but the Federation takes the final decision. An agreement between Russia and the EU is thus a prerequisite for strengthening Kaliningrad's role in international cooperation. The draft title for such an agreement could be 'On Kaliningrad *oblast* as a pilot area of cooperation between the Russian Federation and the EU'. It is important that representatives of regional organs and experts from the region, as well as from the federal centre, are involved in drawing it up.

Any such agreement should address two kinds of tasks. First, it should facilitate convergence between Russia and the EU by setting up new cooperation mechanisms in Kaliningrad, adopting examples of best practice in EU–Russia cooperation from elsewhere in Russia. Second, the agreement should take into account the region's status as an exclave surrounded by the EU, and should create the conditions for its socio-economic development and integration into the Baltic Sea region and European markets as a 'vanguard' of Russia.

Such an arrangement would be based on the Agreement on Partnership and Cooperation between the EU and Russia (PCA) of 1994. However, its provisions should be adapted to incorporate the concept of an EU–Russia pilot region of cooperation. It should also take into account the Common Strategy of the EU towards Russia, the Medium-term Strategy for Development of Relations between the Russian Federation and the European Union 2000–10, and the results of further negotiations between both parties on this question. It should also take into account recommendations made by relevant international conferences and consultations.[1] The document should be as specific as possible, should define clear-cut obligations for the parties, and should avoid becoming just a statement of intent. In addition to the agreement itself, addenda will need to be drawn up which elaborate the general provisions.

Conclusion

Russia and the EU have adopted partnership and cooperation policies. Due to its geographical location, Kaliningrad should become a region of cooperation between Russia and the EU. Within the Baltic Sea region, integration processes and mutually-beneficial cooperation in the economic, cultural and environmental spheres can flourish. Moscow should regard the fulfilment of such a regional strategy as a matter of federal concern. This strategy should both overcome the drawbacks and exploit the advantages of Kaliningrad's geopolitical location. By interacting with Western partners in Kaliningrad, the region's role within Russia would grow. The standard of living of the local residents would rise, and separatism would lose its appeal.

Implementation of the cooperation strategy would enhance the region's economic security, but this is not tantamount to making Kaliningrad self-sufficient. Three essential factors will determine the level, structure and speed of Kaliningrad's economic development, and consequently Kaliningraders' standard of living:

1. The diversification of Russia's economy, with a focus on new sectors like technology and the service industry; and the extensive development of the Kaliningrad market.
2. Reliable and inexpensive communication and transport networks linking Kaliningrad to the rest of Russia.
3. Mutually beneficial relations between Kaliningrad and its neighbours.

Kaliningrad's economy requires restructuring to reflect the changes in the *oblast's* external economic environment in the wake of EU enlargement. The interests of Kaliningrad, the Russian Federation and foreign partners need to be taken into account.

If the strategy's proposals are implemented, the target is that Kaliningrad's gross domestic product (GDP) will double by 2010 compared with 2002; there could be a three-fold increase in industrial output; agriculture and transport could expand; and standards of living could rise significantly. To meet these challenges, major increases in investment and foreign investment, currently at a very low level, will be needed. Key factors in this regard are: improving the operational framework of the SEZ, regional economic laws and the federal programme for regional development; a new Russia–EU agreement on Kaliningrad as a pilot region for cooperation; and the creation of an international financial-investment corporation for regional development.

Without the effective implementation of such a strategy, Kaliningrad will remain a depressed region, a double periphery of both the Russian Federation and of Europe, isolated and without prospects.

Note

1 One useful example is the conference 'Northern Dimension and the Kaliningrad Region', held in May 2000.

14. Commercial Prospects for the Kaliningrad Region

Hans Jeppson

The development of Kaliningrad has attracted attention as a consequence of the enlargement of the European Union (EU).[1] Kaliningrad has aroused special interest among academics, foreign-policy experts and EU officials. Its fate has not, however, featured high on the business agenda. The reason for this is simple: Kaliningrad does not play an important economic role, and is not seen as a particularly interesting or promising place either to trade with, or to invest in.

Background

At the beginning of the 1990s, Kaliningrad was regarded as a military powder-keg. Many Soviet Army units withdrawn from East Germany and Poland were redeployed there. Although this transfer of troops was not as large as some Western experts claimed, and the redeployments were often no more than administrative, the EU began to make efforts to assist Kaliningrad.

For Kaliningrad, an important result of the collapse of the Soviet Union was that Russia no longer saw any justification for maintaining the strict barriers against foreigners visiting Kaliningrad. This had several effects. Curiosity among former Koenigsberg inhabitants and their descendants led to a wave of visitors from Germany. This inflow of visitors also generated some foreign investment, particularly in joint ventures in tourism-related fields such as hotels. The border between Kaliningrad and Poland became open, and could be crossed by individuals of both countries without any special permission. This quickly gave rise to a border trade based on differences in taxation and market prices for some consumer goods. The same type of 'grey' border trade also started with Lithuania. During the second half of the 1990s, Kaliningrad saw substantial change. Most collective and state-owned enterprises and properties were dissolved, a Free Economic Zone was proclaimed and special customs rules were applied to imports.

However, there was very little foreign investment. The EU gave assistance to Russia mainly as loans, and through the Tacis programme, but only a small proportion of Tacis money was allocated to Kaliningrad.

More recently, the situation in Russia has improved considerably. The economy is much more stable, the president is in a position of strength, and is able to follow a consistent policy course and important reforms have been enacted. In Kaliningrad, there have been beneficial changes in the administration, and a deputy to the representative of the president is in place. The Russian government has signalled its special interest in Kaliningrad through, for example, its Development Plan for Kaliningrad presented in June 2002. In 2002–03, the Kaliningrad question was overshadowed by changes in the conditions for travel to and from Kaliningrad in the context of EU enlargement. Although visa requirements and the expected reduction in the 'grey' border trade will affect economic conditions in Kaliningrad, several other factors will have much more impact on the development of trade and manufacturing in Kaliningrad.

Great expectations

To some extent, Kaliningrad's development has been harmed by over-ambitious and unrealistic expectations. Notions of Kaliningrad as a 'gateway' or the Hong Kong of the Baltic are unrealistic. It is sometimes claimed that Kaliningrad has a strategic position as a transport hub. However, this perception seems to be based on an unrealistic assessment of contemporary transport patterns and market conditions; geography and political boundaries are not favourable. Although Kaliningrad will have useful and hopefully profitable port facilities in the future, this will have only a limited impact on the region's economy. The same is true for Kaliningrad's prospects as a transit route from the Baltic countries to Poland.

Another approach that seems to have some proponents in Kaliningrad is to seek a return to sectors that were important either during the Soviet period or before the Second World War, such as fishing and agriculture. Although there is no doubt that improvements could be made, the potential for large-scale development in these areas is limited. Fishing resources are becoming depleted in the Baltic and North Seas, and Kaliningrad is not a viable base for fishing in tropical waters. Agricultural products are heavily protected and subsidised in the EU, and so Kaliningrad's production would have to be sold mainly in Russia, competing with many other agricultural areas in the country. The case for Kaliningrad as a tourist destination is quite strong, not least because, for many Russians and Belarusians, it is a cheaper beach destination than other seaside resorts in the Baltic states, the Mediterranean or the Black Sea. The problem, however, is that the tourist season in the Baltic is short.

Major investment

It is a common assumption that large-scale investment will solve most problems. Kaliningrad does indeed have great investment needs in both the public and the private sector, but the crucial issue is limited resources. This is commonly understood as a 'lack of financing'. Most financing is in the form of loans, albeit on favourable terms, which thus should be paid back. Hence, all private investment has to generate revenues sufficient to make repayments, and loans for public sector investment have to be paid by increased public sector revenues.

Another assumption is that foreign investment will 'rescue' Kaliningrad. Foreign investment can be a very important factor in development, bringing in capital and, more importantly, know-how. Hence, even small-scale investment is useful because it provides the business community with useful contacts and knowledge. However, expectations of large-scale investment appear to have been unrealistic. Several schemes have been discussed, but few have materialised.

One such project concerned a KIA car factory, which eventually became an assembly plant used by a Russian-owned company, Avtor, under contract with BMW. This is the largest foreign investment in Kaliningrad, according to officials. It is often assumed in Kaliningrad that the investment was made possible thanks to the Special Economic Zone, and thus the lower local-content requirements for cars. This is true, but it does not explain why other car companies have not come to Kaliningrad if conditions really are so favourable. One negative factor is the cost of producing in Kaliningrad. Wages are low, but there are other costs. Nor is the BMW plant universally welcome; there is no general understanding of how to make Kaliningrad an attractive place for foreign investors. Throughout, BMW was plagued with visa problems for visiting experts. It took an unnecessarily long time to obtain permission, and some middle-ranking officials have pressed BMW for money by threatening to close the factory for non-fulfilment of some 'requirement'. The local infrastructure has not been sufficiently upgraded (the plant had to operate with only two telephone lines, and permission to install a satellite communication link was denied), and the local police was unwilling to provide special security for the plant or for foreign experts. The experiences of BMW are not unique in Russia; many companies with similar investments report the same type of problems. However, there are also examples where support from local governors or mayors significantly reduces the problems. If the Kaliningrad administration and the Russian government are serious about attracting foreign investors, they must do more than express their delight and support – they must create a conducive environment.

Even if conditions for foreign investors changed, and even if many foreign companies found compelling reasons to invest in Kaliningrad, this would not solve all of the region's problems. Foreign investment alone cannot propel a country or a region into development. It requires a dynamic domestic business sphere. Indeed, foreign investors need energetic domestic businesses, with efficient local companies that can act as sub-contractors and service providers. A number of regions, territories and provinces with peculiar geographical locations are sustained by generous transfers of money, mainly from central government, or are given tax and/or duty privileges. Examples in the Baltic Sea region include the Swedish island of Gotland, which receives large amounts of support; and the Åland Islands which enjoy tax and duty exemptions.

Kaliningrad is also a beneficiary of such schemes in the form of the Special Economic Zone. There seems to be a hope that the federal government will provide money for some of the large projects envisaged in the government's development plan for Kaliningrad.

The SEZ is opposed within ministries in Moscow, on the grounds that the government is losing revenue and because it is causing distortions between Russian regions. To what extent the government will give priority to transferring money to Kaliningrad is hard to predict; Kaliningrad accounts for just 0.6% of the Russian population and is relatively well-off by Russian standards. Another possible source of subsidies would be the EU. So far, comparatively small amounts have been spent on Kaliningrad, but as Kaliningrad attracts increased attention post EU-enlargement, it is likely that more EU financial assistance will be allocated to it. However, Tacis – or the new instrument promised by the EU – is likely to be a temporary arrangement, and its purpose is to provide assistance to development, not to function as a permanent source of revenue. Dependence on such politically determined funding does not encourage a growth-conducive environment. A high degree of uncertainty and low efficiency can be expected.

The real and the 'grey' economy

Although there is poverty and deprivation, and despite slow development, Kaliningrad's economy is providing opportunities. Kaliningrad's inhabitants have contacts with other countries, albeit sometimes superficial contacts, and sometimes illegal. According to official statistics, Kaliningrad has more enterprises per inhabitants than other parts of Russia. The statistics also claim a positive growth rate for the region. Understanding the real economy is not always easy in Russia. The 'grey' border trade in its various forms is not recorded in tax records. It is only possible to make guesses and rough estimates about the income people in Kaliningrad can derive from such trade. But it is obvious that 'grey' border trade and related activities constitute an important 'industry' in Kaliningrad. However, the prospects do not look positive.

The general presumption is that the travel restrictions that may result from the Schengen visa requirement will make cross-border travel more difficult. It is also assumed that Polish and Lithuanian customs officials will become more efficient, restricting the amount of goods that can be carried across the border.[2]

An approach to development

Kaliningrad cannot expect to base its future on its geographic location, or build on traditions and knowledge in historically important sectors of the economy. Nor can it expect large amounts of foreign investment, depend on subsidies and special privileges, or expect the 'grey economy' to provide growth opportunities. No 'big-bang' or simple solutions are available. This raises two possible scenarios:

1. *'Muddling through' without any major policy changes*
   - The present power structures in public administration remain in place.
   - A small group of local businessmen enjoy comfortable conditions.
   - Most other people face stagnant or falling incomes. Kaliningrad becomes more dependent on Moscow.

2. *Efforts at reform*
   - Key players unite behind the need for development.
   - More people find work and income increases over time.
   - Kaliningrad grows closer to neighbouring regions.

The following are some of the elements that would form part of such a reform package:

Russia-wide reforms, or Kaliningrad as a pilot region
Kaliningrad is part of Russia, and its development can never be separated from what happens in the rest of Russia. A precondition for positive development in Kaliningrad is that there is general economic development in Russia. Over the last couple of years, a number of positive steps have been taken by the Russian government. These have increased economic activity and revitalised Russia's industrial sector. Russia has also become more interesting from a foreign investor's perspective. A number of foreign companies are building plants to supply the Russian market. Nevertheless, there are still deficiencies in the economic and legal framework that discourage both domestic and foreign investment.

While the development of Kaliningrad has to be part of general development in Russia, this should not prevent Kaliningrad from acting as a pilot region, i.e. a region where changes and reforms can be introduced and implemented earlier than elsewhere in Russia. This falls into two categories: first, changes that can be made by local and regional authorities in Kaliningrad without waiting for decisions in Moscow; and second, reforms that have been approved by the ministries and the state Duma, and introduced first in Kaliningrad. The problem with the pilot region concept is that there has to be a pilot – there has to be leadership, whether by a person or a structure. This is the challenge facing Kaliningrad's administrators and politicians. Leadership has to be paired with prudence and knowledge. Kaliningrad is the most westerly part of Russia, so there ought to be more contacts and better understanding of economic and social conditions in neighbouring countries and Western Europe.[3]

- The Kaliningrad governor and other politicians should set a clear aim to create a more business-friendly setting in Kaliningrad.
- The Kaliningrad administration needs to recruit experts with experience gained from working in the federal Russian government, to find suitable fields for regional reforms with due respect to federal legislation.
- A forum should be created where top-level decision-makers can discuss problems and take advantage of information about similar problems in other countries.
- The federal government should instruct ministries and agencies, within the framework of legislation, to develop better administrative routines for Kaliningrad.

Russian business
The key to economic progress in Kaliningrad lies with the growth and development of domestic firms. There are numerous small companies in Kaliningrad, and many are hard pressed. They bear the high costs associated with compliance with regulation. These can be direct such as fees, fines as well as bribes, or indirect, such as the cost of delays or extra stocks. Officials may, for instance, present firms with impossible demands, and indicate that paying a 'fee' would be a simpler alternative. The business environment is characterised by a lack of short-term credit and risk capital, inadequate training and unpredictable levels of competence in business and business ethics. Some of these problems are difficult to address at a political or administrative level, though some measures should be considered. These include:

- a general review of administrative procedures;
- simplifying and abolishing unnecessary elements;
- setting up a small business gateway, to help small businesses to find out how to fulfil their requirements;

- small-business education, helping new entrepreneurs to make business plans and frame realistic assumptions; and
- establishing a business organisation with sufficient standing to criticise the administration and politicians. This role may possibly be fulfilled by existing organisations such as Chambers of Commerce if they are willing to act on controversial issues.

There are larger companies in Kaliningrad. Some, such as the shipyard Yantar, have ventured into the export market. Others try to work for the domestic market. As Kaliningrad is not an ideal location for production in Russia, most companies will face a hard test in a few years' time. Even some of the larger companies have a weak financial base. This is not a problem that can be rectified easily. An idea often heard in Kaliningrad is that, if foreign banks established themselves in Kaliningrad, this would change things radically. However, although foreign banks often have a positive effect on financial markets, mainly through their introduction of know-how, they are not normally direct routes to foreign credit markets. The larger companies need well-educated key personnel who can implement structural and organisational changes in order to gain productivity. Companies also need help to seek out opportunities in nearby export markets.

Export efforts
Kaliningrad's companies need help to export. Companies themselves are normally unknown by their potential customers, and Kaliningrad itself is relatively unknown. This makes exporting a real challenge. There is a need for a structure to assist and promote exports to help companies to make themselves 'presentable', and to help them understand EU markets. This could be a small organisation consisting of individuals with experience of West European markets, as well as Russian conditions.

Foreign companies
Kaliningrad has not attracted many major foreign investors. There are several reasons for this. The conditions under the SEZ were intended to attract investors, but this has not been sufficient. Kaliningrad lies far from the main Russian markets for both consumer goods and investment goods.[4] Most foreign-owned companies use legal ways to avoid paying high taxes in any country, hence tax incentives are often inefficient attractions. The bureaucracy is 'expensive', transport to and from Kaliningrad is subject to delays at the borders and the business communities in other Baltic Sea regions are more diversified, so it is easier to secure fast access to services. Labour costs in Russia and in Kaliningrad are lower than in the EU new member states, yet it is often more costly to

produce in Russia. The way to attract foreign firms to Kaliningrad is to show that lower wages actually translate into lower production costs. Hence, efforts to reduce bureaucracy are important. Some production would benefit from the SEZ, and companies expect the SEZ to remain in place and to be regularly implemented. The Kaliningrad authorities should try to attract foreign investment. These efforts should involve all spheres of administration:

- Planning for new plants should take place. Basic infrastructure should be made available, as well as security.
- Any reasonably large investor should be assisted in understanding and meeting the various demands upon it, through some kind of legal service.
- Special fast and reliable customs procedures should be arranged, as should a simplified visa system for company staff coming to Kaliningrad.
- The Kaliningrad authorities should make every effort to encourage the Polish airline LOT to continue to operate on the Warsaw–Kaliningrad route. One move would be to separate ownership of the airport from the regional airline company.

The number of risks associated with investing in Russia, and in Kaliningrad in particular, is high. Russia does not have a free-trade agreement with the EU, and hence there is an additional risk when manufacturing in Russia. Nevertheless, as outlined above, there are many steps that can be taken to improve the region's chances of attracting investment. It is to be hoped that Kaliningrad can succeed in these challenges and present a new image of itself abroad.

Notes

1 This chapter was first written for a seminar at the Carnegie Endowment for International Peace, Moscow Office, on 5 September 2002. It should be read in conjunction with *Recommendations for Increased Trade and Investments in the Kaliningrad Region*, from the Business Advisory Council, BAC. That document was presented to the Tenth Ministerial Meeting of the Council of Baltic Sea States (CBSS) in Svetlogorsk, Kaliningrad, on 6 March 2002. BAC, a body under the framework of the Council of Baltic Sea States, is an advisory council. Representatives are nominated by national business organisations and appointed by each government. BAC does not receive any funding from CBSS. This chapter constitutes the author's own reflections and views, and does not represent the views of the members of the BAC or of the Stockholm Chamber of Commerce.

2 The 'grey' trade concept is larger than just bringing vodka and cigarettes across the border. At one extreme is clearly criminal large-scale smuggling, at the other potentially legitimate trade in second-hand equipment and vehicles.

3 At the Ministerial Meeting in Svetlogorsk, the CBSS supported establishing a Business Support Group for Kaliningrad (BSG), consisting of experts from the other CBSS countries. However, later discussions revealed a lukewarm attitude in Kaliningrad to such a concept. Although the BSG scheme was not sufficiently developed, Kaliningrad would benefit if senior politicians and officials devoted more attention to economic conditions in the countries close to Kaliningrad. It is not clear if any kind of advisory body for the commercial development of Kaliningrad will be established.

4 The bulk of the foreign direct investment in Russia comprises the provision and distribution of imported consumer goods; local production of consumer goods and durable consumer goods intended for the Russian market (most foreign direct investment in Russia falls into this category); or production of goods to be exported from Russia. Only minor investment falls into this latter category.

15. Kaliningrad's Economic Growth Problem

Natalia Smorodinskaya

As a result of the accession of Lithuania and Poland to the European Union (EU) on 1 May 2004 Kaliningrad *oblast* is directly exposed to the tough competitive requirements of globalisation.[1] It will struggle to cope with them on its own. The major challenge for Kaliningrad, therefore, is not the crossing of borders or transit traffic to and from Russia, but rather, its inability to compete economically in European markets. There are two major risks. First, that the development gap between the region and its fast-developing neighbours will be increasingly asymmetrical. And second, that a dividing line will run through part of Europe.

Kaliningrad's vulnerable economy
Kaliningrad's economic system is extremely vulnerable, not only in comparison with its European neighbours, but also with Russia and the Russian north-west. Soviet-era industry and infrastructure was designed in complete disregard for market principles, and is unable to function efficiently. More fundamentally, the region's economy suffers from underlying shortcomings, which are further aggravated by its exclave position.

On the one hand, Kaliningrad is dependent on externally supplied power (97% of its electricity comes from United Energy System of Russia, via Lithuania), and on imports of basic consumer goods, raw materials and semi-finished items for industrial production. On the other hand, its local market is too small to generate effective demand. The region is unable to rely for its development either on the mass export of raw materials, as can the rest of Russia, or on its harbour facilities, which cannot compete with other Baltic ports, including those in Leningrad *oblast* and St Petersburg. Moreover, large-scale trade between Kaliningrad and mainland Russia is impracticable because of distance (1,000 kilometres separate Kaliningrad from other Russian regions), and the costs of crossing the borders between Latvia and Lithuania or Belarus and Lithuania; such trade can be maintained only by special non-market-based incentives provided by the state. It is clear that there is no chance of Kaliningrad becoming a 'bridge' for investment and commodity flows, either between the EU and Russia, or between northern and southern Europe.[2]

These factors will make it difficult for the region to develop its economy in a sustainable and self-supporting way. Post-Soviet Kaliningrad needs well-directed state support. However, the current system of federal support for the region is counterproductive.

There are three main dimensions to the system. First, since the early 1990s, along with subsidies and direct federal budget allocations, Kaliningrad has enjoyed the exclusive right to engage in tax-free trade, known as the Special Economic Zone (SEZ) regime. Local enterprises are exempt from paying customs duties, value-added tax (VAT) and some excise taxes, both when they are importing foreign merchandise and when they are shipping abroad or to the rest of Russia items 'considered to be produced in the SEZ'.[3] Such benefits – originally granted to Kaliningrad to compensate it for the burdens associated with its exclave position and for the extra haulage costs connected with trade with mainland Russia – are now worth 10.5 billion roubles a year, or one-third of the Gross Regional Product (GRP). Second, Kaliningrad receives seven billion roubles a year (over one-fifth of its GRP) from the local branch of the Russian Ministry of Transport in the form of special subsidies for the movement of cargo by rail. Third, the region is granted special advantages due to artificially low domestic energy prices in Russia as a whole, as compared to those on the world market.[4]

Although this system offers some social support, it simultaneously generates powerful incentives against market modernisation. The SEZ regime is a fundamental deviation from the global practice of creating free-trade zones. By taking an industrialised and densely populated area out of the national customs territory, it has automatically produced large-scale institutional and structural distortions in the local economy. Furthermore, exclusive foreign-trade privileges, unavailable to economic actors in the rest of Russia, give local enterprises an artificial monopoly and have led to their involvement in rent-oriented practices from the outset.[5] In addition, individual privileges in regard to railway cargo fees create further unfair competition, while artificially low energy prices signal to foreign investors that inflationary pressure is mounting throughout the country, as well as in its regions. For a decade, Kaliningrad's economy has been performing in an unhealthy, resource-wasteful manner; it is farther from genuine market-based development than is Russia as a whole.

Thanks to its tax-free trading benefits, Kaliningrad's economy is extremely open to the rest of the world. In 2003, the value of its foreign trade was equivalent to nearly $2.7bn, or 162% of GRP, whereas for Russia's other regions it is generally between 50% and 60% (see Table

15.1). This astronomical trade turnover is, however, generated not by a rise in exports, but by a large-scale expansion of imports. The SEZ regime and the whole system of federal incentives are working in such a perverted way that, instead of stepping up export production and selling goods to neighbouring European states, Kaliningrad is concentrating on increasing the inflow of tax-free imports and reselling them to remote Russian markets.

Kaliningrad's exclusive right to tax-free trade makes the rouble stronger in this region than in other regions of Russia. Hence import deals and the servicing of imports have become more lucrative activities in Kaliningrad than elsewhere in the country. When Russia was pursuing a 'currency anchor' policy and the rouble was artificially overvalued, prior to the 1998 devaluation, the relative benefits of Kaliningrad's tax-free import-trading status were multiplied many times. As a result, imports were expanded on a scale exceeding the value of GRP and far surpassing local demand for imported commodities – up to $1–1.2bn a year, as it was in 1997 (see Table 15.1).

Of interest here is the fact that 80–90% of these imports are not raw materials or semi-finished products (as is typical for imports into export-processing zones), but rather finished consumer goods, mostly foodstuffs, cars, tobacco and petrol. These items are either resold to other Russian regions and neighbouring countries on an 'informal basis' (shadow trans-border transactions that involve high-excise goods and where money is made on differences in prices) or, mainly, officially dispatched to mainland Russia after minimum processing (upon adding to them only 15–30% of value) labelled as goods produced in the SEZ.[6]

Compared with other companies in the rest of Russia, which are also making money on the servicing of imports, Kaliningrad businesses have a double advantage. First, they can purchase foreign consumer goods tax-free. And second, they can assemble and repackage the goods and then resell them as their own, also tax-free.[7] Furthermore, high shipping costs are covered by reduced federal tariffs on energy supplies and regional cargo traffic. This all means that the expansion of imports remains commercially beneficial under virtually any macroeconomic conditions and any exchange rate of the rouble.

By 1998, Kaliningrad was ranked third out of Russia's 89 regions in terms of per capita imports.[8] The system of federal incentives is such that, after the rouble was devalued in 1998, import expansion in Kaliningrad grew even more significantly, despite the increased cost of imports. Since then, as Kaliningrad's economy entered a phase of rapid recovery, the region's imports have risen to as much as 130% of GRP, attaining a value of $1.6bn in 2002 and $2.1bn in 2003. Meanwhile, contrary to this upward trend, over the past decade Kaliningrad's total exports have remained at

Table 15.1 Kaliningrad's trade transactions as a percentage of GRP

	1997	1999	2000	2001	2002	2003
Value of foreign trade	118	177	154	140	173	162
Total exports	24	58	52	46	43	33
Exports proper*	–	–	26	19	17	15
Total imports	92	125	94	94	130	128
Trade balance	-70	-89	-50	-48	-87	-95
Deliveries of goods to Russia*	–	–	49	56	60	67

* Refers to commodities with the status 'produced in the SEZ', which are exported abroad or delivered to mainland Russia tax-free. The category of exports proper does not cover transit export deliveries through Kaliningrad.

Sources: Smorodinskaya, N. and Zhukov, S., *The Kaliningrad Enclave in Europe: Swimming Against the Tide. Diagnostics of the State and Potential of Economic Development* (Moscow: East–West Institute, 2003); *Kaliningradkomstat; Usanov, Kaliningradskaia Oblast v 2003 godu. Analiticheskii obzor sotsial'no-ekonomicheskogo razvitiya* [The Kaliningrad Region in 2003: Analytical Review of Social and Economic Development] (Kaliningrad: Regional Development Agency, May 2004).

the low level of $500 million a year on average, with its exports proper, excluding Russian transit flows, accounting for only half of this sum. Between 2000 and 2004, the relative volume of exports has been steadily declining – down to 33% of the region's GRP regarding total exports, and to 15% regarding exports proper (see Table 15.1). This suggests that Kaliningrad's economy has an import-led pattern of growth, with the *oblast's* dependence on the expansion of imports rising. The SEZ regime has transformed Kaliningrad into a mere transit point for the channelling of all kinds of consumer imports, regardless of their quality, to Russian markets.

In 2001, the region's tax-free deliveries to Russia were worth as much as $619m, three times greater than tax-free exports (that is, exports proper). By 2003, these deliveries had doubled to $1,118m, four times as much as exports proper, or 67% of GRP.

The upward trend in regard to Kaliningrad's deliveries to Russian markets is usually treated both in Russia and in Europe as a positive phenomenon, preserving the *oblast's* economic links with the rest of the country and increasing its role in import substitution.[9] However, even if SEZ consumer goods (including television sets, vacuum cleaners, refrigerators and automobiles) are able to compete with Russia's original imports on the basis of price, they are still unable to generate true import substitution in macroeconomic terms. The more imports of final-demand goods are resold to Russia for roubles, the more hard currency Kaliningrad needs to pay for imported components. As a result, the region has built up an enormous foreign-trade deficit. In 2003, it amounted to $1.5bn, accounting for 95% of GRP. There are no macroeconomic constraints to hinder its further expansion.

This macroeconomic bias means that both Kaliningrad and Russia as a whole are paying a high price for maintaining the existing pattern of market interaction. Kaliningrad's mounting trade with mainland Russia is actually an absurdity in market economic terms, at best a dead end; it is making the region's economy ever more vulnerable and inflicting rising financial losses on the national economy.

The shadow economy

Kaliningrad has an equally unprecedented turnover in the realm of the grey economy. It accounts for 60–95% of officially recorded GRP, as compared with the Russia-wide average of 25–50%.[10] But this is not the consequence of a bloated criminal sector (illegal operations make up less than 30% of the region's non-legitimate (or informal) economic activities); rather it is the result of the region's legitimate benefits. Customs favours and expansion of imports have led to the proliferation of additional legal and semi-legal businesses that generate shadow earnings. In Kaliningrad, most of this revenue is accumulated in the redistribution sphere, as opposed to that of production, primarily through the servicing of commodity and financial flows which allows tax evasion on any trade deals.

The region's shadow economy can be broken down into at least three discrete categories, defined according to how shadow rents are extracted. The first is the 'shuttle' (or small-scale cross-border) traders, who smuggle taxable goods between Lithuania, Poland and Russia, working for themselves or for trade companies. These semi-legal markets function as a 'built-in social shock absorber' for the Kaliningrad economy, because they satisfy the basic and consumer-oriented needs of the local population and provide livelihoods for half of the labour force.

The second category is import processing in the real sector of the economy. Operating under the SEZ regime, local enterprises extract shadow incomes not only by concealing the true volume of their total production, but also, on a far larger scale, by overestimating the 'value added' to imported goods. Such items are easily turned into, and labelled, merchandise 'produced in the SEZ', and thus delivered tax-free to the Russian mainland. Any legally operating company, small or large, can utilise such fake import servicing and false upgrading on a massive scale.

The third category is 'virtual' foreign-trade contracts, where Kaliningrad is used merely as a point for compiling customs documentation. Because several customs regimes co-exist in this region, Kaliningrad is a convenient place for doing paperwork on export and import operations. Transactions related to contracts that have been formally concluded in Kaliningrad can actually take place anywhere abroad, so that such dealings may serve to disguise complicated false import and export chains, or to cover the tracks of money launderers.

It is clear that Kaliningrad's economy can be brought out of the shadow economy only through drastic modification of the SEZ regime. Meanwhile, the redistribution-based focus implies that the bulk of transactions are virtual, in other words, they cannot be legalised and included in regular turnover. If it becomes impossible to enter into such dealings, then real production and the trade operations behind it will also lose much sense. Contrary to common expectations, therefore, the contraction of informal activities is unlikely to lead either to an inflow of capital and additional labour into the official sector of Kaliningrad, or to a substantial increase in GRP.

Financial insolvency

In parallel with the growing trade imbalances, the emphasis on imports has created a similar vicious circle in the sphere of the region's finance. The higher the rate of economic growth in Kaliningrad, the greater its servicing of tax-free imports to Russia, and the larger the share of the region's GRP that is derived from minimum processing. This factor, as well as the simultaneously increasing proportion of shadow turnover, contribute to a reduction of taxation revenue.

This sequence leads to severe shortages of local finance, and thus to higher demand for extra federal assistance. In fact, since 1995, Kaliningrad has run high budget deficits (although they were sometimes hidden); and in 2001, the ratio of deficit to the volume of budget receipts proper (total receipts less transfers from the federal budget) almost reached the critical benchmark of 15% – the permissible limit for Russia's regions, as specified in the Russian Federation Budgetary Code.[11] The region is unable to repay its debts either to the Russian Federation Ministry of Finance (400m roubles) or to foreign lenders ($15m for a 1997 Dresdner Bank loan); in 2001, the Russian Clearing House declared Kaliningrad bankrupt. It is no wonder that, over the past decade, Kaliningrad has become increasingly dependent on subsidies from the federal treasury. It is now officially recognised as a recipient region in terms of federal budget allocations after a long period of being considered a net donor.[12] As long as an import-led pattern of growth is maintained, the region is doomed to rely increasingly on the federal treasury. No additional federal privileges or new amounts of federal subsidies will be able to break the cycle.

The fact that the trade deficit amounts to 50–95% of GRP, and the budget deficit is also high and continues to grow, implies that, for many years, Kaliningrad has been in a chronic state of default, regardless of its outstanding external debts. Under market conditions no territory would survive if it had a zero level of creditworthiness. If Kaliningrad were a sovereign state it would automatically face default and a crucial devaluation of its currency. But as a part of Russia, the federal centre covers its foreign-exchange shortages. This inflicts mounting losses on the national economy: the region consumes an increasing share of the current-account surplus of Russia's balance of payments (estimated at 0.7% in 2000, and a total of 8% in 2002–03), and of Russia's net inflow of foreign-currency assets (1% in 2000, and as much as 14% in 2003). Although at the moment these losses are not tangible, they will be a problem for Russia if it faces reduced export earnings, especially in the light of national debt payments.

Macroeconomic trends and recurring structural distortions
By 2003, Kaliningrad's per capita GRP – a good general indicator of social and economic development – had reached $4,300 (calculated at relative 2001 prices and at purchasing power parity based on the 2001 Eurostat).[13] This amounts to only 56% of the all-Russia level, and 45% and 42% respectively of the average level in the Baltic States (Estonia, Latvia and Lithuania) and in Poland. The gap between Kaliningrad and the developed Baltic economies is six- or seven-fold; it looks like Kaliningrad will never catch up with its neighbours. After the 1998 financial crisis and a deep transformational recession, the whole of Russia began to enjoy an economic recovery. Likewise, Kaliningrad has shown rapid rates of growth (9.7% on average between 1999 and 2001, 10.1% in 2002, and 9% in 2003), much higher than in Russia (4.7% in 2002 and 7.3% in 2003) and in the Baltic countries. Kaliningrad's fixed capital investment has been rising at an even faster rate (a record 68.8% in 2003).[14] This might give the impression that the region is advancing economically in leaps and bounds. However, its development is neither sound nor sustainable. Rather, higher growth rates have been accompanied by worsening structural distortions.

Since Kaliningrad is free of tight budgetary constraints as a result of the SEZ regime, its industrial structure – in terms of both production and employment – is evolving independent of, and largely contrary to, the requirements imposed by market rules, globalisation, and actual opportunities and limitations in the region. As trade and other services continue to generate shadow earnings and to attract increasing numbers of employees hoping to make such incomes, employment in Kaliningrad is growing faster than recorded output, thus taking structural adjustment in the wrong direction. The tertiary sector, although it has absorbed the bulk of the local workforce (nearly 65%), contributes much less to GRP (45%) than it does in the rest of Russia (53%) or in the Baltic States (60–70%). Meanwhile, the relative size of Kaliningrad's mining and manufacturing sectors (40% of GRP), compared both to Kaliningrad's optimal industrial proportions and to structural shifts in transition economies towards service-based economic systems.[15]

Half of the region's economy is involved in serving imports and this has a negative impact on the structure of GRP. Some industries (machinery, furniture and food, for instance) operate exclusively on that basis and are demonstrating the most rapid rates of growth.[16] Yet their contribution to Kaliningrad's economic development is considerably smaller. In 2003, for example, the machinery sector grew by 38%, but accounted for only 6.7% of total industrial investment and just 24% of total industrial production.[17]

As time passes and the SEZ regime orients Kaliningrad towards expansion of imports, this artificial growth is resulting in the local economy becoming increasingly distorted. If Kaliningrad's dependence on non-market-based federal incentives is reduced even slightly, the *oblast's* present economic recovery might turn sharply into a deep industrial slump. Clear proof that this scenario is realistic was provided in January 2001, when the temporary abolition by the Federal Customs Service of the VAT-free terms vis-à-vis the region's deliveries to Russia led the majority of local businesses to cease production and to make their workers redundant. A similar and perhaps much greater systemic shock may be provoked by any of a wide range of external factors: a drop in international oil prices; a rise in domestic energy tariffs in Russia; or Russia's preparations for membership of the World Trade Organisation (WTO). This implies that Kaliningrad's economy is more than just unstable: it is operating despite at systemic risks typical of a 'bubble economy'.

Alienation from Europe

In parallel with this increasing dependence on federal assistance, Kaliningrad is facing growing alienation from EU trade and capital markets. The combination of these two tendencies is creating a fundamental threat to Kaliningrad's future development. First, unstable economic growth prevents the region from making visible progress towards economic integration in the Baltic Sea region or in the EU economic space. Second, although Kaliningrad's major trade partners are EU member states including the new members (accounting for 70–75% of Kaliningrad's trade turnover), the *oblast's* pattern of trade relations with Europe (high imports and low exports) is hampering its participation in Baltic industrial and business networks. Kaliningrad faces chronic trade deficits with its leading business partners (Germany, Lithuania and Poland) and has no export niches in Baltic markets.

As shown in Table 15.2, by January 2004, Kaliningrad had attracted only $106m of foreign direct investment (FDI). Between 1999 and 2002, the flow of FDI to Kaliningrad virtually stopped ($5m a year on average); in 2003 it amounted to $14m, or just $15 per capita. This is in stark contrast to the substantial sums invested in the neighbouring new EU member states in the same period: Estonia and Poland attracted 82 and six times as much respectively. The share of FDI in total foreign investment in Kaliningrad is steadily declining and now amounts to only 4.8%. Moreover, the leading investors (Germany, Sweden and Switzerland) are withdrawing their capital; Germany accounts for $21m of total foreign investment in Kaliningrad (FDI plus equity, portfolio investment, etc.).

Kaliningrad is currently experiencing an increasing inflow of investments from American and British offshore territories (the capital is mostly of Russian origin, and the primary source is Cyprus), as well as from medium-sized Lithuanian and Polish companies. All this capital goes mostly to the trade sector, in other words, to the sphere of imports servicing (53% of FDI in 2003). This means that, in the post-EU enlargement period, the region is likely to remain a duty-free entry point to Russian outlets for the least competitive European merchandise, rather than become a gateway for Russian goods to European export markets. In any case, if Kaliningrad's economic development continues to proceed along its present trajectory, the region will remain of marginal interest to the multinational corporations and strategic investors whose activities are shaping the international division of labour in the Baltic Sea region. Thus Kaliningrad will be at risk of self-isolation, and hence of persistent backwardness.

The path of inertial development

What will happen now, following EU enlargement? Unfortunately, existing vested interests in and around Kaliningrad will automatically keep it on the course of inertial development. Lithuania and Poland, in particular, have an objective economic concern in preserving Kaliningrad's specialisation in import intermediation. These states will likely focus on Russia and the Commonwealth of Independent States (CIS) in the course of their export expansion, so as to minimise the costs of joining the EU.[18] To this end, they will exploit the benefits of the Kaliningrad SEZ, using the region as a potential launch pad for duty-free exports to Russia through 'joint ventures' established with Kaliningrad-based partners. In addition, in light of the unfavourable macroeconomic situation in developed European nations, a number of other transition economies in the Baltic Sea region and Central Europe, whose development depends on export demand, will follow the example of Lithuania and Poland in utilising the Kaliningrad SEZ. Finally, the EU as a whole will welcome the resulting splash of trade and investment in Kaliningrad, in the (misplaced) belief that it represents some stability on the Union's new eastern border.

Table 15.2 Foreign investment in Kaliningrad *oblast*

	1999	2000	2001	2002	2003
Total inflow ($m)	18.3	19.1	24.6	47.7	56.2
Per capita ($)	17	20	26	51	60
FDI inflow ($m)	4.1	6.6	3.2	5.9	14.0
Per capita ($)	4	7	4	6	15
	0.3	0.5	0.2	2.4	1.3
FDI as a share of total foreign investment (%)	22.4	34.6	13.0	12.4	4.8
Total accumulated stock ($m)	-	-	-	-	105.8
including from:					
Cyprus and other offshore sources (%)	-	-	-	-	44
Germany (%)	-	-	-	-	21
Poland (%)	-	-	-	-	14
Lithuania (%)	-	-	-	-	9
Accumulated FDI ($m)	-	-	-	-	42

Sources: Smorodinskaya, N. and Zhukov, S., *The Kaliningrad Enclave in Europe: Swimming Against the Tide. Diagnostics of the State and Potential of Economic Development* (Moscow: East–West Institute, 2003); Usanov, *Kaliningradskaia Oblast v 2003 godu. Analiticheskii obzor sotsial'no-ekonomicheskogo razvitiya* [The Kaliningrad Region in 2003: Analytical Review of Social and Economic Development] (Kaliningrad: Regional Development Agency, May 2004).

This will, in turn, encourage Russian companies affected by the 'Dutch disease' (whereby the economy is driven by energy exports but manufactured goods are not competitive on world markets) to link up with Kaliningrad as a channel for importing into mainland Russia. Russian bureaucrats might well embrace such a course of events, because it would help to preserve the status quo in regard to relations between the region and the centre. Therefore, in the near future, due to further widening of imports servicing, Kaliningrad may enjoy a massive inflow of investment and a consequent industrial boom. It may even double its per capita GRP and in this term move closer to its European neighbours. However, its convergence with Europe in terms of the level of development will remain strictly formal, since its divergence from the EU in respect of quality of growth and technological set-up will automatically widen. Sooner or later, the course of inertial development will produce a formidable systemic shock in Kaliningrad's bubble economy. When this happens, radical reforms will be unavoidable, regardless of vested interests. The later such reforms begin, though, the higher will be their cost for Russia and for the region itself, and the more difficult it will be to narrow the development disparity between Kaliningrad and the EU.

Economic policy for Kaliningrad

The SEZ and other federal economic policies resulted from bargaining between the region and the centre, or between different federal ministries and business groups. No surprise then that most of the Ministry of Economic Development and Trade's repeated attempts to formulate a sensible economic strategy for Kaliningrad usually ended in meeting just another set of local demands for further favours and budget allocations. The decisions were never followed by any assessment of the macroeconomic implications of the policies.

Moreover, despite all of the rhetoric about rapprochement with Europe and the idea of Kaliningrad being a pilot region for EU–Russia cooperation, in reality, the federal economic course being pursued with regard to Kaliningrad continues to prioritise security and geopolitics. This classic security approach implies that all of the major local life-support systems of the exclave (infrastructure, power supply, and transportation and communication networks) should be tied centripetally to Russia. Moscow has two main concerns about Kaliningrad. First, it does not wish to relinquish its transport links with Kaliningrad's ports because of the transit problem; it wants the economic viability of the Baltic Fleet to be maintained and the region to continue to have a strong strategic military function. Second, it does not wish to lose economic control over Kaliningrad in the era of EU enlargement and a potential encroaching Western presence in this territory. It is these considerations that lie behind Russia's negotiating position on Kaliningrad transit and its energy and transportation investment projects. These considerations are spelled out in the renewed 2001 version of the Federal Target Programme for Kaliningrad Until 2010,[19] as well as in the new edition of the 1996 Federal Law on the SEZ, submitted to the federal government for consideration in April 2004.[20]

The revised Federal Law on the SEZ sets the objective of ensuring the stable development of the exclave in the enlarged EU by means of attracting respectable investors to the region and boosting the rate of investment and production. To this end, three kinds of measures are to be introduced. First, the SEZ regime will be amended by limiting the present customs privileges to a maximum term of ten years and to type of user (newly registered firms will not be entitled to these benefits). Second, large investment projects in non-oil sectors, no less than €10bn in the first three years, are to be encouraged through the provision of extensive and specially tailored tax advantages.[21] Meanwhile, the SEZ will be governed by a Federal Commissioner (in order to block the formation of any kind of internal off-shore zone). Third, administrative procedures for investors will be simplified in order to improve the investment climate.

These initiatives have not been welcomed in the region: the local authorities are unhappy with the placing of any restrictions on their ability to act, and the local business community fears that competition with large Russian or foreign companies will result in them losing their market share. However, this is not the crux of the major problem with the measures. Rather, the federal attempt to adjust Kaliningrad to the new economic reality is constrained by an old politicised logic: the centre sees its primary task not as bringing Kaliningrad closer to Europe, but instead preventing its possible breakaway from Russia in the event that the growing socio-economic disparity between Kaliningrad and its EU neighbours gives rise to local separatism. In this context, the proposed economic policies for the region represent little more than trivial compromise solutions; they might formally boost the level of development (in terms of per capita GRP) but they do not address fundamental issues concerning Kaliningrad's economic modernisation.

Instead of improving the quality of economic growth, the new SEZ law places the emphasis on its acceleration, as well as on replacing one type of privilege (customs) with another (taxes) and extending the customs concessions for another ten years. Rather than promoting efficient small businesses, the document tries to entice large companies; this ignores the fact that global and major overseas investors are unlikely to be enticed with tax favours. Meanwhile, speculative investors engaged in imports servicing will continue to come to Kaliningrad in any case. Instead of functional reform of government aimed at export promotion, the bill will create more bureaucracy, particularly on the federal level. This policy will not help Kaliningrad to enhance its competitive power, but, rather, it will preserve its unhealthy state of development.

The EU has adopted two special documents for Kaliningrad: in January 2001, a communication from the EU Commission, *The EU and Kaliningrad,* and, in summer 2002, a report from the EU Commission, *Russia–EU Partnership for Kaliningrad Region.* Neither focuses on the problem of Kaliningrad's growing development gap or on the related issue of policies to make European financial assistance to the region more productive. At the moment, the volume of this aid and its allocation are mostly determined by Europe's awareness of environmental and humanitarian threats emanating from the region, rather than by its willingness to engage with Kaliningrad's economic-growth problem.

Hence the Kaliningrad authorities have prepared their own long-term development strategy for the exclave and a mid-term programme for its implementation.[22] Their plan is to make Kaliningrad a 'region of cooperation' with Europe and to double its GRP by 2010. Nevertheless, no matter how ambitious and righteous the goals the local community will be unable to alter the irregular pattern of Kaliningrad's economic development. For as long as the SEZ regime is in operation, the regional administration will never be able to manage such problems as the growing turnover of the shadow economy, fiscal shortages, or Kaliningrad's lack of competitive power. Under the existing and renewed set of federal incentives these troubles will reoccur time and again.

All that the Kaliningrad authorities can do is to continue to seek additional money, benefits, and powers from the centre under the guise of improving the investment climate. Their main concern is to ensure that the business community has enough federal favours today, fearing perhaps that, in future, for one external reason or another, the advantages of the current system of benefits may be lost.

What is to be done?
The prospect of moving Kaliningrad away from inertial and risky development raises a crucial question about replacing the ten-year-long regime of exclusive customs favours with a more productive system of governmental support, focused on market-based incentives. A new set of policies must enable the region to curtail import expansion, reorient its economy towards European export markets, and find a place in the international division of labour in the Baltic Rim. In other words, Kaliningrad has to be transformed into an export-led economy and this is dictated by strict market logic. The main driving force behind Kaliningrad's economic growth must be external demand (as the local market is too small); the region is much closer to Baltic and West European markets than it is to the rest of Russia. And Kaliningrad's present growing dependence on federal subsidies and favours must be replaced with a larger contribution to the national tax base and foreign currency earnings.

For at least two reasons the task of reorienting Kaliningrad towards European export markets cannot be carried out by either the EU or Russia alone. One reason is that the local economy is in the ambiguous position of being simultaneously inside and outside the EU. The other is that all vested interests, in Russia and in Europe, will wish to see import intermediation continue. But Kaliningrad's economic backwardness – to say nothing of possible economic collapse – is not in anyone's interest. Brussels and Moscow, therefore, have no alternative but to treat Kaliningrad as a common challenge, and to make it a pilot case for cooperation.[23] As an immediate step in this direction, the EU and Russia should explicitly acknowledge the following three points. First, Kaliningrad has no positive alternative to export-oriented integration into the EU economic space. Second, this prospect is a win-win strategic option for all parties involved and the only responsible solution to Kaliningrad's problem. In order to achieve it, the two sides need a common strategy and a concerted (preferably joint) action plan for economic reforms in the *oblast*. Third, an action plan for Kaliningrad's modernisation should be focused on its volte-face structural turn from an import- to an export-led economy. This will require a specially tailored industrial policy, which will differ from the standard reform procedures applied earlier in Lithuania and Poland during their accession to the EU. The main economic justification for a unique industrial policy is that the local economy has become so dependent on exclusive privileges, and has accumulated such deep distortions as a result of them, that it will be unable to undergo drastic modernisation based on shock therapy.

Consequently, the EU and Russia would be advised to seek joint and innovative policy measures for Kaliningrad's economic modernisation, avoiding serious social and market shocks in the process. In particular, the region's industrial policy must ensure a two- or three-year transition period, allowing local actors to prepare themselves institutionally for the scheduled revision of the SEZ regime (in favour of export-oriented produces and efficient SMEs), higher energy tariffs, and the subsequent structural shifts. For its part, the federal centre must be ready to modify both the 1996 Federal Law on the SEZ and the Federal Target Programme for Kaliningrad Until 2010 in a way that could really restrain import expansion while stimulating local exports. The European Union, meanwhile, should launch special programmes and offer special incentives that ease access for Kaliningrad's exports to EU markets.

At present, the prospect of Kaliningrad's reorientation towards exports does not appear realistic. This is partly because the region will probably not be able to rely on traditional items of merchandise. Yet, a realistic approach seldom sits well with a strategic vision. Concerted action by the EU and Russia to reform the region may present an opportunity to reshape its economic profile anew. And it cannot be ruled out that Kaliningrad will find a place in the Baltic technological set-up on the basis of the mass-scale export of services. Tourism is one potential sector where investment in knowledge and human capital could occur – transportation and communications technology are two others. Kaliningrad could find its place in the knowledge-based economy of the Baltic Sea region, which is currently being promoted by Denmark, Finland and Sweden.[24]

Kaliningrad's economic vulnerability benefits neither Europe nor Russia. Furthermore, its unsustainable economic growth may generate tensions and risks that neither party can prevent or manage alone. Nonetheless, despite the fact that both Brussels and Moscow have often affirmed their willingness to find a positive solution to the Kaliningrad issue, the crucial problem of the region's asymmetrical development in relation to its neighbours has never been seriously flagged as an independent subject for official discussion. As a result, there has been practically no meaningful European–Russian dialogue on the socio-economic future of the *oblast*.

The Pilot Region project would improve this situation. EU–Russia dialogue on Kaliningrad would not then be limited either to the problem of 'soft security' risks, or merely to the allocation of more money to the exclave. Rather, it will focus on seeking ways of stopping Kaliningrad from inertly 'swimming against the tide'. This will spare Europe from new divisions and tensions. What is more, in light of the cooler relations between Brussels and Moscow on the eve of enlargement, such a project looks promising for their strategic partnership, as well as for the Common European Economic Space.

Notes

1   This chapter is an updated and abridged version of Smorodinskaya, N., 'Analysing the Kaliningrad Situation: The Economic Growth Dimension', in Birkenbach, H.M. and Wellmann, C. (eds), *The Kaliningrad Challenge: Options and Recommendations* (Munster: LitVerlag, 2003), pp. 169–205. It is published here with the permission of the publishers and the editors.

2   Smorodinskaya, N. and Zhukov, S., *The Kaliningrad Enclave in Europe: Swimming Against the Tide. Diagnostics of the State and Potential of Economic Development* (Moscow: East–West Institute, 2003); Stockholm Chamber of Commerce, *Recommendations for the Expansion of Trade and Investment in the Kaliningrad Region: Position of the Business Advisory Council of the Council of Baltic Sea States*, submitted to the Conference of Ministers of Foreign Affairs of the Council of Baltic Sea States (CBSS), Svetlogorsk, Russia, 6 March 2002.

3   The SEZ regime has been in force since 1993 when the region was granted the status of Free Economic Zone. The latter was legally transformed into a Special Economic Zone as a result of the 1996 federal law 'On the SEZ in Kaliningrad Region'. See Smorodinskaya, N., Kapoustin, A. and Malyguin, V., 'Kaliningradskaia *Oblast* kak svobodnaia ekonomicheskaia zona (otsenka uslovii i rezul'tatov razvitiya v 1994-1998 godakh)' [The Kaliningrad Region as a Free Economic Zone (Assessment of Conditions and Results of Development in 1994–1998)], *Voprosy ekonomiki*, No. 9, 1999, pp. 90–107.

4   With regard to electrical power, local households pay half of the tariff charged in Lithuania, while enterprises pay around 40% of the equivalent charge in Poland. Data for 1999 are from *Kaliningrad Oblkomstat*, European Bank for Reconstruction and Development, Transition Report, 2001.

5   The Kaliningrad SEZ regime can be considered to be the most evident regional case of politically created rents in post-Soviet Russia. See Smorodinskaya, N., 'Rent-seeking in the Regions: The Politics of Economic Privilege in Kaliningrad', in Segbers, K. (ed.), *Explaining Post-Soviet Patchworks, Volume 3: The Political Economy of Regions, Regimes and Republics* (Aldershot: Ashgate, 2001), pp. 56–82.

6   According to the 1996 federal law 'On the SEZ in Kaliningrad Region', any imports can be deemed goods 'produced in the SEZ' and delivered to mainland Russia tax-free if at least 15–30% of their value is added in Kaliningrad during processing. In practice, this entails very little added value.

7 It is noticeable that flows of food products, which dominate both the structure of Kaliningrad imports from abroad and its deliveries to mainland Russia, are virtually identical in value: in 2000, imports amounted to $356.3 million, while shipments to Russia amounted to $340.8m. Vinokurov, E., 'Development of Trade with Mainland Russia in Trade Balance of Kaliningrad Region', in *Russia–European Union On the Eve of EU Enlargement*, special issue of *Les Cahiers de l'Espace Europe*, Autumn 2002.

8 After Moscow and the Republic of Ingushetia.

9 Samson, I., Lamande, V., Eliseeva, I., Burova, N. and Fedorov, G., *A New Look at Kaliningrad Region*, UPMF-FINEC Working Paper, Université Pierre Mendes France (UPMF), Grenoble, France, October 2002; Samson, I. and Eliseeva, I., 'Novyi obraz Kaliningradskoy oblasty' [A New Image of the Kaliningrad Region], in *Voprosy ekonomiki*, No. 2, 2003, pp. 40–52.

10 Eliseeva, I. and Burova, N., 'The Measurement of the Shadow Economy in St Petersburg and Kaliningrad', paper presented at the Russian–European Centre for Economic Policy (RECEP) conference 'Russia's Opening to the World Economy and the Building of a Common European Economic Space', Moscow, 20–21 September 2002;

Samson, I. and Eliseeva, I., 'Novyi obraz Kaliningradskoy oblasty' [A New Image of the Kaliningrad Region], op. cit.

11 *Ekspert North-west*, No. 9 (70), 4 March 2002.

12 According to the Russian Center for Fiscal Policy, whose estimates are based on official data from the federal financial authorities, in 2001, federal budget transfers to the Kaliningrad region exceeded regional allocations to the centre for the first time in the post-Soviet period, with the net inflow of federal resources (the inflow less the outflow) amounting to 2.1% of the region's Gross Regional Product (GRP).

13 The figure of $4,300 for Kaliningrad's GRP is calculated at relative 2001 prices and at purchasing power parity based on the 2001 Eurostat method for comparing purchasing power parities. Although it differs from our previous estimation based on the 1999 Eurostat version ($6,900 – see Smorodinskaya, N. and Zhukov, S., *The Kaliningrad Enclave in Europe: Swimming Against the Tide. Diagnostics of the State and Potential of Economic Development*, op. cit.), this does not alter the revealed scale of Kaliningrad's development gap.

14 Ibid and Usanov, *Kaliningradskaia Oblast v 2003 godu. Analiticheskii obzor sotsial'no-ekonomicheskogo razvitiya* [The Kaliningrad Region in 2003: Analytical

Review of Social and Economic Development] (Kaliningrad: Regional Development Agency, May 2004).

15 Ibid.

16 In the assembly of passenger cars, TV sets, vacuum cleaners, refrigerators 70–85% of the components are imported.

17 Usanov, *Kaliningradskaia Oblast v 2003 godu. Analiticheskii obzor sotsial'no-ekonomicheskogo razvitiya* [The Kaliningrad Region in 2003: Analytical Review of Social and Economic Development], op. cit.

18 The prediction that Lithuania and Poland will expand their exports to the East is based on the macroeconomic need of these countries: to compensate for the anticipated crowding out of goods from domestic markets by agricultural and other imports from the developed European countries; to acquire recompense for future constraints in EU export markets due to slow economic growth in Europe as a whole; and to reduce the currently profound trade deficit with Russia.

19 There are a number of costly federal projects in Kaliningrad of questionable economic expediency: the construction of a new large-scale regional thermal power station that will cost $1 billion (while fuel would come from 1,000 kilometres away); the hasty development of a ferry from Kaliningrad to St Petersburg; and the injudicious construction of an access railroad to a civil port site in Baltiisk, even though the port has not been built.

20 The document was prepared by a working group headed by Igor Shuvalov, the assistant to the president of the Russian Federation. The revised bill is expected to pass through the Duma in 2004 and to enter into force in January 2005.

21 Large investors are exempt from corporate property tax for a period of seven years, while the rate of profit tax that they have to pay is set at zero for the first six years and at 12% for the following six years. See Prihodko, S., 'Kaliningrad as a Pilot Region for Russia–EU Cooperation' paper presented at the Turku School of Economics and Business Administration, Finland, 1 April 2004.

22 'Strategy of the Social and Economic Development of Kaliningrad Oblast as a Region of Cooperation up to 2010', adopted in March 2003, and 'Programme for the Social and Economic Development of Kaliningrad Oblast for 2004–2007', adopted in September 2003.

23 See Smorodinskaya, N., *Kaliningrad Exclave: Prospects for Transformation into a Pilot Region* (Moscow: Institute of Economics, Russian Academy of Sciences, 2001); Smorodinskaya, N., 'Kaliningrad v usloviyah ob'edineniya Evropy: vyzov i

otvet' [Kaliningrad Under the Unification of Europe: Challenge and Response], in *Voprosy ekonomiki*, No. 11, 2001, pp. 106–127; Kiel International Ad-hoc Group of Experts on Kaliningrad, *Kaliningrad in Focus: Policy Recommendations in the Perspective of Problem-solving*, Kiel, SHIFF-texte, No. 67, October 2002.

[24] The main theme at the fifth annual Baltic Development Forum summit (in Riga, Latvia, in October 2003) was how to turn the Baltic Sea region into a global front-runner, exploring the mixture of old and new democracies, and mature and emerging markets.

Socio-economic indicators of Russia's north-west regions

Regions of Russia	Territory (in kilometres squared)	Total Population & percentage of urban residents	Ethnic Composition	Gross Regional Product (in US dollars) 2002	Average income per capita per month 2002	Distance from Moscow	Head/Governor	Date of next election
Kaliningrad oblast	15,100	946,700 76.9%	Russian 78.5% Belarusian 8.5% Ukrainian 7.2%	$910m	$126	1,289km	Governor V. Egorov (since November 2000)	2004
Republic of Karelia	172,400	1,760,600 74.3%	Russian 53.6% Karelian 10% Belarusian 8.3%	$1bn	$159	925km	Head of Republic S. Katanandov (since May 1998)	2006
Leningrad oblast	85,900	1,659,100 66%	Russian 90.9%	$2bn	$155	651km	Governor V. Serdiukov (since 1999)	2007
Murmansk oblast	144,900	988,500 91.9%	Russian 82.9% Ukrainian 9%	$2bn	$249	1,967km	Governor Yu. Evdokimov (since December 1996)	2004
Pskov oblast	55,300	789,500 66.8%	Russian 94.3%	$596m	$103	689km	Governor E. Mikhailov (since October 1996)	2004
St Petersburg	1,400	4,627,800 100%	Russian 89.1%	$7bn	$183	651km	Governor V. Matvienko (since October 2003)	2007
Arkhangelsk oblast	587,400	1,422,700 74.6%	Russian 92.1%	$2bn	$173	1,1733km	Head of administration A. Efremov (since March 1996)	2004

Republic of Komi	415,000	1,126,100 73.9%	Russian 57.7% Komi 23.3% Ukrainian 8.3%	$2.5bn	$224	1,515km	Head of Republic V. Torlopov (since December 2001)	2005
Nenets autonomous district (okrug)	176,700	45,000 59.3%	Russian -65.8% Nenets -11.9% Komi -9.5%	$315m	$268	2,230km	Governor V. Butov (since December 1996)	2004
Novgorod oblast	55,300	719,400 70.9%	Russian 94.7%	$736m	$122	606km	Governor M. Prusak (since 1991)	2007
Vologda oblast	145,700	1,311,300 68.4%	Russian 96.5%	$2.4bn	$157	497km	Governor V. Pozgalev (since 1996 – re-elected December 2003)	2008

Source: *Sotsialno-ekonomichiskoe polozhenie severo-zapadnovo federalnovo okruga v 2002g.* (Moscow: Goskomstat, 2002). *Regiony Rossii. Sotsialno-ekonomichiskoe pokazateli 2002. Statisticheckii sbornik* (Moscow: Goskomstat, 2002)

Index

Chernobyl accident (186) 87
Chinese migration 134
Chizhov, Ludvig 218
Chizhov, Vladimir 78
CIS (Commonwealth of Independent States)
  23, 42, 60, 69, 124, 183
Clinton, President Bill 54
Committee of Contributors 26
Common Agricultural Policy (CAP) 119
Common European Economic Space *see*
  CEES
Common Foreign and Security Policy *see*
  CFSP
common spaces initiative 2, 3, 6, 23, 25, 42,
  59, 61, 74; economic *see* CEES; education
  23, 59; and security field 23, 59, 68–71, 74
Common Strategy on Russia 5, 18, 19–21, 24,
  25, 54, 73, 97, 104, 121
Constitution of the Russian Federation 140
Contact Group 68
Cooperation Programme for Non-
  Proliferation and Disarmament in the
  Russian Federation 27
Copenhagen Summit (2003) 67
corruption 128
Council of Baltic Sea States *see* CBSS
Council of Europe 52, 57, 108
Council of Interior Ministers 86
Council for Mutual Economic Assistance 52
crime 91, 227; border regions 91, 92, 227;
  comparative regional statistics 92; *see also*
  organised crime
crisis management: EU–Russia political
  dialogue on 26

Dalai Lama 140
Danilova, Elena 123
drug-trafficking 89–96; measures taken to
  combat in Russia 94; registered crimes in
  Russia 95; routes through Russia 93;
  Russia sees itself as victim of 91; statistics
  89, 91

'Eastern Dimension' (ED) 41–2, 89
economic convergence *see* CEES
Economic and Currency Union (ECU) 109
economic relations, EU–Russia 105–6,
  115–19; common interests and objectives
  116; deterioration in 2004 115; energy
  dialogue 124–7; impact of enlargement on
  trade 118–19, 122; limitations 128–9;
  negotiations over Russia's entry to WTO
  119–21; and trade 117–18; *see also* CEES
education: common space of 23, 59
Egorov, Vladimir 146
electricity 125

energy: EU–Russia relations over 60, 124–6,
  128
energy exports 3, 117, 118, 120, 124
energy prices 120–1
enlargement, eastern 51–64
environmental issues 61, 88, 89, 228–9
ESDP (European Security and Defence
  Policy) 3, 7, 17, 27, 28, 68, 69, 155, 211
Estonia: accession to EU 35, 58, 178–9, 211;
  amphetamines factory in 94; borders of 77;
  illegal migrants 83; impact of EU accession
  on Pskov 181, 183, 186–7, 190; principles of
  European policies 211–12
Estonian–Russian border 75, 214–18
Estonian–Russian relations 4, 179, 211–20;
  border treaty negotiations 72, 79, 216–18;
  on eve of enlargement 212–14; impact of
  EU enlargement on 218–20; and trade 213;
  and visa regime 214–16
EU: comprehensive review of its Russia
  policy (2004) 16, 18, 21, 23–5; enlargement
  (2004) 1, 17, 35, 67; Russian foreign policy
  in 1990s 52–6
EU–Russia Cooperation Council 73
EU–Russia Joint Statement on Transit (2002)
  201
EU–Russia Partnership Council 7
EU–Russia relations: breakdown in 1999 52;
  challenge of ensuring greater convergence
  between 1–3; changes brought about by
  eastern enlargement 44; common interests
  and objectives 116; and common spaces
  initiative see common spaces initiative;
  creating a more favourable environment for
  trade and promotion of interests by EU 6;
  crisis in at end of 2003 60; economic 105–6,
  115–29; factors forcing EU to comes to
  terms with Russia as a neighbour 17–18;
  factors to be taken into account in devising
  a new strategy for 5–13; main problems 55;
  obstacles to 10–11, 16; opportunity for
  cooperation after enlargement 62–4;
  perception of 'strategic partnership' in
  different ways 43; political dialogue 25–9;
  pre-enlargement negotiations 3; serious
  issues of discord between 60–2
EU–Russia summits 7; (May 2001) 103; (Oct
  2001) 155; (Nov 2002) 74, 79, 248; (May
  2003) 2, 23, 42, 59, 68, 85, 142, 155; (Nov
  2003) 24, 61, 74, 85, 103, 105; (May 2004)
  25, 74, 112
Eurocities 142
European Commission 21; Communication
  on Relations with Russia (2004) 24–5
European Economic Area (EEA) 5, 104, 111,
  123